THE GREAT WAR
THROUGH PICTURE POSTCARDS

THE GREAT WAR
THROUGH PICTURE POSTCARDS

Guus de Vries

Pen & Sword
MILITARY

First published in 2014 by S.I. Publicaties BV
Postbus 188, 6860 AD Oosterbeek, Netherlands

Reprinted in this format in 2016 by Pen and Sword Military,
an imprint of Pen & Sword Books Ltd
47 Church Street
Barnsley
South Yorkshire
S70 2AS

ISBN 978 1 47385 668 4

Typeset by Pen & Sword Books Ltd
Printed and bound by Replika Press Pvt. Ltd.

Translated into English by Britta Nurmann.

Pen & Sword Books Ltd incorporates the imprints of Pen & Sword Archaeology, Atlas,
Aviation, Battleground, Discovery, Family History, History, Maritime, Military, Naval,
Politics, Railways, Select, Social History, Transport, True Crime, and Claymore Press,
Frontline Books, Leo Cooper, Praetorian Press, Remember When, Seaforth Publishing and
Wharncliffe.

For a complete list of Pen and Sword titles please contact
Pen and Sword Books Limited
47 Church Street, Barnsley, South Yorkshire, S70 2AS, England
E-mail: enquiries@pen-and-sword.co.uk
Website: www.pen-and-sword.co.uk

Contents

Introduction

PICTURE POSTCARDS from the First World War offer a multi-layered source of information, which researchers have only mined to a small degree up to now. The postcards sent by and to soldiers not only mirror the events in the different theatres, but also give a unique view of the daily life both on the front line and at home, in all warring countries. They transport the dreams, wishes and desires of the men on the battlefields and paint a picture of the changing role of women in everyday life. In this way, not only do they offer a complex picture of reality, but also allow deep insights into the minds of the artists, publishers and producers, as well as the people who sent the cards in the first place.

Collecting picture postcards had been a popular pastime since their introduction in 1869 and so many of the cards had survived in albums and boxes along with military mail. The German Reich recognised the positive effects of home contacts on morale, therefore the letters and postcards

Let the little children come unto me!!!
Picture postcard from 1915 with an illustration by the Swiss graphic artist Pierre Châtillon (1885-1974). He depicted Emperor Wilhelm II as God, chopping off children's hands. During the war, stories such as this of atrocities allegedly committed by German soldiers were repeated again and again. Even though these rumours would later turn out to be completely unfounded, they still were a popular motif for postcards in order to emphasise the huge guilt of the German troops.

LAISSEZ VENIR A MOI LES PETITS ENFANTS !!!

Heranschleichende indische Gurkhas.

Indian Gurkhas sneaking up.
Among the troops of the British Commonwealth were several battalions of Gurkhas. These professional soldiers from Nepal were feared among their enemies, not least because of their skills in wielding the heavy, curved, all-purpose knife called the Kukri. Motifs portraying the enemy as respectable and even dangerous, such as on this German picture postcard, are relatively rare.

motifs of the picture postcards, not the private messages of the senders, which were astonishingly consistent across all countries and often only served to communicate that personal health was still maintained and to express gratitude for received mail and comforts. Critical reports are rare and perhaps more likely to be found in letters, which are not as easily censored as postcards.

The postcards are grouped into twelve chapters in which accompanying texts provide the reader with an overview of the warring states and their armies, the developments at the front and at home, and the weapons in use. The scope of this book allows only glimpses at the four years of the 'war to end all wars', and military historians will hopefully forgive the author and the publisher for occasional generalisations.

All postcards shown in this book are from the collections of S.I. Publications and VS-BOOKS.

Guus de Vries, September 2014

delivered by the field postal service were subsidised as 'soldiers' mail', handled by special field post offices called *Feldpostexpedition* and carried between the front and home by the millions. The designs were diverse, ranging from lithographed and sometimes even embossed works of renowned artists, to pictures taken by the writer as a personal 'greeting from the field', and sent back to loved ones at home.

The aim of this publication is to document how the First World War was portrayed by and through picture postcards from three different vantage points:
- How were the real events pictured?
- How were emotions and perceptions of the war communicated?
- Which artistic and stylistic devices were used to influence and manipulate public opinion?

This research is based exclusively on the various

Chapter 1

War and Picture Postcards

Mail and Morale

During the First World War, the most important people in a soldier's life were the cook and the postman. The distribution of mail and comforts from home were the emotional highlight of the day, and contacts with the outside world were an important support, helping the soldiers to bear many deprivations. Knowing that there was a

'normal' life outside the theatre of war, receiving mail meant a connection to home and was extremely important to the soldiers. It meant that their minds could, temporarily at least, flee the hell they were captured in. On the other hand, receiving military mail from the front was at least a sign of life, and so the daily visit of the postman was eagerly anticipated by those at home.

The military authorities were aware of the massive influence mail had on the morale of the troops. Consequently, sending mail was often very cheap or even free of charge for active soldiers, even though it required extensive and costly organisation. In 1918 for example, the

The soldier's two friends.
'Whenever he sees them, he gives them a smile, as both provide him with nourishment. One satisfies his hunger, the other his heart, mind and soul.' A nice example of the broad range of postcards picturing the cook and the postman.

LES DEUX AMIS DU SOLDAT.
Quand il les voit, il leur sourit,
Car l'un et l'autre le nourrit
L'un apaise son appétit,
L'autre son cœur et son esprit.

PATRIOTIC
1104

A sorting room of the German field post office. In 1918 around 13,000 civilian and military personnel worked carrying mail, transporting around 16 million shipments daily. The mailbags in the foreground are labelled with their destinations, from left to right the 29th, 25th, 26th and 27th Infantry Divisions. The numbers below the division information are the regimental numbers, in the case of the 26th ID this would be the 119th, 121st, 122nd and 125th Infantry Regiment. This division initially fought in Belgium and northern France, but was later moved to the East.

German Army's field post offices were staffed by about 8,000 mail clerks and 5,000 supporting troops, while in 1917, the British Field Post Office employed about 4,000 personnel. Of course, the number of picture postcards, letters and parcels transported by the various field post services is beyond imagination.

In Germany alone, about 16.7 million shipments were transported daily between the various fronts and the home country (altogether the volume of mail between August 1914 and November 1918 amounts to 28.7 billion individual shipments); in France it was around 4 million shipments per day (amounting to 10 billion over the course of the war); the British Field Post Office processed 2 million shipments a day (5 billion altogether). The combined volume of mail items for these three countries alone

A typical photographic postcard not produced for commercial sale, but ordered by one of the soldiers in the picture or a comrade. It shows French soldiers in a dugout somewhere behind the front line, whose appearance betrays their experiences. This everyday situation also shows the importance of mail: two of the four men are writing and two picture postcards are fixed to the shelf over their heads.

amounts to almost 45 billion. With a cautious estimation of 5 billion each for Austria-Hungary, Russia and the US, and without even allowing for the other nations taking part in the war, the end result is around 60 billion postcards, letters and parcels sent over the four years.

According to estimates, roughly half the shipments were picture postcards, meaning at least 30 billion postcards were sent by or received by a soldier between August 1914 and November 1918.

This inconceivable number was the result of a desire for communication between the millions of soldiers, who were often away from home for years, and their families at home. Picture postcards were the best means for this; they were readily available and cheap. Active soldiers could often mail them free of charge and they were prettier to look at than letters and could be written faster, as they needed less text. By choosing the image, the sender could perhaps convey his feelings or sentiments more easily than by putting them into words. Moreover, in

The war letter.
An overjoyed young German woman reads a letter from her husband or fiancé serving in the army. The old man in the background smiling contently is most likely the father of the far-away soldier. At the very least, receiving a postcard or a letter meant that the sender was alive recently, even though it usually took a couple of days for military mail to arrive.

Der Feldpoſtbrief.

the years leading up to the war, a time without telephones and radio broadcasts, the picture postcard was the most important means of communication.

A happy hour. Mail from home is distributed to Austro-Hungarian troops.
This card is a retouched and coloured photograph by the *K.U.K Kriegspressequartier*, the Austro-Hungarian press information office, established at the beginning of the war. The joy of the soldiers in the picture is therefore not artificial.

Serie 45/2   Nr. 240. Eine frohe Stunde. Verteilung der Poſt aus der Heimat bei öſt. ung. Truppen.

Searching for a pen pal.
'Young soldier with a free heart, searches for a friendly and loving pen pal.' The typically French phenomenon of the '*Marraine de Guerre*', which appeared in Spring 1915 and can loosely be translated as 'wartime godmother' or 'wartime foster mother', shows one important influence of mail on morale. The idea behind it was to establish contact for the duration of the war between soldiers without family, or whose family lived in the occupied and therefore unreachable parts of France, and a female pen pal.

Correspondence Cards, Picture Postcards and Military Postcards

The first ever postcard, at that time called a correspondence card, was mailed in Austria in 1869 and reached unforeseen popularity almost immediately. Soon images were added to the postcards and the picture postcard was born. At the turn of the century the picture postcard was not only an important means of communication but also an art form and a phenomenon. Furthered by technical progress in the field of printing, producing and publishing postcards had become an important branch of the economy.

Collecting picture postcards was a popular pastime at the beginning

A group of exhausted German soldiers pose for the camera. The picture was most likely taken in echelon quarters a couple of miles behind the front line, to which the troops were moved for rest and recreation after spending time in the forward positions and where they could also resupply and receive replacements. The ledge is decorated with a great number of postcards, the majority of them showing women.

A letter home.
Often sketches, drawings or watercolours made by soldiers were used as motifs for postcards. Style and artistic quality ranged from simple to high-end. This card, with the writing on the front side and dated 9 April 1917, was actually printed.

events. The onset of the war allowed them to prove their efficiency, as the first cards remembering the '1914 campaign' were up for sale only a couple of days after the first shots were fired.

The demand for information about the war was enormous, not least or perhaps exactly because millions of young man were mobilised and deployed to the field. No publisher considering himself a serious businessman could

of the twentieth century and was a singular and inexhaustible source of information, as every corner of the earth and almost every human activity could be pictured. The picture postcard had an important influence on the development of our visual culture and the communication of art and beauty, especially as from the late nineteenth century, an increasing number of well-known artists were tasked with creating 'artist postcards', which introduced the stylistic language of the Art Nouveau to a wider audience.

Current events also formed motifs; train accidents and natural disasters were favourite topics and publishers reacted quickly to such

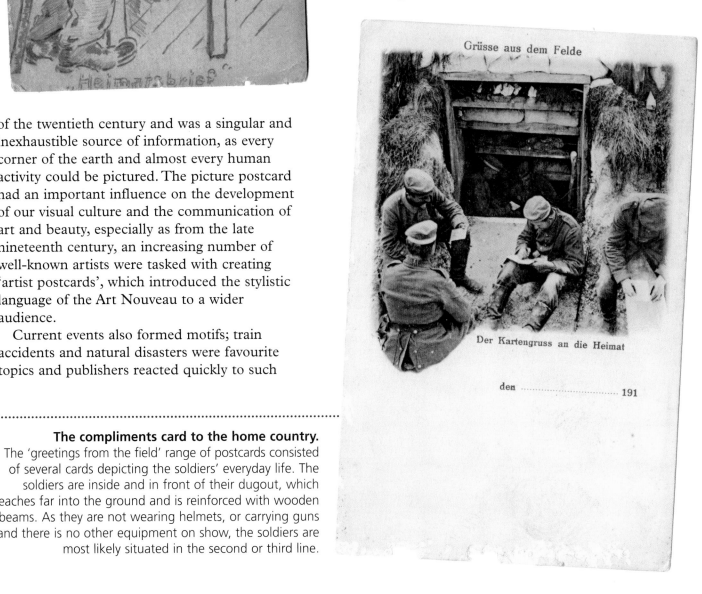

The compliments card to the home country.
The 'greetings from the field' range of postcards consisted of several cards depicting the soldiers' everyday life. The soldiers are inside and in front of their dugout, which reaches far into the ground and is reinforced with wooden beams. As they are not wearing helmets, or carrying guns and there is no other equipment on show, the soldiers are most likely situated in the second or third line.

One Line From France.
This text is not exactly logical, as the picture shows an American soldier in France receiving a card from home. Perhaps the publisher, J.M.T from Paris, did not speak English. As many French publishing houses produced uncountable numbers of cards for the British and American troops, typographical errors were a common occurrence.

Gut geht es dem Soldat,
Der sieben Bräute hat.

A soldier with seven brides will fare well.
The rations of the soldiers at the front were supplemented by shipments from home, the most favourite surely being tobacco, followed by various foodstuffs and warm clothing in winter. These parcels, in Germany known as *'Liebesgaben'*, literally 'gifts of love', were usually sent by families and spouses – hence the piece of wisdom that the more brides, the more parcels.

ignore this development, so in no time at all, numerous series of picture postcards showing military images were published.

Although billions of postcards were sent between the front and the home countries between 1914 and 1918, the end of the war also marked the end of the heyday of the postcard. This was mainly due to demobilisation, increased postage costs for postcards and new means of communication, like the telephone and the radio. Even though the picture postcard has survived until today, it reached its high point in both quality and quantity in the time between 1898 and 1918.

Postcards produced during the First World War can be categorised by their production methods. The most important variants are printed photographic cards, artist cards and real photographic cards. The printed photo card is a card with a printed image based on a photograph. The picture can be taken in a studio or outside; photo montages are also possible. Artist postcards are also printed, but depict drawings, watercolours, woodcuts or reproduced paintings. A real photo postcard is printed from a negative onto photographic paper, which has postcard markings printed on the reverse.

FRED™ SPURGIN

CAN'T WRITE MUCH AT PRESENT.

Je ne puis écrire long cette fois.

Can't write much at present.
A drawing by Frank Spurgin (1882 –1968), for decades one of the best known British illustrators. During the First World War he published many series of postcards, usually of a humoristic or patriotic nature. He often depicted children taking on the roles of adults. This motif illustrates one of the advantages of the postcard: the sender can give a sign of life but does not have to use many words.

This picture of the German Crown Prince Friedrich Wilhelm Victor August Ernst of Prussia, shows the heir in a field tunic and with the cap of the *Leibgarde-Husaren-Regiment* household light cavalry regiment. It was issued by the *Heeresgruppe Kronprinz für Verwundetenfürsorge* army group for casualty support. Emperor Wilhelm II had six sons, who all served in the war and survived. The Crown Prince was the best known of them and very present in the media; his image decorated countless picture postcards of the Germans and their allies.

Printed photo cards and artist cards were produced by commercial publishing houses and sold in much higher numbers than real photo cards, which were manufactured in small batches. Amateur and professional photographers took their studio equipment to the front line and found motifs that are rarely seen on commercial cards. Apart from these three main types, there are also the rather rare cards with hand-painted motifs or with woven or embroidered appliqués. The latter two variants were apparently made mainly in northern France and sold predominantly to British and American soldiers.

Pre-printed military correspondence cards form a category of their own. They had room for a short personal message or were already printed with pre-worded messages, so that the sender only had to strike out the non-applicable parts. As these cards are not illustrated, they are not included in this book.

Censoring
Immediately after the outbreak of the war, the governments of the nations involved passed censoring laws. These also applied to picture postcards. The messages on the postcards were

A typical real photo card. Two German soldiers had their picture taken in a gun position hit by an artillery strike. The picture shows the destroyed gun with the entrance to a dugout behind it. The ammunition is stacked to the right. Picture postcards with motifs like this were supposed to record the soldiers' experiences for their own memory and allowed them to share them with a small group of others.

1914 campaign, French infantry, machine-gun section.
This printed picture postcard is based on a photograph and was published by *Neurdein Frères* from Paris, one of the biggest publishers of cards of this kind. The label '1914 campaign' dates it to the early months of the war. The mules of the machine-gun section carry special pack saddles for ammunition boxes.

usually censored, the illustrations, however, were of lower priority to the officials and thus received less scrutiny. In 1914, authorities in Germany had already recommended approving pictures whenever possible, 'even if they show the whole seriousness of war (combat scenes, the dead and the severely wounded)'. In 1915 the *Kriegspresseamt* press information office added to these instructions: 'Exaggerated depictions of the

CAMPAGNE DE 1914
132 *Infanterie Française, Section de mitrailleuses* N.D. Phot.

A German salute.
In the decade leading up to the First World War, German publishing and printing houses dominated the international market for picture postcards in both quality and quantity. More than half of the cards produced in Germany were exported. This card, with the crests of all German federal states printed partially in relief and decorated with gold, is a good illustration of the quality of workmanship delivered by German printers. The bottom line shows the crests of Alsace and Lorraine, which were also recognised in France.

Honour and Homeland. France despite everything!
Cottage industries were widespread in northern France, and so cards were made that sometimes featured woven or embroidered appliqués or were painted by hand, such as this one. They were mainly sold to foreign soldiers. The flags of the Allies were popular motifs: this card depicts those of France, Belgium, Russia and Britain. They symbolised solidarity and also made a colourful motif.

horrors of war, or those which our enemies could interpret in a way that hinders our warfare, are to be prevented.'

Two more designs were also forbidden by the German authorities. One was the wide range of jingoistic pictures that flooded the market in the first months of the war, ridiculing the enemy or portraying him as inferior. One of the best known of these designs is most likely the card with the words '*Jeder Schuss ein Russ! – Jeder Stoß ein Franzos! – Jeder Tritt ein Brit'!*' – 'Each shot a Russian! – Each thrust a Frenchman! – Each kick a Brit!'. The text is accompanied with variations of the same drawings; a German soldier shooting a Russian whilst simultaneously clubbing a Frenchman with the stock of his rifle and kicking a British soldier.

The Bavarian Ministry of War had already banned the card in September 1914, with the Prussians and other federal states following suit shortly after as, 'they are likely to impinge on the reputation of German culture, as well as the

German Army and its military achievements.'

Also hit by the anathema of the censors were the so-called 'hunger postcards' that were published in Germany from late 1916 and early 1917, and commented on the deteriorating food supply situation in Germany. But even the rather lenient rules for images on picture postcards issued by the German censoring authorities were not implemented stringently. The number of mailed postcards was simply too large, the rules not clear enough, and the opinions of the different level of authorities in charge too diverse. What was banned by one censor could,

Jeder Schuss Ein Russ! – Jeder Stoss Ein Franzos! – Jeder Tritt Ein Brit'!

ges.gesch:1513.   Druck v. Verlag v. Ad. Harth Mainz.

Each shot a Russian! – Each thrust a Frenchman! – Each kick a Brit!
This card appeared in several variations. They all show a German soldier who not only beats his three opponents, but also humiliates them. Although the topic was very popular at the beginning of the war, this and similar motifs were already banned in September 1914 by the Bavarian Ministry of War, as 'they are likely to impinge on the reputation of German culture as well as the German Army and its military achievements.'

for example, be cleared somewhere else.

In France, censoring started in March 1915 with an assessment of picture postcards, after the office responsible had been reorganised and began its work under the name *Service de press du ministère de la Guerre* – Press service of the Ministry of War. This authority developed guidelines that demanded the banning of cards, if their wording or pictures could have a negative

influence on the morale of the troops or the general population, or if they depicted new weapons and equipment.

While press releases were censored before publication, picture postcards were only censored after they were published. Often cards were only officially cleared months after being published, without having any negative effects on the publisher. The cards cleared by the authorities

A Close Shave.
'Tommy: "If they comes much nearer – I shall cut meself."'
This cartoon was drawn by Lieutenant Frank Osborne and the card was transferred by Field Post Office H.3, after censor 3934 had cleared the contents of the card. Theoretically, every card or letter going from the front to the home country was subject to censoring, and had to be read officially to make sure it did not contain military secrets.

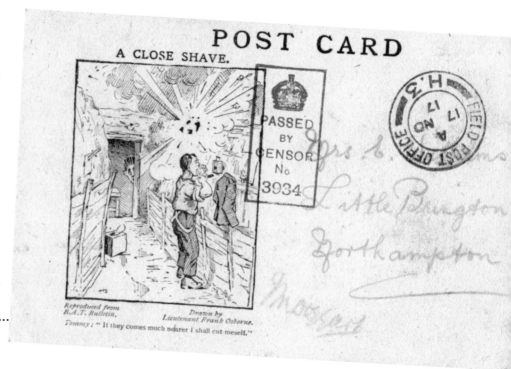

POST CARD

A CLOSE SHAVE.

PASSED BY CENSOR No 3934

Reproduced from B.A.T. Bulletin.   Drawn by Lieutenant Frank Osborne.
Tommy: " If they comes much nearer I shall cut meself."

"18 and 80"

Youth and Age in a British Shell-filling factory.

Help us win! Sign war bonds.
National authorities and offices only published picture postcards on a small scale during the war. The multitude of cards produced for the various war bonds were an exception. One of the most famous is the 'man with the steel helmet' by Fritz Erler (1868-1940), whose image became a symbol for the whole war. The bonds were very important for the war effort. Germany issued nine war bonds during the First World War, which raised 98 billion Reichsmarks and so paid for 60 per cent of the German war effort.

Youth and Age in a British Shell-filling factory.
This card was most likely published by order of the British government to raise awareness that the whole population contributed to the war effort of the home country. This was actually true, as over the course of the war the defence industry became increasingly dependent on female workers and men, who for age reasons, could not serve in the armed forces.

were labelled *visé*, followed by the location where the approval was given.

As in Germany, the French censors also disliked cards that portrayed the enemy as a bunch of cowards or were demeaning in other ways. This was less due to a fear of damaging the French reputation, but rather because of the possibility of undermining the morale of the troops, who might not take up the fight with the necessary determination. Consequently, a number of French cards were banned in the spring of 1915. However, the ban was rarely implemented, and many cards that derided the Germans in various and often highly unflattering ways were still published up until the end of the war.

With the 'Defence of the Realm Act', passed on 8 August 1914, the UK paved the way for extensive censoring. The press as well as incoming and outgoing mail were monitored in an ever-increasing scope over the course of the war, but the motifs of picture postcards were of little interest here, too. A ban on demeaning depictions of the enemy was most likely unnecessary, as the genre was virtually unknown in Britain. However, if the weaknesses of new weapons could be given away, the authorities took action. During the introduction of the new tank, for example, increased attention was paid to ensure that picture postcards did not show any tanks. Therefore all cards showing military equipment had to be presented to the censoring authorities for approval from 15 September 1916 onwards.

Propaganda

Information, especially of a biased or misleading nature, which is used to promote a political cause or point of view – the Oxford Dictionary

ARMÉE ALLEMANDE
SOLDAT DU RÉGIMENT DU
KRONPRINZ (TENUE DE
CAMPAGNE)

definition of propaganda – was widely used during the First World War. Initially used only by certain groups and associations, over the course of the war civilian and military authorities also began to distribute propaganda. Departments were especially established to influence the opinion of the local population, as well as foreign nations. Government propaganda was heavily text-based and mainly aimed at the daily newspapers, as well as other printed media. Flyers dropped from aircraft or balloons over enemy positions praised the achievements of their own forces and encouraged the enemy to drop their weapons.

Pictures were less important in terms of propaganda. Although the military authorities of all nations established special departments for press and photography over the course of the war, pictures were rarely used for immediate propaganda purposes as they were still not considered to be convincing enough. The German *Bild- und Filmamt* picture and film authority provided series of photographs of the various theatres for publication, but they mainly served as illustrations for public lectures.

The authorities only used picture postcards as a means of propaganda on a small scale. Although pictures were provided to commercial publishers to make sure that their own forces left a good impression, the authorities rarely published cards themselves. Postcards promoting the country's war bonds or emphasising the important role of women in the wartime economy were among the exceptions to this rule.

German Army. Soldier of the 'Crown Prince' Regiment (campaign dress).
A satirical card referring to the looting allegedly committed by German troops in northern France, in this case the 'Crown Prince' Regiment (which incidentally, did not carry the number 171). The drawing was made by Jean-Jacques Waltz (1873-1951), who was born in German-occupied Alsace and worked under the pseudonym of 'Hansi' in favour of a reconnection to France even before 1914. He was incarcerated in Germany several times for this, and was wanted for treason as a *Landesverräter* (traitor) by the German Gestapo during the Second World War.

The ambulance dog.
Germany had already banned picture postcards denigrating enemy soldiers in September 1914. Similar regulations were passed in France, but they were applied less frequently. According to the French authorities, one card that took things too far was the ambulance dog urinating on a German soldier, and it was banned in Spring 1915. The censorship of images was, however, completely arbitrary. A great number of much more insulting and debasing images were cleared.

LE CHIEN
AMBULANCIER

Adventures in stockpiling. A critical moment!
Apart from cards insulting the enemy or capable of damaging the German Army, the so-called 'hunger cards' were also banned in Germany. They were published from the end of 1916 onwards and drew their motifs from the increasingly difficult supply situation for civilians, for which the British naval blockade was a major contributing factor. This example of a banned card shows a smuggler whose bag opens on a railway platform, spilling the stockpiled food under the watchful eye of a policeman.

Hamster-
Erlebnisse.

Ein kritischer Augenblick!

LES BONS AMIS
Tommy britannique et enfants français

S 6

The good friends. British Tommy and French children.
A typical propaganda card showing how well British soldiers got along with French children. The card was printed and distributed early in the war by the British government, as no publisher or printing house is mentioned on the reverse.

"DO YOUR DUTY BRAVELY. FEAR GOD. HONOUR THE KING."
(Signed) KITCHENER Field Marshal

Do your duty bravely. Fear God. Honour the King. (signed) Kitchener, Field Marshal.
Printed by a commercial publisher, this card shows a prominent protagonist becoming a symbol of patriotism and securing commercial success. Kitchener was appointed Secretary of State for War in 1914 and was one of the few contemporaries to foresee a long and hard war. He succeeded in raising a large volunteer army, but died in 1916, when the ship that was carrying him to Russia for negotiations struck a German mine and sank.

Uhlan patrol.
German Uhlans in field grey uniforms watch a train on a railway embankment. The uniforms in this 1914 drawing are very accurate and the steel tube lance was also still in use. The most important piece of 'equipment', however, is the pack of Leibniz biscuits fixed to the saddle! Entrepreneur Herrman Bahlsen founded his biscuit factory in 1889 under the name of *Hannoversche Cakesfabrik* and published a number of patriotic advertisement cards during the war. The artist, Walter Georgi (1891–1924), was a member of the *Deutscher Werkbund* (German Designers' Association) and created twenty-five Leibniz motifs for postcards.

La Carte à payer

London buses at the front.
The French company, Dubonnet, used picture postcards to advertise their aperitif. Here the advertisement is on a London double-decker bus full of Scottish soldiers, who according to the text, are on their way to the front. Dubonnet published a number of promotional cards that all showed scenes from the soldiers' daily lives, and an advertising panel was always part of the motif.

Offered by Phoscao. The bill.
Phoscao produced a cocoa-based drink and published a number of cards that carried the company name in addition to the motif (Offert par Phoscao, Edition Phoscao or Collection du Phoscao). This rather unsubtle card shows a French and Scottish soldier presenting the bill for the actions of the German Army against the cities of Louvain, Dinant, Reims, Senlis and Arras, to the German Emperor Wilhelm II.

A more indirect form of government propaganda was the publishing of postcards depicting paintings or watercolours by official war artists or with the motifs of propaganda posters, for example Kitchener's famous recruiting poster. These were marketed by commercial publishers in large numbers.

On top of this, a large number of patriotic organisations felt a loyalty to their home country and used propaganda actively and knowingly to further their goals. These included *La Crosaide des Femmes Françaises*, the *Ligue Maritime Française*, the *Ligue Républicaine pour la Défense nationale*, the *Order of the White Feather*, the *Kolonial-Krieger-Spende* or the *Verein für das Deutschtum in Russland*, as well as the numerous associations that took care of prisoners of war, the wounded and other victims.

Finally, 'commercial propaganda', such as advertising cards, also deserve a mention. Many

For King and Country. Our Defenders on Land and Sea.
Cards carrying the pictures of heads of state and leaders of armies were very popular at the beginning of the war, but lost their standing the longer the war carried on, as people lost faith in their leaders. This motif can be dated to the beginning of the war by the persons pictured, as Field Marshal French and General Smith-Dorrien were relieved of their commands in 1915, and Kitchener died in 1916.

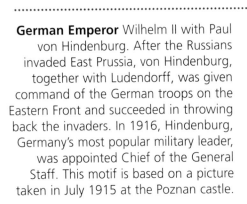

German Emperor Wilhelm II with Paul von Hindenburg. After the Russians invaded East Prussia, von Hindenburg, together with Ludendorff, was given command of the German troops on the Eastern Front and succeeded in throwing back the invaders. In 1916, Hindenburg, Germany's most popular military leader, was appointed Chief of the General Staff. This motif is based on a picture taken in July 1915 at the Poznan castle.

companies had cards produced to advertise their products, and these were usually handed out free of charge to ensure the most wide-spread distribution possible.

The Picture Changes
The visual language of the picture postcards slowly changed over the course of the war.

Initially, the landscape was dominated by patriotism, the invincibility of the respective country's forces and those of its loyal allies, the inferiority of the enemy and the certain and swift fall of Paris or Berlin. However, the pictures began to change after the Western Front became a stalemate.

An increasing number of cards were published

The savages. Their methods of warfare.
Georges Scott (1873–1943) was a war correspondent and illustrator for the French magazine, *l'Illustration*. His drawings that were also marketed on picture postcards sold in large numbers in France and were often copied. This drawing was created in 1914 in response to the atrocities committed by the German Army in Belgium. 'Dear Camille – do not forget, my little one, the war of 1914', the sender Victor writes to his daughter, '– and if I am killed, plot revenge'.

aiming to ridicule the enemy and spread hatred. In the countries of the 'Entente Cordiale', atrocities committed by the Germans in Belgium and northern France were pictured in great detail.

The German Reich answered this by producing pictures of German soldiers sharing their rations with local children or images of exemplary prisoner of war camps, where the enemy was well looked after. There were also cards that shed a poor light on the Russian Army, the colonial troops of France or the United Kingdom, adding more fuel to the *Gott strafe England* (May God punish England) campaign.

In the first year of the war, postcards with pictures of 'great men' were quite popular

'We barbarians' Captured Frenchmen are treated by the Red Cross.
To counter accusations of acting like savages and barbarians in the occupied territories, Germany published cards with humanitarian motifs, for example citizens receiving aid, children being fed, or enemy soldiers being given medical assistance.

Gott strafe England!

'May God punish England!'
For many Germans, Great Britain was mainly to blame for the outbreak of the war, which swiftly led to a campaign of which the title literally translates as 'May God punish England!' This rather catchy slogan was coined by Ernst Lissauer, who also wrote a 'Hymn of Hate against England'. The British soldiers made light of the sentence by adapting it to everything they did not like: 'Gott strafe the barbed wire.'

including emperors, kings and generals, who by their overwhelming powers, were expected to lead their own armies to a swift victory. But as these quick successes failed to materialise, enthusiasm continued to wane, as did the number of these cards produced.

This also held true for cards depicting the enemy as an idiot, coward or wimp. Most soldiers' experiences at the front were that their enemy fought as bravely and tenaciously as they did. What's more, if the enemy was a coward, then why was the war not already won? The pictures of women and children in uniform, initially in favour with the publishers, also saw a steady decline in popularity as the war went on.

The soldiers' everyday lives in the trenches became a key aspect of the pictures, as were elements of life behind the lines, such as field kitchens, bakeries, casualty stations and army hospitals, which were necessary to help supply armies now numbering in the millions.

The Home Front also received increased attention, making great sacrifices to keep the machinery of war running, by delivering ammunition and other goods, whilst still suffering from constant food and supply shortages itself. Only two topics never changed in popularity from the beginning of the war to its end: sentimental and romantic pictures as well as pin-ups.

Chapter 2

Themes: From Hatred to Love

First World War picture postcards can only be grouped not only by their methods of production, but also by the themes of the motifs. Almost all cards fall into one of the following eight categories.

Reality

The image in question shows an incident, situation or object. From time to time these may be portrayed truthfully, but often parts or the whole image are carefully arranged and staged. The accompanying text may also either tell the truth or not. These cards were aimed at distributing information about certain events, without being coloured by propaganda.

Cards of this type are almost infinite in number and variety. They can show scenes from combat, destroyed houses, devastated villages or towns, prisoners of war, wounded or dead soldiers, displaced civilians, military equipment, scenes from the soldiers' everyday lives and portraits or group photos, to name just a few.

Photographic postcards were among the most fruitful sources, as they could be produced quickly and, important to the soldiers, showed their situation and their environment. Being produced locally and in small numbers, they usually went uncensored and were often bought to serve as a memento rather than be sent. Many artist postcards also fall into this category.

Almost all warring nations had official war painters (primarily artists who already had some reputation), who were tasked with creating pictures of the military actions of the respective

La Marmite – Grenade impact.
A nice example of the very realistic illustrations by Ernest Gabard. A grenade hits close to the front of a trench and the soldiers duck for cover in alarm. The face of the *poilu* to the right shows fear. Gabard had lived through these horrors and as he was a renowned artist, his works could be much closer to reality than most other picture postcards could.

Colour photography from the Vosges Mountains. Destroyed houses (upper Alsace).
A colour photograph capturing the destruction in one of the disputed provinces. Many motifs were coloured by hand, but there was also, although in a very small scope, real colour photography, mainly in Germany. The picture shows a group of German soldiers in a village that has been heavily damaged by artillery fire.

forces. These paintings were not only presented in exhibitions, but also often printed on postcards. Pictures created by more or less talented amateurs were also distributed this way, as were impressions painted by artists serving at the front, such as Ernest Gabard (1879–1957).

Gabard was a multi-talented French artist who served as a sergeant in the *270e Régiment d'Infanterie* during the war and created a series of forty-two watercolours showing the life of the *poilu*. The picture postcards depicting Gabard's realistic and truthful snapshots were quite popular and printed in high numbers, as soldiers liked to buy and send them to their families, so they had an idea of life at the front.

The images on this real photo card show the cruel reality of war. The upper picture shows a large number of fallen soldiers, the corpses stacked. In the lower picture, French soldiers load the bodies of the fallen soldiers onto a transport carriage under the supervision of a medic. Although large publishing houses sold postcards showing fallen soldiers – with the permission of the authorities – the images on these were far less drastic than this motif, which would never have passed a censor's desk without objection.

558 La Grande Guerre 1914-15

En Haute-Alsace. — Allemand surpris par un territorial
dans une tranchée abandonnée   A. R.

The Great War 1914-15. In upper Alsace a territorial soldier surprises a German in an abandoned trench.
A good example of the many motifs showing obviously posed situations, which were no less popular than real pictures featuring everyday reality at the front.

A coloured German picture postcard showing a group of French soldiers, some of them wounded. Among them is an African and sitting in front a *Chasseur Alpin* (mountain trooper) wearing a beret. A German NCO can be seen in the background. The red trousers and kepis put the date at the beginning of the war, the less eye-catching 'horizon blue' uniforms were introduced from spring 1915 onwards. Even though there is no caption to the picture, showing captured enemies in this way was a form of propaganda.

For Freedom and Liberty.
The flags of Japan, Belgium, the UK, France and Russia symbolise the nations who, in their understanding, fought for freedom. Flags were an easy motif – they were colourful and everybody understood them. They therefore appear on many patriotic cards, especially if the solidarity of the respective countries was to be emphasised.

Patriotism

Cards in the patriotism category often show national symbols (flags and colours, lions, eagles), generals, heads of state, determined soldiers and loyal spouses. They were supposed to strengthen the love of country and the morale of the population, as well as further combativeness.

Pictures of the emperor in his various uniforms, followed by those of his sons and other family members, were extremely popular in Germany. In the federal states, pictures of the kings, princes and dukes were equally favoured. Generals also graced many picture postcards, foremost Hindenburg, followed by Ludendorff, Moltke, Falkenhayn and a multitude of army and division commanders. In France, the list was topped by Generals Foch and Joffre. Another often published patriotic topic was the lost provinces of Alsace and Lorraine that were usually symbolised by women and children in regional costume.

Cards with patriotic images were usually printed by commercial publishers, however, in the early days of the war they were so popular that they were also published by organisations collecting money for social or national causes. These organisations included the Red Cross, widows and orphans, refugees, prisoners of war and disabled former servicemen, or those who worked for patriotic causes, like the *Ligue maritime Française*, the *Verein für das Deutschtum in Russland* or the *Deutscher Flotten-Verein*. Governments also published a series of patriotic cards, usually aimed at selling the respective national war bonds needed to pay for the war.

This category also includes a large group of motifs confirming the strong and unshakeable bond between the allies, and always uses the same symbols. They were meant to foster solidarity and show the population that they were not alone in difficult times. Whenever a new state joined the war, for example on the side of the Entente, the market was inundated with new cards spreading the good news. The Central Powers obviously published fewer of these cards.

The images on patriotic cards brimmed over with pathos and heroism, especially where German and French examples are concerned. One hundred years later it is difficult to judge

Honour. Homeland. Unity is Strength.
A card from 1914 with text, flags and the pictures of the Allied heads of state. To the upper left, the French President Poincaré, to the upper right, the Russian Tsar Nicholas II, the bottom left shows the British King George V and the bottom right, the Belgian King Albert I.

EN ALSACE !
Par Georges SCOTT

Le vrai Plébiscite

This text-free postcard was published in late 1915. It shows three demurely clothed ladies with the flags of the Central Forces; Bulgaria, Germany, Austria-Hungary and Turkey.

The real plebiscite.
This drawing by Georges Scott shows a young woman wearing Alsacian costume clutching to the breast of a French officer. A boundary post of the German Empire is lying in the foreground, while in the background, the French Army advances. The lady symbolises Alsace, which after the Franco-Prussian War of 1870/71 had been annexed by Germany.

the public perception of these cards, but the substantial amount of surviving specimens indicates that they were produced and mailed in high numbers. The longer the war carried on, however, they became less and less popular, as the number of casualties rose and there appeared to be no end in sight.

Sergeant O'Leary advances ahead of his comrades, shoots the five men manning 1st machine gun, then three of the second and returns with two prisoners.
The patriotism category also includes depictions of personal bravery. The event described here actually happened. On 1 February 1915, close to the French village of Cuinchy, Lance-Corporal Michael O'Leary, 1st Battalion, The Irish Guards, received the highest award for valour in the British Army; the Victoria Cross. The only mistake in the description is his rank. Motifs of this kind wanted to suggest that the human will is strong enough to defeat even machines.

D'après The Sphere — *par Matania*
Le Sergent O'Leary devançant ses compagnons fusille les 5 servants d'une Iʳᵉ mitrailleuse puis 3 de la seconde et revient avec 2 prisonniers.

Humour

Cards in this category almost always carry drawings showing funny situations or self-mocking motifs. They are meant to brighten the receiver's mood or create a bond by sharing a joke. Although there are quite a number of cards from France and Germany in this category, the majority of them are British. Reg Carter, Donald McGill and Hayward Young were well-known artists in this genre, but the most popular by far was Bruce Bairnsfather.

Bairnsfather served as an officer in the Royal Warwickshire Regiment and was transferred to the War Office in London for health reasons in 1915, after the Second Battle of Ypres, where he

'A covering movement by the right wing to protect the rear.'
A humorous motif by the English illustrator, Donald McGill (1875-1962). It shows a Scottish soldier whose kilt has developed a dangerous life of its own due to strong wind. The cards of all nations show saucy humour, but only the British motifs could also be self-mocking.

Cordial agreement. The French always liked skirts.
This card also uses a kilted Scotsman as a humorous motif, but it belongs in a rare category: French self-mockery. The French and Germans only had a few cards that poked fun at themselves – most cards of this category are of British origin.

was officially designated, 'Officer, Cartoonist'. He created sketches and cartoons that were published in *Bystander* magazine and on postcards, portraying the bulb-nosed and walrus-moustached front soldier, 'Old Bill', and his muddy and dangerous life in the trenches.

The combination of realism, self-mockery and black humour made Bairnsfather's cards extremely popular. Although difficult to measure, this type of humour contributed substantially to keeping up morale in the fighting troops. Even the German Army Command was convinced of his contribution; after the war the defence ministry, now called *Reichswehrministerium*, published a report that included a number of Bairnsfather's cards.

The self-mockery and black humour that were mainly found in the UK during the First World

No possible doubt whatever.

Sentry: "'Alt! Who goes there?"
He of the Bundle: "You shut yer ------ mouth, or I'll come and knock yer ------ head off!" Sentry: "Pass, friend!"

And if it freezes tonight? Well, pal, then we can sit down.
Dry humour by Francisque Poulbot (1879-1946), one of the best known French war artists. He created a huge number of designs for postcards, many of them showing children or scenes intended to fuel hatred.

No possible doubt whatever.
When it comes to humorous postcards, Bruce Bairnsfather was the best-loved artist of all. He served at the front for a long time and so his cartoons are often based on his own experiences. A typical example of his work carries the text: 'Sentry: "Alt! Who goes there?" He of the Bundle: "You shut yer ------ mouth, or I'll come and knock yer ----- head off!" Sentry: "Pass, friend!"'

War, may at least partially be explained by the fact that the war was not fought on British soil. In addition, the civilian population was not directly affected except for bombardments by zeppelins and air planes.

In Germany and in France and Belgium especially, things were different. People fought for survival, as parts of the country were occupied and the population lived under foreign rule. No doubt self-mockery and humour were part of their national traditions, but they were not popular in these difficult times.

Many humorous cards were published in Belgium, Germany and France, but except for astonishingly few examples, their level of humour is restricted to tripping soldiers and

Thinking of you all! Napoleon said 'I am France'. I feel the same way, with all this French mud on me.
This cartoon by Fergus McKain pokes fun at the unbearable living conditions in the trenches. In south-western Belgium and northern France, especially where most of the British troops were deployed, whole sections of the front line could turn into muddy wastelands.

Napoleon said: " I am France ".
I feel the same way, with all this French mud on me.

LE CONFLIT EUROPÉEN EN 1914
Les voilà, les deux qui voulaient dévorer l'Europe

CHARGEZ !!!...

Charge!!!

Not much is known about Mass'beuf, a graphic artist who was active between 1900 and 1930. During the First World War he created at least two series of satirical illustrations intended to ridicule the German army. This card shows an exhausted Prussian uhlan who is certainly no longer capable of charging on his emaciated horse.

The European conflict of 1914. Here they are, the two who wanted to swallow Europe.

Frédéric Regamey (1849-1925) drew this French colonial soldier (a Turco from Algeria) holding the emperors of Germany and Austria-Hungary in a headlock. Soldiers from the overseas territories of France and of course the UK were a popular motif for picture postcards. On the Allied side they were supposed to document the potential for more soldiers and perhaps also show that even 'colonial' troops were a match for the German Army. The German versions depicted the enemy as using non-European, i.e. 'uncivilised' soldiers.

Schach! Schach!

Check! Check!

Given command of the armed forces of the Central Powers at the Eastern Front, von Hindenburg and von Hötzendorf have checked the Allied leaders. The latter are represented by Tsar Nicholas II, sitting at the table, and standing behind him from left to right; the Serbian King Peter I, the British General Smith-Dorrien and the French Commander in Chief, Joffre. This caricature is actually close to the truth, as the German/Austrian duo could turn the tables after the Russians invaded Germany in 1915 and even gain about 500km of ground.

harmless innuendos, motifs that of course were also present in Britain.

Finally, in all warring nations there were of course numerous cards making the enemy the target of jokes ranging from the subtle to the plain rude. Such motifs have to be counted in the following category.

Satire

The common denominator for this type of card is that they are supposed to ridicule, denigrate and lampoon the enemy. In the illustrations, usually drawings, the enemy often appear lazy,

stupid, dull, mollycoddled, uncivilised, barbaric, cowardly, prone to drinking, dishonest, starved, exhausted, unclean, too old, too young and so on. The manner and standard of the illustrations

.à Berlin-
à Berlin˙

Serie N° 5

'To Berlin, To Berlin'.
German propaganda often portrayed the French as effeminate and shabby, which this card nicely documents. The soldier's uniform consists of only a kepi and a patched-up jacket, under which he only wears underpants. His footwear consists of a slipper and a lady's boot.

I COLLABORATORI DELL'INGHILTERRA

The allies of the British.
A rather nasty caricature of Italian origin, which has to be dated to before May 1915, as Italy entered the First World War on the British side after that. The UK is symbolised by a Scotsman in a kilt, accompanied by an Indian depicted as a headhunter and a black African portrayed as an uncivilised drunk, dressed only in a skirt and carrying a bottle of aquavit.

range from amusing to downright bawdy.

Picture postcards with satirical motifs were mainly published in France and Germany, but were also common in Belgium and Italy. The French and Belgians often aimed their mockery at the German emperor, whereas German publishers rarely dared to ridicule enemy dignitaries. The only exception here was the King of Serbia, who was disparaged as the ruler of an uncivilised nation.

German postcards liked to show the French soldiers as sissies, the British as cowards and the Russians as unkempt, drunk and full of lice. Although rarely subtle in their choice of motifs, the illustrations on these cards are usually not as malicious as those of their British and French counterparts, which humiliated and lampooned the Germans in all manners imaginable.

There are untold numbers of heavy-handed motifs showing Emperor Wilhelm II or his soldiers as piglets on their way to the slaughterhouse. Colonial soldiers who fought for the Entente were often the subject of caricatures by both friend and foe. In Germany the aim was to show more or less bluntly that one fought an 'uncivilised' enemy, whereas the Allies laid the emphasis on presenting the enormous number of potential troops and their supremacy over the Central Powers.

This group of motifs contains a large number of cards showing French colonial troops guarding German prisoners, or leading them to PoW camps. In an indirect way, they illustrate that colonial soldiers 'sufficed' to deal with the army of Emperor Wilhelm II.

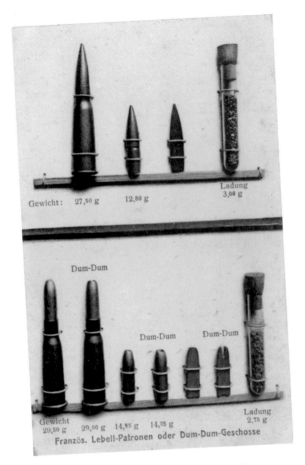

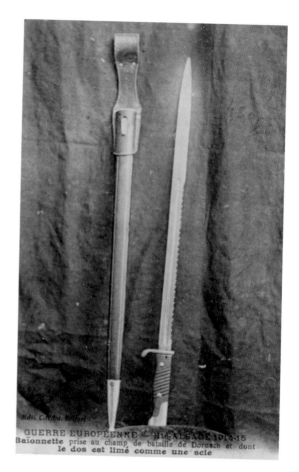

GUERRE EUROPÉENNE – HTE-ALSACE 1914-15
Baïonnette prise au champ de bataille de Dornach et dont
le dos est limé comme une scie

French Lebel cartridges or dumdum bullets.
A German card showing French cartridges with alleged dumdum bullets. These were soft-pointed or hollow-pointed bullets that expanded on impact and created especially severe wounds, and were banned by the Hague Convention of 1899. The pictured cartridges, however, are exercise rounds with a shortened trajectory used for exercises at close distances or on insufficiently secured ranges. The German Army captured a large stock of these rounds in 1914 at Lille, and subsequently used them to show the world that the enemy employed illegal means.

European war. Haute Alsace 1914-15. Bayonet with back edge sharpened to a saw, taken from the battlefield of Dornach.
This French picture postcard shows a German *Seitengewehr* 98 bayonet, of which more than half of the back edge has been given saw teeth. This would certainly inflict even more severe wounds than a regular bayonet, but it is not the main reason for this special cut – it was meant to be used as a tool and issued to NCOs in small numbers.

Hatred

Most motifs in this category originated in Belgium and France and were supposed to demonise the enemy and fuel hatred for him. As with the previous category, the main reason for this may be that the war was fought on these two nations' territory and that parts of the civilian population were subject to occupation. The German soldiers were portrayed murdering women, children and clergymen, raping, stealing and pillaging, with all the offences, whether real or fictitious, being depicted as luridly as possible.

It is telling that the most dramatic images in this group were created by Raemaekers and Châtillon,

both artists from neutral states (the Netherlands and Switzerland, respectively). Their motifs often showed the suffering of the civilian population and depicted proven or alleged atrocities.

If the enemy could be harmed, truth was the first victim, and an easy one. Rumours were spread that the Germans had shot a young boy pointing a wooden toy gun at them, or had chopped off captured children's hands. Both tales had no base in reality, but nevertheless were used by many artists and published in huge numbers.

Some historians argue that the manifold motifs of the French hatred postcards did their share in demonising the enemy, adding to the increasing French rejection of post-war Germany and in the

LES DEUX WILLY.
LE CLOWN PRINCE. SÉRIE C. Nº 4.

MAINTENANT, PETIT WILLY RACONTE-NOUS CE QUE TU SAIS DE NOS HAUTS FAITS D'ARMES.

EH BIEN!.... NOUS AVONS DÉMOLI BEAUCOUP D'ÉGLISES ET D'HOPITAUX; TUÉ BEAUCOUP DE FEMMES ET D'ENFANTS; RUINÉ.........

CHUT! PAS ÇA.......PAS ÇA...

LE MANNEQUIN TERRIBLE DU VENTRILOQUE.
TOUS DROITS RÉSERVÉS.

The two Willies. The Clown Prince. The ventriloquist's terrible dummy.
This series of cards with French language texts were produced in England. They show Emperor Wilhelm II with his son, the crown (clown) Prince Wilhelm Victor August Ernst, as a ventriloquist's dummy. 'Now, little Willy, tell us all you know about our great feats of arms.' 'All right. We have destroyed many churches and hospitals, killed many women and children, we ruined…' 'Shhhh! Not that… Not that…'

.... 1914 !
es Officiers Prussiens - Attends, ne le tue pas tout de suite, laissez-le souffrir encore.
e Germans Officers: Wait, a minute, don't kill him directly, let him suffer a little longer.

The Prussian officers: wait, don't kill him right away, let him suffer for a while!
This drawing from 1914 was created by Jack Abeillé. It is meant to illustrate the cruel nature of the German officers, who take pleasure in the death throes of a severely wounded French soldier sitting defenceless on the ground and waiting for a bullet to the head instead of receiving medical attention.

were almost exclusively aimed against Britain. Shortly after the outbreak of the war, a public campaign was organised in Germany against the UK, with many Germans considering them responsible for the conflict. The slogan, '*Gott strafe England*' – 'May God punish England', was created and quickly entered into everyday vocabulary, even decorating various picture postcards. Its creator, Ernst Lissauer, even added a poem to it called '*Hassgesang gegen England*' – 'Hymn of Hate against England'.

end furthering the rise of fascism. This may be a controversial point of view, but the way the German enemy was portrayed in France must have had its influence on the perception of Germany by the French population.

Germany only published a few cards that fall into this category, and they

The killing of the wounded.
This motif is part of a series of cards that also includes *L'Orgie* and *Bouclier Humain* among others and depicted alleged atrocities by German troops in Belgium. The Allies made an example of the international uproar following the invasion of a neutral country, and the brutal behaviour of some German units whenever possible.

Die schönsten Karten, die es gibt,
Schickt gern man denen, die man liebt.

Sentiment and Romanticism

This category mirrors the feelings of parting from family or the longing for fiancés/fiancées, spouses, children, peace and the home country. Even though no accurate numbers are available, one can easily see that the motifs addressing the issues of sentiment and romanticism make up the largest group of picture postcards by far.

At a time when only a few people ever left the place where they were born, the war forced millions of men to part from their families and homes. Many soldiers had received only basic

The nicest cards that can be bought, you love to send to those you love.
'*In Treue fest*' – 'Firm in Fidelity' was the motto of the Bavarian Army, but was often also used to demonstrate the solidarity between the German Empire and that of Austria-Hungary and could also be perfectly projected onto the connection between husband and wife at the front and at home. This picture postcard was sent from Cologne to a musketeer of the *12. Kompagnie, III. Bataillon, Infanterie-Leibregiment Großherzogin 117* (12th company, 3rd battalion of 117 Großherzogin household infantry) on 16 May 1915. At that time, this Hessian unit was deployed close to the French village of Roye on the Somme and later fought at Verdun, among other places.

schooling, meaning the ability to read and write could not be taken for granted in every country; a number of soldiers will have even been illiterate. Picture postcards with romantic images on them were a good way of communicating the intense emotions the soldiers felt, which were hard to put into words, or were forbidden from revealing.

The means of transporting emotions via picture postcards varied from country to country. The majority of the French postcards showed sickly sweet photo montages, usually a pretty girl on a light brown background. Often the marital bed is also pictured, either with the soldier and his wife, or without, but a helmet or kepi is always part of the picture. These rather outspoken images were unique to France and almost unheard of in other countries.

German and Austro-Hungarian motifs conveying sentiment or romanticism used a completely different visual language, which could be called an innocent romanticism. They are often quite matter-of-fact and feature patriotic symbols, such as oak leaves and flags, as additional decorations.

Patriotic lullaby. For France! For the home land!
Cupid plays romantic music, while under the canopy, a fervent mêlée ensues between a soldier, represented by a steel helmet and boots, and his wife. The patriotic aspect of this was the possibility of children, who might become soldiers – for France, the home country.

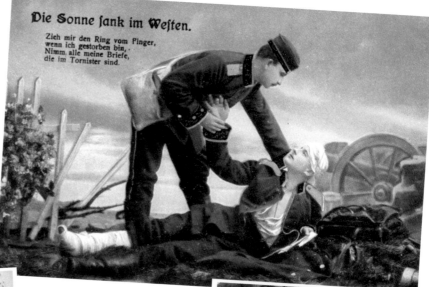

The sun sets in the West.
Motifs depicting the farewell from a heavily wounded comrade are almost exclusively German. They are usually portrayed in a heavy flowery-kitschy pseudorealism and often based on well-known soldiers' songs, like here the fourth stanza of 'The Sun sets in the West', a piece by an unknown author.

When the ebb tide flows.
The farewell to spouses, family and relatives was an often repeated motif. Between 1914 and 1918 countless millions of men left their home country, usually not by choice, and headed into an uncertain future. Most cards depict the soldier saying goodbye to a young and beautiful wife, but here, a British sailor gives comfort to his old mother.

Be brave. I'm thinking of you!
Sitting at her sewing machine, she thinks of her husband. He can be seen as a shadow in the upper-left corner, charging with a bayonet. The words on this card are not empty, as a wife wrote it to her husband after he had finished his home leave and rejoined his unit. She writes that the time after his departure was difficult, but that she is better now.

An almost exclusively German variant are the cards that depict saying farewell to a mortally wounded or fallen comrade. Their slogans include '*Die Sonne sank im Westen*' – 'The Sun set in the West', '*Ich hatte einen Kameraden*' – 'I had a comrade' or '*Stolzenfels am Rhein*' – 'Stolzenfels on the Rhine', and were borrowed from folk songs or other popular prose from Germany. Other nations' cards rarely show romanticised images of fallen soldiers, but still picture cemeteries and graves.

It appears that picture postcards with sentimental or romantic motifs were far more widely used in Germany and France than in the UK. The images from these countries do portray stronger emotions, whereas British cards in this category are far more restrained and less romantic, especially in their choice of motifs.

Nina with a jewellery box by Raphael Kirchner (1876-1917). Kirchner was born in Vienna but worked in Paris from about 1900 onwards, for *La Vie Parisienne* magazine amongst others. Shortly before his death in 1917, he emigrated to New York. His nudes painted in the style of the Art Nouveau were extremely popular during the war and soldiers collected them. After his early death, his wife, Nina, who modelled for all his pin-ups, tried to commit suicide. She was not successful and became addicted to opium, the use of which eventually killed her.

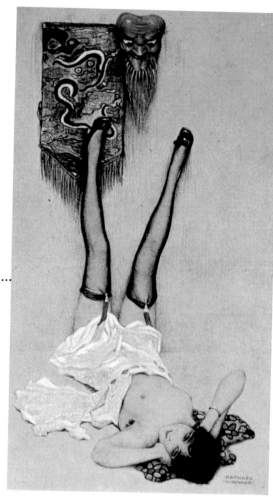

The dispassionate mask. Another illustration by Raphael Kirchner which clearly shows why he was so popular, especially with his male audience. This motif was published in late 1914 and was part of a series with similarly erotic images.

Pin-ups

Due to the war, millions of young men found themselves cooped together in barracks, tents, trenches and dugouts. This understandably resulted in an increased requirement for pictures of women in different stages of undress. These needs were mainly met by French publishers, photographers and artists, who for some time had been allowed more freedom in this genre than their colleagues in other countries; both Germany and the UK were far more puritanical in these matters.

The motifs of pin-up postcards (although the term 'pin-up' had not been coined yet), range from the very innocent, through unabashedly erotic to the clearly pornographic. Of course, these cards were not meant to be sent to families but were collected by the men, either to carry with them or to decorate the walls of their dug-outs.

Perhaps the best known artist of this genre is Raphael Kirchner. He was born in Austria, worked in Paris for several magazines, among them *La Vie Parisienne* magazine, where the pin-up was actually invented, and died in New York in 1917. He became famous for his nude portraits of his wife, Nina, which were inspired by Art Nouveau. Other renowned artists of the genre were the two Frenchmen, Xavier Sager and Ney, and the Italians, Mauzan and Rappini.

The Swedish illustrator, Byrnoff Wennerberg, was quite popular in the more reserved Germany and first worked for the well-respected magazines, *Lustige Blätter* and *Simplicissimus*. During the war he created two series of postcards from the Home Front, which pictured attractive and well-groomed young ladies of better standing, showing special interest and admiration for a soldier who was also in the picture. Wennerberg liked to model the young women after his daughters.

Postcards of pin-ups were most likely far more

Vorpoſten im Feuer.

Miss Lieutenant.
During the First World War, real pin-ups (the word was not even invented yet…) were only published in France, where the attitudes towards public displays of female beauty were much more laid-back than in Germany or England. Germany rather favoured this type of starry eyed, romantic and rather kitsch-ridden depictions of young ladies.

Fräulein Leutnant

Picket under fire.
Real pin-up postcards with erotic images were rarely published in Germany, and if they were, they were not available through normal shops. Here gentlemen had to be content with modestly dressed but not lesser attractive ladies. These two were painted by Brynoff Wennerberg (1866-1950), who created illustrations for magazines as famous as *Lustige Blätter* and *Simplicissimus* among others. He mainly drew illustrations of women on the home front, most likely often using his daughters as models.

belongings, if the soldier in question was wounded or killed. This was especially true for cards with motifs of an obvious sexual nature.

popular than the surviving examples lead us to believe. The number of cards in circulation was enormous, but they were hidden carefully from outside view. Several sources report soldiers destroying their collections before a large attack, so they would not be sent to their families with their

Amorous decorations.
A pin-up by the French artist, Ney. The millions of young men, often parted from their homes, young ladies, fiancées or wives for the first time, desired female beauty. The painted pin-ups by Fontan, Kirchner, Sager or Ney, to name only a few French artists, decorated the walls of almost every accommodation or dugout. Picture postcards like this one were almost never mailed, they were collected and guarded as treasures by their owner.

Meinen Einzigen gab ich dem Kaiser.
„Andacht für den Sohn im Felde."

I gave the emperor my only one. Devotions for a son in the field.
A German mother holding a bible prays for her only son, who is deployed with his regiment. In a time mostly without telephones, the post was the only means of communication. Cards with motifs that did not romanticise or glorify the war were rather uncommon, especially in Germany.

Anti-War Propaganda

The cards in this category bear witness to the horrors of war and its consequences, without taking sides or trying to point out a guilty party. They are quite rare, were usually published in neutral states, and were sold in larger numbers, mainly in the Netherlands and Switzerland.

The warring countries most likely had limited need for motifs of this kind and the authorities will not have encouraged their distribution. Although no general bans were issued, cards with clear anti-war messages could be censored, as it was presumed they would have a negative effect on public morale and the fighting power of their own forces.

Most anti-war postcards showed the suffering of the population, the agonies of the soldiers and several other cruelties inflicted by war. This could either be done ostentatiously or by quite subtle means. A good example of the latter are the images of grieving parents, spouses and children at a soldier's grave – a motif that appears in many guises in Germany, France and Belgium.

These cards may have been published for a number of different reasons, which are difficult

Grieving Europe.
The Greek goddess Europa, shown on the right of the card, grieves that her whole continent has become a battlefield, while the devil, on the left of the picture, now reigns. This apocalyptical picture from 1915 by the Swiss artist, Weiss, takes no sides, but shows the torments of the rank and file and the horrors of the civilian population, against the backdrop of a burning city.

Sur la tombe des martyrs.

At the martyrs' grave.
This Belgian card shows a family grieving their loss at the grave of their husband, father and bread-winner. The surroundings are shown in devastation, which spells out the hardships of the civilian population near the front lines in Belgium and northern France. On the Eastern Front and in the Balkans, the situation was often even more desperate.

to determine today. They could be used as a quiet protest against the war, as well as a special form of motivation, urging the need to continue the fight now more than ever.

The anti-war category also contains the hunger cards published in Germany from 1916 onwards, which portrayed the increasingly difficult food situation at home and therefore indirectly criticised the war policy of the German Reich. As this had a negative impact on the civilian population's will to persevere, not to mention the morale of the troops, they were eventually banned.

Wir haben den Krieg nicht gewollt!

We did not want the war.
An interesting German real photo card with a collection of unexploded shells of different calibres. Without knowing the context of the picture, it is impossible to judge whether the text is supposed to mean that the instigators oppose the war in general or only want to point out that Germany is not at fault.

LA TOMBE DU FILS.

The son's grave.
A French officer grieves at the grave of his son, who was buried in a field. The simple wooden cross with the kepi on top marks his last resting place. The drawing by A. de Broca was also published in *L'Illustration* magazine.

Chapter 3

The First World War

The First World War lasted from 28 July 1914 to 11 November 1918. It was fought by almost thirty countries, with the loss of 20 million soldiers and non-combatants. This worldwide struggle caused unspeakable sorrow, drastically changed the map of Europe and laid the foundation for even bloodier murder, twenty years later.

An Unnecessary Catastrophe

This was an unnecessary conflict and unlike the Second World War, none of the parties involved were eager to fight. However, the long-standing distrust and suspicions surrounding the intents of the others involved started a downward spiral of sabre-rattling and ultimatums, finally leading to the catastrophe, as each state involved feared losing face if it backed out. After the war broke out, it quickly became clear that modern

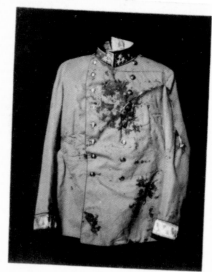

Das Geschoß drang durch die Naht auf der rechten Kragenseite ein und durchschlug die Halsschlagader. Diese tödliche Wunde wurde nicht sofort entdeckt; die Ärzte durchschnitten, da sie einen Herzschuß vermuteten, die linke Seite des Rockes und dann den ganzen Rock an der Rückseite. Erst nach Entfernung des Kleidungsstückes konnte der Ort der Verletzung festgestellt werden,

Tunic of Archduke Franz Ferdinand.
Together with his wife, Sophie, the Archduke and heir to the throne of the Austro-Hungarian Monarchy was shot by the Serbian nationalist, Gavrilo Princip, on 28 July 1914. The archduke bled to death after the bullet had penetrated the collar of his tunic and severed the carotid artery. The doctors cut him out of his tunic which, still covered in his blood, is now on show in the collection of the *Heeresgeschichtliches Museum* (Museum of Military History) in Vienna, together with the car in which he was riding.

... Serbien muss sterbien!

Serbia must die!
This motif was published shortly after the assassination and mirrors the sentiments of the time. Serbia is depicted as the archetypical terrorist with a bomb and a knife, smashed by a strong Austrian fist. The assassination was in fact convenient for Austria-Hungary, as its military had been searching for an occasion to settle scores with Serbia for a while, and considered them responsible for the continuing unrest in the Balkans.

LO CZAR DELLA PACE.

The tsar of peace.
This Italian propaganda card shows the Russian tsar plucking the feathers from an angel of peace. Tsar Nicholas II (1868-1918) was one of the initiators of the The Hague Peace Conference of 1899, but his loyalty to the alliance with Serbia made him a key factor in the outbreak of the First World War, which would indirectly cost him his life. Although he had abdicated the throne in March 1917, he and his family were murdered by the Communists in July 1918.

and unspeakable suffering had been caused.

The first shot of the First World War fell in Sarajevo on 28 July 1914, when the heir to the Austrian throne, Archduke Franz Ferdinand, was assassinated by a Serbian nationalist. This political murder started a chain reaction of ultimatums and declarations of war, finally resulting in a bloodshed of previously unknown dimensions that affected the majority of the world's population. The reason behind the assassination lies in the situation in the Balkans, where for years, the territory of the weakened Ottoman Empire had been disputed both openly and in secret.

The war began on 28 July 1914, when Austria-Hungary declared war on Serbia, resulting in the mobilisation of Russian forces. Immediately afterwards, the German Empire mobilised its forces, with France following suite the next day.

technology had radically changed the rules of warfare. However, by the time the high commands had acknowledged this and changed their tactics, millions of soldiers had already died

Lieb' Vaterland magst ruhig sein!

Dear fatherland, no fear be thine!
A German card typical for the beginning of the war. A German soldier happily smoking his pipe sorts out the three most important opponents of his home country: Russia, the UK and France. The card was printed in the first few weeks of the war, as it was already being posted in September 1914.

ADORATION

THE WISE MEN
OFFER THEIR PRESENTS

LES PRÉSENTS
DES ROIS MAGES

Adoration. The Wise Men offer their Presents.
A drawing by the Dutch artist, Louis Raemaekers, showing the emperors of Germany, Austria-Hungary and the Sultan of Turkey as the three wise men, but instead of gold, incense and myrrh they present weapons and ammunition to the divine child. Raemaekers was extremely anti-German and came to worldwide fame with his drawings, which mainly documented the sufferings of the civilian population.

....

On 3 August, Germany declared war on France and invaded neutral Belgium the following day (4 August). This act led to the UK declaring war on Germany, meaning it had taken only eight days for two large coalitions to be at war with each other.

On one side were Germany and Austria-Hungary (later joined by Turkey and Bulgaria), who due to their central location in Europe, were called the 'Central Powers'. The opposing side was made up of Serbia, Belgium, France, England and Russia, who were called 'Entente' or 'Allies'. Over the course of the war, this second coalition would be reinforced by Portugal, Japan, Italy, Romania, Greece, Brazil, Cuba, Panama and the USA.

Considering the large number of states involved, the various front lines and the fact that the soldiers fighting it came from all over the globe, the struggle between the European states swiftly developed to a conflict that warranted the designation 'World War'. The First World War was also a total war, affecting all aspects of social life, the economy and the role of women in society.

The war was primarily fought in western Europe, but many other places also became battlefields, such as eastern Europe, Russia, the Balkans, the Italo-Austrian border, Africa, Asia, the Middle East and even the high-seas. Many soldiers from colonies or

....

We stand together firm and loyal!
Four officers of the Central Powers walking arm in arm. From the left to the right: Bulgaria, Turkey, Austria-Hungary and Germany. The term Central Powers can be explained by the geographical location in Europe of the two original allies, Germany and Austria-Hungary.

Wir halten fest und treu zusammen!

LA SAINTE ALLIANCE — HET HEILIG VERBOND

The Holy Alliance.
This Belgian card refers to the alliance between the French Republic and tsarist Russia, which was forged in 1894. Even though the two countries had little in common, they still agreed on being wary of Germany. Both profited from massive French investment in the expansion of the Russian railway system; France especially from the fact that in case of mobilisation, its ally could move its army into action on the German border much faster by rail.

Reasons and Causes

A question that has been researched for almost a century is, 'how could things come to this?' Undoubtedly, tensions between some European states were running high at the beginning of the twentieth century; high enough that some saw the outbreak of war as an act of liberation. The hope was to gain victory over the enemy in a swift and energetically led campaign, gain positive influence on international relationships and thus secure a bright future. This was the view of many Germans especially, among them leading military men, manufacturers, scientists and government officials – but only a few Frenchmen saw it this way. Germany wanted colonies, overseas markets, power and prestige, whereas France was still very aware of the loss of Alsace and Lorraine. In the UK, the German bid for more influence in world politics – and on the high-seas – caused great discomfort, and there

overseas territories fought for the UK and France. Forces from India, Canada, Australia, New Zealand and Nepal, for example, fought for Britain, while soldiers from Algeria, Morocco, Senegal, Madagascar and former Indochina (Vietnam, Laos and Cambodia) fought and died for France.

This Italian card portrays the warring countries as dogs having sunk their jaws into a map of Europe. The caricature was created before Italy entered the war in May 1915, as the dog with the green-white-red neckerchief (Italy) is still sitting on the side, watching the turmoil. At first, the initial neutrality of Italy led to very different motifs: in favour of staying neutral, for or against the Entente and for or against the Central Powers. After Italy joined the war, the majority of caricatures were criticisms of Austria-Hungary.

United against the Barbarians.
'Barbarians' was a common term for all Germans, followed by the French term '*boches*' and the English 'huns.' The term 'huns' originated from an address by Emperor Wilhelm II, given when German troops embarked to East Africa, supposedly to put down the Boxer Rebellion. From left to right, the three soldiers symbolise the UK, Belgium and France. The Frenchman is purposefully shown with his hands on the Belgian's shoulders in a supportive gesture. The upper third of the picture shows a Russian cavalry squadron on the move.

L'Entente Cordiale – Cordial Agreement.
The Alliance between France and England was forged in 1904, not least to lay to rest colonial issues and also to indirectly assure mutual support against the mounting power of the German Empire. Three years later, the UK also signed a treaty with Russia, who had been allied to France since 1894. Thus, the Triple Entente was formed.

was little desire to accept a power shift on the continent and on the oceans.

The Balkans had recently seen two wars that had shifted the borders of the crumbling Ottoman Empire and Austria-Hungary now wanted to occupy Serbia and finally put an end to the unrest on its south-eastern borders. This played into the hands of Russia, who hoped to gain access to the Mediterranean Sea by assisting

its Slavic brother nation. To Germany and Russia, the outside enemies were also a welcome distraction from domestic problems. Other countries who joined the war later on (Bulgaria, Italy, Greece, Japan and Romania), hoped to gain something from the war and enlarge their national territories.

The danger stemming from the low-key conflicts was increased by the alliances formed by various European states, causing a chain reaction. The rather weak Austria-Hungary first formed an alliance with its strong neighbour Germany, as Serbia relied on its alliance with

91   GUERRE DE 1914. — De bons alliés !
A good shake hand !
Reproduction interdite

HANS IST DABEI·ER KOMMT·ER KOMMT ZURÜCK MUTTER!

A good shake hand! – The war of 1914. – The good allies! A good handshake!

Pictures that showed good cooperation and friendship between allies were quite common. This picture was most likely taken in Autumn 1914, in south-western Belgium, and shows from left to right a British naval officer, a British sailor, a Belgian soldier and a *Spahi Algériens* from the French colony, Algeria. For commercial reasons the texts on these postcards were often bilingual (or tri – or even quadrilingual). The quality of the English text on French cards ranged from relatively sloppy to almost unreadable.

Hans is among them – He's coming – He's coming back mother!

From their window, a mother and daughter are waving at the German soldiers parading through the city, their son and brother amongst them. Perhaps this was meant to refer to the swift end of the war and the safe return of their loved ones, which was still the general expectation in 1914. Some form of worry was nevertheless discernable and it was clear that even a short war would not be without casualties.

Russia, which in turn was allied with France. Belgium was a neutral state, and its neutrality was guaranteed by the UK, which was allied to France by the 'Entente Cordiale', although the two states had no actual military relations. Nevertheless, the UK had forces that could be immediately deployed across the Channel to Belgium in order to intervene, should Germany attack France.

Technology played a further role in the drama, especially the network of railways that had continued to expand since the middle of the nineteenth century. Complex plans had been developed to deploy armies to their staging areas swiftly and on time, by moving soldiers and materials to their designated positions by train. Once this machinery had been set in motion, it could not be stopped without giving a potential opponent valuable information and strategic advantages. If mobilisation was started late, there was the risk of the enemy arriving on the doorstep before your own forces were ready for action.

Japanese infantryman.
Together with Bulgaria, Greece, Italy and Romania, Japan was among the countries that entered the war in order to enlarge their territory. Japan actually did this by annexing parts of China and a number of islands in the Pacific Ocean. The watercolour belongs to a series by Emile Dupuis.

A long round of Skat, Berlin-Paris.
During the long train ride from Berlin to Paris, German soldiers play a round of *Skat*, one of the most popular card games in Germany. This picture illustrates the role of railways as the most important means of transporting troops to the front, and the graffiti on the railway carriages mirror the opinion shared by all powers involved that this would be a short campaign. The card bears a postmark from 29 August 1914, one week before the First Battle of the Marne, during which the German Army would actually come dangerously close to Paris.

Emperors, Kings and Generals

In 1914, the question whether – and when – to mobilise was not answered by democratically elected politicians, who would make an informed and rational decision after consulting with capable and well-informed military leaders. At the beginning of the twentieth century, political and military decisions lay in the hands of a few 'great men', who usually owed their position to their last name. They were primarily emperors, kings and tsars, followed by marshals, generals and admirals, and last but not least, a small group of professional politicians, who in addition to their titles, also had considerable financial means at

Cordial Agreement.
The Allies of 1914 at work: three British and two French soldiers demonstrate their understanding of each other for the photographer. The picture was taken at a train station, as a railway carriage can be seen to the right. One of the British soldiers has looped his bandolier over his arm and carries two canteens. Considering the soldiers' equipment they have not just arrived by train.

CROQUIS DE GUERRE 1914

Mobilisation - Dans toutes les gares, le départ fut enthousiaste.
c'est au cri de « Vive la France ! » que tous ont répondu à
l'ordre d'appel.

Mobilisation. Departure was enthusiastic at all stations, the enlistment orders were answered with cries of 'Long live France'.
Frenchmen, still in civilian clothing, depart from a train station. There are at least two variants with differing texts of this card from the *Croquis de Guerre* series. One claims the station to be that of Meaux, the other describes the scene as the arrival of foreign volunteers.

their disposal. The majority of the population looked up to these important men and were convinced that their skills, traits and views would decide the course of history.

This was a common attitude among the citizens of the Central Powers especially, i.e. those under the German Emperor Wilhelm II and his Austro-Hungarian counterpart, Franz Joseph, as well as in Russia, where Tsar Nicholas II ruled absolutely. His nephew, George V, had substantially less power as king of the United Kingdom, but like the Belgian king, Albert I, remained an important national symbol.

The main roles in the development of the conflict, however, were played by the two emperors and the tsar. After the assassination of his heir,

Franz Ferdinand, Franz Joseph issued a pro forma ultimatum to Serbia, requesting it eliminate all anti-Austrian propaganda and separatist efforts. Serbia generally accepted the ultimatum, but refused to tolerate interference in its domestic affairs, and immediately started to mobilise its forces, forcing Austria-Hungary to declare war on Serbia. In response, the Russian tsar mobilised his forces, with Germany giving similar orders soon afterwards. And so a combination of years of tension, a system of alliances and their mobilisation schemes, and irresponsible behaviour by high-ranking personalities carrying politicians and military

Infanterie auf der Fahrt nach dem Kriegsschauplatz.

Infantry en route to the theatre of war.
Once again, the railway is the most important means of transporting troops and the picture was certainly taken during the early phase of mobilisation. The soldiers waving from the railway carriage wear *Pickelhaube* spiked helmets and or peaked caps. The carriage is decorated with laurel wreaths, oak leaves and flags.

Germany and Austria. We stand together firm and loyal.
This simple drawing by Anton Hoffmann, from Munich, shows a German and Austrian soldier side by side with the often quoted motto '*Fest und Treu zusammen*' – 'firm and loyal together.' However, it was not an alliance of equals, as the German Army was much stronger and had to bail out its Austro-Hungarian allies again and again.

Isn't it annoying, Papa? It's more difficult than we thought.
A card by the well-known British illustrator, T. Gilson, that was also supposedly for the French market. It shows Emperor Wilhelm II and his eldest son, Crown Prince Friedrich Wilhelm Victor August Ernst. To the average German, the emperor was a demi-god – to his enemies a perfect target for ridicule and hatred.

leaders in their wake, finally resulted in the inevitable outbreak of war.

Tactics and Technology

On the eve of the First World War, almost all general staffs regarded an offensive as their best choice: a massive attack with strong infantry forces, who were well armed and determined, simply had to result in a swift victory. Certainly, the effects of modern small arms and the use of mobile artillery in defence were hugely underestimated. This was most likely due to the fact that the European military leaders had mainly used the Franco-Prussian War of 1870-

71, as a reference for future wars and was predominantly of the opinion that France had lost the war by using its forces too defensively. This may have been true, but in the forty years since the war a revolution had taken place in the field of weapons technology, meaning they were now capable of immensely more firepower. During the Boer War and the Russo-Japanese War, it became clear that modern rifles, machine guns and artillery pieces had a far bigger influence on the outcome of a battle than the unshakeable belief in the full-frontal assault. Personal qualities such as courage, enthusiasm or a death-defying attitude no longer decided the outcome of a battle. War

LES MONSTRES DES CATHÉDRALES Nº 2

François-Joseph. Le sinistre vorace qui non content d'avoir étouffé la Bosnie, l'Herzé-govine, le Trentin et Trieste voudrait encore dévorer la Serbie.

The cathedral monsters, No. 2, Francis-Joseph. The sinister glutton who, not content with having suffocated Bosnia, Herzegovina, the Trentino and Trieste, now wants to swallow Serbia.
On the list of the most despicable European rulers, the Austrian Emperor Franz Joseph was second only to Wilhelm II. This card also mentions the Trentino and Trieste, both territories desired by Italy, and the means by which the UK and France drew Italy into the war on the side of the Entente.

had now become mechanised by machine guns, rapid-fire guns, tanks, airplanes and gas. Means of transportation and communication such as railways, cars, telegraphs and radio sets, complemented defensive means like trenches, barbed wire and concrete bunkers.

After the armies had fought each other using modern equipment and old tactics for three and a half years, and suffered immense losses for no real territorial gains, in the spring of 1918 the German offensive used a new tactic that appeared to be effective. It mainly consisted of a short, very strong and well-aimed artillery barrage, followed by assault troops who crossed no-man's-land as soon as the barrage stopped, and entered the enemy trenches, taking their lines as far as possible. The Americans and the growing number of French and British tanks are to be thanked for stopping the German advance. A few months later, the combination of the arrival of the USA, the tank, and eventually the new Allied tactic of the 'all arms battle' (a perfect coordination of infantry, artillery, tanks and aircraft), finally tipped the balance of this war of attrition in favour of the Entente.

Logistics

As well as tactics and technology, logistics also played a very important role in the war. The high

Armée belge   La garde de l'aéroplane.

The Belgian Army. The aeroplane guard.
This card is part of a series published in around 1912, and symbolises the progress that would cause a warfare revolution. Two Uhlans on horses guard a Farman aeroplane. Soon after the outbreak of the war, this unarmed pusher aircraft was replaced by more powerful planes that could carry machine guns and bombs. The Farman was also among the first aircraft used for military purposes in France and the Netherlands.

3. LA POMPELLE — Tank allemand capturé devant le Fort
German captured Thank

La Pompelle. German tank captured before the fortress.

From 1917 onwards, the tank took over an increasingly important role in warfare. England and France spearheaded the development of this new weapon, whereas the German high command pursued its development only half-heartedly. Therefore, most tanks used by the Germans were British vehicles that had been captured, like the one abandoned here in front of La Pompelle fortress, which was most likely taken out of combat on 1 June 1918. La Pompelle was an important fortress in the ring of fortifications guarding Reims.

commands were confronted with various problems of previously unknown proportions; millions of soldiers with a multitude of different weapons, their transport towards the front or the

A German machine gun with additional armour for the cooling jacket on a sled mount. The crew wears gas masks. At the outbreak of the war, the German Army had about 5,000 machine guns at its disposal, roughly the same number as the French Army. The German MG 08 was an improved version of the 1888 Maxim (almost identical models were introduced in Belgium, Bulgaria, the UK and Russia) and could fire about 600 rounds per minute. Without much effort, a couple of cleverly placed machine guns crewed by well-trained soldiers could bring even a large scale infantry attack to a screeching halt.

rear, the evacuation of casualties and prisoners of war, not to mention the enormous amount of ammunition, food, water and other supplies that had to be brought up. Some aspects had already been meticulously planned in advance, for example, the deployment of troops by railway, following mobilisation. In other areas, the new developments caught the authorities completely unprepared, including the artillery's massive use of ammunition. In 1914, 1,000 to 1,500 rounds per gun were considered absolutely sufficient, but during the war it

An ammunition supply train in marching order shortly before battle.
Although the military leaders had meticulously planned the mobilisation and transport of millions of soldiers to the front line, they had apparently completely underestimated the amount of ammunition necessary for the small arms and artillery. It took enormous efforts to not only produce, but also to transport the ammunition for armies of this inconceivable size, efforts that tied up resources and personnel.

The war in the North. On the main roads. The hunt for the Taube.
Built by the Rumpler factories, the Taube was one of the first German military aeroplanes and thus its name became synonymous for all German planes. The new weapon of the military aeroplane necessitated new means of defence, which led to the development of anti-aircraft machine guns and anti-aircraft artillery. This image shows a French Hotchkiss machine gun, which were sometimes mounted on cars. Meanwhile, the driver serves as spotter and searches the skies with his binoculars.

LA GUERRE DANS LE NORD
6 Sur les grandes routes - La Chasse au Taube

544

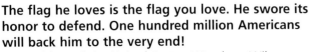

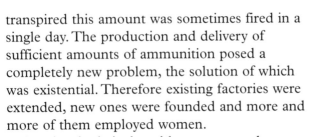

The flag he loves is the flag you love. He swore its honor to defend. One hundred million Americans will back him to the very end!

As president of the United States, Woodrow Wilson seemed determined to keep the USA out of the war for a long time, which led to his re-election on 7 November 1916. However his country was never really neutral, providing huge amounts of strategic supplies to the Allies, which were partially funded by American bonds. Wilson declared war against Germany on 2 April 1917.

The United Forces.

This British card shows the ideal role models of the First World War: two handsome youths, he a dashing army officer, she a nurse. Several hundred thousand young women registered to serve with relief organisations during the war, usually without any medical training. They worked in one of the many casualty clearing stations, at aid posts or in civilian or field hospitals and homes for recuperating soldiers. Many women served under dangerous conditions close to the front line and a number lost their lives due to the fighting.

transpired this amount was sometimes fired in a single day. The production and delivery of sufficient amounts of ammunition posed a completely new problem, the solution of which was existential. Therefore existing factories were extended, new ones were founded and more and more of them employed women.

Another logistical problem was petroleum

supplies, the crucial fuel for an increasingly industrialised warfare. The various powers tried to cut off their opponents' supply lines using mutual blockades to prevent the importation of petroleum, coal, and other resources such as food and in doing so, force them into surrender. The British blockade caused major supply problems in Germany, while the

Community service act. The new orderly.
The Central Powers also suffered from a lack of human resources as the war went on, which Germany tried to address with the *Civildienst-Gesetz*. From 1916 onwards, this law involved compulsory community service for men not serving in the army and a voluntary community service for women. This card by the artist A. Gumbart, is part of a series that includes at least two more motifs. The lady, who looks a little embarrassed here, also served as a clerk and cook.

A French Sergeant-Chef poses for the camera with his wife. In order to leave a picture with those they left behind, many soldiers had themselves photographed (with or without a fiancée or spouse), before they were sent to the front. One in five *poilus* was not to return from the war, so a picture postcard was often the last tangible memory.

increasing use of German submarines from 1917 onwards almost brought down the British economy. Only the power of the US Navy, the massive number of ships they could build, and the introduction of sailing in convoys could prevent a defeat.

Total War

The First World War can be considered a total war, as it had substantial impact on all aspects of social, political and economic life. In the best case, the mobilisation of millions of young men meant only the temporary loss of a son, brother, husband and provider. The price of food and all basic supplies increased drastically, if they could be had at all. Over the course of the war, diseases and epidemics caused huge losses amongst the weakened civilian population. Trucks, buses and

horses were considered strategic supplies and were commandeered by the authorities (who calculated one horse per three soldiers), civic rights were restricted and emergency laws passed. Substantial areas suffered from displacement or occupation by enemy troops.

One of the few positive aspects of the World War, if the word can be used in this context at all, was female empowerment. As virtually every man was in the trenches, there was a massive lack of labourers. Many positions previously only open to men were increasingly filled by women, giving them an independence they had not known before. Although after the war most positions were taken over again by men, the huge number of working women had still initiated a change in the mentality of the population.

Miss Field Grey.
One of the many motifs showing a woman in uniform. Apart from a handful of exceptions, women did not take direct part in the fighting, but often carried out dangerous work behind the front line, as well as unhealthy work in the factories at home, producing strategic goods. These cards were supposed to give the men at the front a distraction and were often used to decorate their otherwise bare accommodations. As the hole left from a drawing-pin proves, this picture postcard also used to be pinned to a wall somewhere.

Chapter 4

Countries and Armies

During the First World War, dozens of countries were at war with each other, at least on paper. In reality, however, the war was decided by the armies of six states: France, Germany, Russia, the UK, Austria-Hungary and the USA. The forces of Belgium, Serbia, Montenegro, Turkey, Bulgaria and Italy also played important roles and whilst Japan, Portugal, Romania and Greece were involved in the fighting, it was only on a limited scale.

The Division

The combat strength of an army is mainly defined by the number of soldiers it can muster, and the measure for this was the division. The majority of the soldiers were infantrymen who could march about 50km per day, carrying 25-30kg of equipment.

The company was the smallest tactical unit, numbering roughly 200 soldiers led by a captain. Four companies formed a battalion, which with the battalion HQ and supporting units would consist of around 1,000 men. A regiment consisted of between two and six battalions. Two to four regiments of infantry and cavalry, artillery and additional technical units formed a division, the key element of tactical formations. The average infantry division numbered about 18,000 soldiers and 5,000 to 6,000 horses. Except for the USA, where divisions were roughly $1\frac{1}{2}$ times as strong, these general numbers are correct for all countries involved in the war.

The armoury of an infantry division was made up of roughly 12,000 rifles, 24 machine guns and 72 artillery pieces. Over the course of the war, the number of soldiers in a division decreased in all countries, whereas the number of machine guns, artillery pieces and other weapons increased steadily. In Autumn 1914, the Entente could muster around 178 divisions as opposed to

Chiché Gve Ouvière
Reproduction interdite
240 - LA TRIPLE ENTENTE
Départ d'un Réserviste
« *SOYEZ SAGE ET A BIENTOT* »
Editeur Barabino, 38, Rue d'Aubagne - Marseille

The Triple Entente. Departure of a reservist. Be brave and see you soon.
After several years of compulsory service, the men of almost all European countries had to be available for military service and could be called up for exercises in wartime even after their fiftieth birthday. This card shows an older French reservist saying goodbye to his two children.

The date on this huge shell proves that the picture was taken during the last phase of the war. The soldier, a *Gefreiter* (a rank comparable to lance-corporal), wears the typical uniform including a Model 1915 field blouse and a Model 1916 steel helmet, which in this picture features the rather uncommon camouflage paint that was only introduced in July 1918. On his shoulder he carries the typical weapon of the German infantry, the Gewehr 98 rifle.

Vorposten – Outpost.
A soldier of the Austro-Hungarian Army in full kit leans on his Mannlicher rifle to make the 25-30kg weight of his equipment more bearable. This load was roughly the same size in all European armies. The painting was created by Hans Larwin (1873-1938), an official war painter of the Dual Monarchy.

In Belgium. Ypres. A trench at the front.
In 1914, Belgium commanded an army of roughly 200,000 men. The combat forces were structured into six infantry divisions and one cavalry division and numbered about 115,000 troops. This picture was most likely taken in November 1914, when the German advance had been brought to a halt south-west of the river Yser.

Déploiement d'Infanterie - Avant l'attaque
Aux abords de la route de Varedde

Infantry deployment before an attack
Along the road of Varredde

Infantry deployment before an attack. Along the road of Varredde. At the point of departure the platoons of a French infantry company take up their positions for an attack. A company numbered about 200 men and was led by a *Capitaine* (captain), four companies formed a battalion. The name of the French village is misspelled on the card, it should be Varreddes, which is located on the Marne, near Meaux.

around 166 divisions for the Central Powers. The numbers of the Entente included twenty-four Russian cavalry divisions, numbering 5,000 cavalrymen each.

Except for the British Army, which up to 1916 consisted only of professional soldiers and volunteers, the majority of soldiers were conscripts. Aged around 18 to 20 years-old, all men were drafted to do from eighteen to thirty-six months of compulsory service, during which they were trained as soldiers. After this, they had to be available for military service up to the age of 40 or even 50 years-old, and could firstly be called upon to serve in the reserve, then the militia and finally the home guard.

All countries with compulsory service had more or less similar regulations, with only the numbers of drafted recruits changing. In Germany, where the numbers of children were high, and even more so in Russia, only parts of the male population theoretically obliged to serve were actually drafted. On the other hand, in France, every man had to serve.

France

In 1914 France had a population of about 40 million and a rather large army; it was the only one of the major warring countries with a comprehensive peacetime national service. After

A French infantry unit marches by. The rank and file march in line, with the NCOs staggered on the side. The officers move on horseback. An infantry unit was expected to cover a daily average of 30km. Even though an increasing number of horses were used and motorisation was continually expanded during the course of the war, short and medium distances were usually covered by foot.

CAMPAGNE DE 1914
Escadron de Dragons en observation

135   ND. Phot.

Campaign of 1914. A squadron of dragoons on observation.
Although the dragoons in the picture have carbines slung across their backs, their most important weapon is the lance. Cavalry charges with couched lances still happened in limited numbers, but on the Western Front they were soon history. This picture postcard had already been published before the war, although at that time the text referred to an exercise. With the text adapted to the circumstances, the reprint most likely took place in August or September 1914.

mobilisation, which included all able-bodied men up to the age of forty-eight, the army grew five to six times its original size. By the end of 1914 it could muster roughly 4 million soldiers (80 divisions). Between 1914 and 1918, around 8.4 million Frenchmen were in service, divided into first line, reserve and militia forces and mainly led by a reserve officer.

The majority of the French Army consisted of infantrymen divided into companies, which were commanded by a mounted *capitaine*. Sixty-seven infantry divisions consisting of roughly 3 million soldiers could be formed after mobilisation. The French infantryman quickly received the nickname '*poilu*', a term loosely translated as 'hairy one', and meaning an energetic, down-to-earth man.

The *poilu* of 1914 was basically a moving target; not only did he wear a rather flashy

The valiant commanders of the glorious French Army.
The Commander-in-Chief, Joffre, surrounded by his generals. Joffre's handling of the initial phase of the war was less than successful, but his leadership during the First Battle of the Marne, which brought a halt to the German offensive, made him a hero in France. Due to the poor preparations around Verdun and the catastrophes on the Somme, he was replaced by Nivelle in December 1916. But Nivelle also had to resign his post after a couple of unsuccessful and extremely bloody offensives that had driven several units of the French Army to outright mutiny.

La Fessée!

En Avant !
Avec ce joujou heureux on embroche
Un echantillon de la race boche.

DIX
312/5

The beating.

This French postcard was published in the first months of the war and could be said to epitomise 'wishful thinking'. Even though the Germans could not successfully carry through their deployment plan, they nevertheless gained a lot of territory and occupied large areas. This picture is interesting, however, for its depiction of uniforms. Whereas the British soldier wears khaki all over, the Frenchman is still in a blue tunic, red trousers and a red kepi, and carries his shiny mess tin on his knapsack – making him an ideal target.

Onwards! With this nice toy we'll skewer an example of the *boche* (German) race.

The 'nice toy' this rather vicious text refers to, is the bayonet for the Lebel rifle. It was 52cm long, sharpened to a point and had a cruciform cross section that made it useful for thrusting. The card was printed in the second half of the war and shows the changed appearance of the *poilu*. He now wears the 'horizon blue' uniform and a steel helmet that was called *casque Adrian*. The mess tin is still sitting on top of his knapsack and most likely gives about the same protection as the rather thin helmet..

uniform consisting of a blue tunic, red trousers and a red kepi, he also carried his metal mess tin on his knapsack. His red garments already drew attention at a great distance and the flashing bowl at the back of his neck gave the enemy a perfect target. One year later, the red trousers were history and the new colour of the uniform was 'horizon blue'. The kepi gave way to the steel helmet called 'Adrian' and only the mess tin remained unchanged.

The French Army also commanded another

important branch of arms at the outset of the war, namely eighty-nine cavalry regiments. The light cavalry consisted of mounted infantrymen and hussars, and was armed with carbines and sabres, while the heavy cavalry at this time still carried lances. In the beginning, the *cuirassiers* wore the *cuirass*, a breastplate, and polished metal helmets, similar to the dragoons.

Among the cavalry's main tasks were reconnaissance, dispatch and courier services as well as flank protection. In addition to this, the

Four older French soldiers with a St Etienne machine gun. The box holding the tools, equipment and spare parts for the weapon can be seen to the front-left. The two soldiers on the right each hold an ammunition strip, which was used to feed ammunition into the gun. On 29 July 1916, a French soldier sent this card to his brother, starting with the words *Je suis toujours en bonne santé* – 'I am still in good health' – a phrase that can be found on almost all French cards sent home from the front.

Decorating the brave.
Joffre presents medals to a *Turco* from Algeria, a *Spahi* from Morocco and a *Chasseur d'Alpin*, most likely from France. The group is flanked by an officer on the left and a private on the right. The motif was certainly supposed to point out the diversity of the French Army, as well as documenting how different nations bravely fought side by side.

28   L'ARMÉE FRANÇAISE. — Dragons. — Manœuvre des Mitrailleuses. — I...

The French Army. Dragoons. Machine-gun exercises.
Although this coloured card was published around 1910 it shows a situation that was still true in 1914. Dragoons, nineteenth century heavy cavalry in colourful uniforms wearing shiny helmets with horsehair plumes, are manning one of the deadliest weapons ever. It perfectly symbolises the change from the brave warrior to a battlefield dominated by technology.

In Alsace. Senegalese riflemen go over the top of their trench in a counter attack.
Roughly half a million soldiers from colonies and overseas territories fought for the French Army during the First World War. Although their name suggests otherwise, the Tirailleurs Sénégalais did not come from Senegal exclusively, but also from other colonies in central and western Africa.

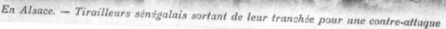

En Alsace. — Tirailleurs sénégalais sortant de leur tranchée pour une contre-attaque

— C'est à nous le 75 !

heavy cavalry was prepared to deliver surprise attacks against weak spots in the enemy lines. Over the course of the war, however, cavalry became less and less relevant and many cavalrymen were transferred to other branches of the service, a fact that benefited the new air force in particular, which had only been formed in 1912. In Summer 1914, France commanded about 120 military aircraft, but the air force would grow rapidly. More information on this can be found in the chapter concerning aerial warfare.

The main weapons of the French Army were the Lebel Model 1886 and the St Etienne Model 1907 rifles and the Hotchkiss Model 1914 machine gun. The backbone of the artillery forces was the 75mm Model 1897 field gun, of which roughly 4,800 were available at the beginning of the war. It was the pride of the French Army and was considered vastly superior

We have got the 75!
The French 75mm Model 1897 field gun was the first gun of its kind that featured a hydro-pneumatic recoil mechanism and consequently had a remarkable rate of fire. The German Model 1896 field gun, which had only been introduced a year previously, was outdated by the 75 and was converted to hydro-pneumatic recoil from 1904 onwards. The *soixante-quinze* was the pride of the French Army and the motif of many pictures.

2

to its German counterpart (77mm M/96 field gun). It was also used as an anti-aircraft gun and main armament of the Sainte-Chamond tank. Around 17,000 more of these 75mm guns were built during the war, 2,000 of which were delivered to the US Army. Almost 200 million rounds of 75mm ammunition were produced between 1914 and 1918, with just shrapnel and high explosive shells at first, but later with gas shells as well.

Other important artillery pieces were the 37mm infantry support gun and the 105mm, 120mm and 155mm heavy calibre guns. For a while, the German Army had better quality and greater quantity of material at its disposal, and it took France until 1917 to deploy sufficient numbers of modern heavy artillery pieces. The static warfare resulted in the introduction of mainly light short-range weapons used against enemy trenches, which were often only a few dozen to a couple of hundred metres ahead. These included rifle grenades, mortars and grenade launchers.

Finally, the weapons for hand-to-hand combat deserve a mention. 'Rosalie' was the nickname of the 52cm long bayonet for the Lebel rifle, featuring a cruciform cross section. As rifles with fixed bayonets were difficult to wield in the confined trenches, bayonets were shortened, sometimes to no more than dagger length. In addition to these, spades, clubs and a multitude of other improvised cut and thrust weapons were used.

This watercolour by Emil Dupuis from the *Nos poilus* (our soldiers) series shows a *Tirailleur Sénégalais*. All in all, almost 200,000 riflemen from central and western Africa served on the French side during the First World War, 30,000 of them lost their lives.

....

French Overseas Territories and Colonies

In addition to continental Frenchmen, the war in the European theatre was also fought by units from French overseas territories and colonies. Around 250,000 'foreign' soldiers took part in the defence of France in 1914, with their number later rising to almost half a million men. The colonial troops consisted of the *Tirailleurs Sénégalais* (from western and central Africa), the *Tirailleurs Malgaches* (from Madagascar), the

The Great War 1914-15. A group of Algerian Spahis.
In 1914 the French Army commanded a total of four regiments of *Spahis* (North-African cavalry): three from Algeria and one from Tunisia, with Arabs, Berbers and also French volunteers serving in them. During the war the majority of the *Spahis* were moved to France and the number of regiments increased to seven until 1918, including one from Morocco. At first they were used as cavalry, but over the course of the war they lost their horses and had to fight in an infantry capacity.

58. La Grande Guerre 1914-15 – Groupe de spahis Algériens · Algeria spahis · Phot-Express ·

1914... a *Tirailleur Algérien* tends to a wounded German.
At the beginning of the war, Germany protested at the UK and France bringing in colonial troops to Europe, and insinuated that the African soldiers in particular were extremely cruel. Cards like this one were published as a reaction, showing a north African soldier who tends to a German casualty.

1914..
Tirailleur algérien soignant un blessé allemand
Algérian sharp-shooter nursing a wonded German

4me Série

A wartime sketch. September 1914. A group of Tirailleurs Marocains.
The Brigade Marocaine, to which these soldiers belong, saw action on the Marne in September 1914. Of its roughly 5,000 soldiers, about 4,300 were killed, wounded or taken prisoner during the battle, reducing the brigade to a strength of only around 700 soldiers.

Tirailleurs Indochinois and the *Tirailleur Annamites* (from Laos, Cambodia and Vietnam), the *Spahis Marocains* (Moroccan cavalry), the *Tirailleurs Algériens*, the *Zouaves* (Zouzous, French citizens born in Algeria) and the *Turcos* (Algeria).

Most north African soldiers came from Algeria, which at that time was not a French colony but regarded an overseas territory. The soldiers from western and central Africa were mainly deployed as attack forces during offensives and did not serve in the trenches as much due to concerns that the soldiers would suffer from the European climate. Consequently, these units were moved to camps in the South during winter.

II Charente-Infre — Les Tirailleurs Malgaches à LA TREMBLADE en 1917
Groupe de quatre tirailleurs malgaches, tous les quatre engagés volontaires, montrant leur dévouement pour la France.
Le 1er à gauche se nomme Ratovo, le 2e Ravotovohitra, le 3e Rainizapindramanana, le 4e Ravoavy

Charente Infantry. Malagasy riflemen at La Tremblade in 1917.
The French Army even received recruits from Madagascar, which was a French colony until 1960. There were several thousand soldiers in all, and about 3,000 of them would lose their lives. Most of these losses occurred in the last phase of the war, and diseases and epidemics such as the Spanish Influenza deserve a particular mention in this case. The caption reads: 'A group of Tirailleurs Malgaches. All four have volunteered for service to demonstrate their loyalty to France. The first on the left is named Ratovo, the second Ravotovohitra, the third Rainizapindramanana, the fourth Ravoavy.'

Don't be Alarmed, the Royal Welsh Fusiliers are on guard.
The Royal Welsh Fusiliers were among the regiments who took part in an informal ceasefire along the front line between German and British soldiers during Christmas 1914. The regiment was also home to a few famous writers who published their experiences during the war, among them Frank Richards, Siegfried Sassoon, Robert Graves, David Jones and James C. Dunn. The illustration was created by C.T. Howard.

Don't be Alarmed, the Royal Welsh Fusiliers are on guard.

Three British officers of the Welsh Regiment pose for the camera on 24 April 1916. They carry the typical British helmet, which had been issued in great numbers shortly before, and are armed with a revolver in a holster on the belt. Incidentally, 24 April 1916 was Easter Monday, the first day of the 'Easter Rising' in Ireland.

The United Kingdom

In 1914, the United Kingdom had a population of around 46 million and at the outbreak of war, commanded a rather small professional army. Nevertheless, an expeditionary corps consisting of four infantry divisions and one cavalry division was immediately deployed to France and Belgium. This 'British Expeditionary Force – B.E.F.' was roughly

THE WORCESTERS GOING INTO ACTION.

The Worcesters going into action.
An image from the very popular '*Daily Mail* War Pictures' series. It shows soldiers of the Worcester Regiment waving on their way to the front. Before the war the regiment numbered eight battalions. This increased to fourteen during the war, of which twelve were on foreign duty. Among other places, they played an important role in the Second Battle of Ypres in 1915. Note the man in the centre of the picture carrying a wooden hammer. This may have been used to set up wire obstacles.

110,000 men strong at first, and was commanded by Sir John French. He was replaced in December 1915 by General Douglas Haig, who later rose to the rank of Field Marshal in 1917. From 1914 to early 1918, the British Army fought on the left flank of the Allied front line in Belgium and north-western France. Roughly seventy divisions were raised during the course of the war, first from reserve forces (members of the Territorial Force) and volunteers, and later on from conscripts as well. The volunteers were mainly raised by the 'Your King and Country Need You' campaign of Field Marshal Kitchener, the Secretary of State for War, which drew in 100,000 new recruits in two weeks. In spring 1915, however, the number of volunteers dropped, while the demand for recruits rose steadily.

The social pressure to 'volunteer' was substantial and it was common to pile the pressure on able-bodied men using rather unsubtle means. For example, Admiral Fitzgerald (who himself did not fight in any battle and died peacefully in his bed at the age of eighty), founded the 'Order of the White Feather' and from August 1914 onwards, this organisation encouraged women to hand a white feather as a sign of cowardice to men not wearing a uniform. At first the success was overwhelming, but despite all appeals to the love of home country and immense social pressures, the numbers of volunteers fell below the necessary amount in 1915. To be able to mobilise sufficient numbers of recruits, conscription was introduced at the beginning of 1916.

A total of roughly 4 million Englishmen, 557,000 Scotsmen, 273,000 Welshmen and 134,000 Irishmen served in the British Army

A souvenir for Tipperary.
This card is part of a series that was created by H. Canivet using the song, *It's a Long, Long Way to Tipperary*, as its topic. This was one of the most popular songs in England during the war, and legend has it that it was sung for the first time when the men of the 22nd Battalion, The Connaught Rangers, stepped onto French soil in Boulogne on 13 August 1914. It is a symbol for a soldier's longing for home. The woman in this picture is *Marianne*, the personification of France and she is pinning a souvenir to the soldier's uniform.

No Gun – No Girl!
One of the hundreds of postcards by popular cartoonist, Don McGill (1875-1962), nicely illustrating the pressure put onto British men to 'volunteer' for service. Whether organised or not, women's and girls' fondness for a smart uniform certainly had a strong influence on the gentlemen. When even this power of persuasion was no longer sufficient, the UK, too, introduced compulsory service in 1916.

during the war. In addition to this were around 3 million soldiers from the dominions, colonies and protectorates of the crown, which made up almost a third of the forces of the British Empire to take up arms in the Great War.

The UK had learnt from the Boer War and so the colourful uniforms had given way to a khaki-coloured field dress. The soldiers carried their personal equipment in the system of pouches and belts from woven materials that had been introduced in 1908 and which distributed the load better than the German or French equivalents. Even though the British soldiers had better uniforms and personal equipment than their French comrades, they had to wait until April 1916 before the introduction of a steel helmet.

The most important weapons of the British Army were the Lee-Enfield rifle, the Vickers machine gun and the 18-pounder (84mm) field gun, which was towed behind a limber and six horses. Six guns formed a battery. In 1914, there were around 1,200 of these field guns available, with 9,900 more following until 1918. In addition to these, the British Army also used a 13-pounder field gun and 4.5 and 5 inch howitzers. Like the other nations involved in the war, the British mainly developed short range artillery during the conflict, the most important innovations being the 3 inch Stokes Mortar and the 9.45 inch Heavy Trench Mortar, the projectile of which was nicknamed, 'Flying Pig.'

LES ALLIÉS

L'INDE MYSTÉRIEUSE
est aux côtés de la loyale Angleterre
pour la défense de la civilisation.

Mysterious India is on the side of loyal England for the defence of civilisation.
This well-designed card from the French *Les Alliés* series, kills three birds with one stone: England is loyal to France, India is at England's side and as one they defend culture and civilisation. The card was sent on 10 October 1916, and the writer had good news to tell; he had a couple of days leave from the front and could come home. *Quelle Joie!!*

Guerre de 1914
Avec les forces de l'Afrique du Sud
En attendant l'appel au Camp de Wanderers

The war of 1914. With the South-African forces. Waiting for roll call in the camp at Wanderers.
Soldiers from South Africa fought under the Union Defence Force in south-west Africa (Namibia), German East Africa, in the Egyptian desert (as part of the Western Frontier Force) and on the left flank of the Western Front in France. Of around 146,000 soldiers, 6,600 were killed in action and 12,000 were wounded.

The war. A unit from New Zealand going to the front.
The first volunteers from New Zealand, around 8,500 soldiers, along with Australian troops, reached Egypt on 3 December 1914. After a good four weeks of training near Cairo, the ANZAC (Australian and New Zealand Army Corps) landed near Gallipoli, in the Dardanelles, on 25 January 1915. In March 1916 a New Zealand division was also formed on the Western Front. Altogether, 100,000 New Zealanders served during the First World War, and almost one in six of them was killed.

British Dominions

Even before the declaration of war on 1 August 1914, the Governor General of Canada offered military assistance to the 'mother country'. During the whole war, Canadians fought together with the British on the Allied left flank and Canada raised a total of five divisions with roughly 418,000 soldiers.

The 'Australian Imperial Force' which received its marching orders in Australia on 1 November 1914, initially numbered 20,000 soldiers. The troops were first used in the defence of the Suez Canal and later took part in the Gallipoli Campaign. At the beginning of 1916 they were moved to the European theatre, forming four Australian divisions that fought in Ypres and on the Somme among other places. All in all, 400,000 Australians fought in the A.I.F., and by the end of the war, more than 60,000 had been

killed in action, while another 156,000 had been wounded or taken prisoner.

At first, the Australians formed the 'ANZAC – Australian and New Zealand Army Corps',

Bravo! Canada.
Even before the official declaration of war on 1 August 1914, the Governor General of Canada had offered military assistance to the United Kingdom, and the first Canadian troops saw action on the Western Front from early 1915 onwards. A total of around 418,000 Canadian soldiers served during the First World War. The card reads: 'From o'er the Sea at England's call, Her brave Colonial Sons, Stand by the Empire one and all, Against the foeman's guns!'

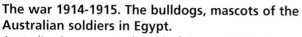

The war 1914-1915. The bulldogs, mascots of the Australian soldiers in Egypt.
Australia also came to the aid of the motherland. Around 400,000 soldiers fought in the Australian Imperial Force, first in the Middle East, then at Gallipoli and finally on the Western Front. 60,000 of them lost their lives.

....

together with the soldiers from New Zealand. The first 8,500 volunteers left New Zealand on 14 October 1914, as part of the 'New Zealand Expeditionary Force'. They joined the Australian troops and reached Egypt on 3 December 1914. After around four months of training, they took part in the Gallipoli landings on 25 April 1915. The New Zealanders were moved to the Western Front in 1916, where a New Zealand division was formed in March of the same year. Around 17,000 soldiers from New Zealand lost their lives in the First World War; roughly one in six of the approximatley 100,000 combatants.

Soldiers from South Africa fought in South-West Africa (Namibia), German East Africa, the Egyptian desert (Western Frontier Force) and on the Western Front. Of 146,000 soldiers, 6,600 lost their lives and 12,000 were wounded.

An Indian Hotchkiss gun at work.
Another motif from the *Daily Mail* series. The reverse is stamped 'Passed by Censor' and the appropriate text explains that the strange kaleidoscope of war results in pictures like this – Indian soldiers wearing turbans, manning a French Hotchkiss machine gun, in a British sector of the Western Front, in France. The Indian units were moved in 1915 and then saw action in Egypt.

....

The Indian Army

Behind the British, the Indian Army provided the largest contingent of soldiers for the British Empire. India took part in the war with 1.5 million soldiers and a large number of auxiliary troops and labourers (from China, Nepal, Egypt and South Africa). India's military contribution consisted of seven expeditionary forces, labelled with the letters A to G for distinction.

The 'Indian Expeditionary Force A', consisting of two infantry divisions and two cavalry divisions, reached Marseille on 30 September 1914. From Autumn 1914 onwards, it was deployed on the Western Front, although the infantry divisions were moved to Egypt in October 1915. The cavalry mainly fought in the trenches on foot as infantry, seeing action at the battle of the Somme and at Cambrai, until they too were moved to Egypt, in March 1918. Of roughly 130,000 Indians who fought in Belgium and France, almost 9,000 lost their lives.

European war 1914. With the Indians. Before returning to the front line trenches.
The Indian Army sent 1.5 million soldiers to war. The majority of them fought in Mesopotamia (today's Iraq), but the soldiers in this picture are among the 130,000 men who disembarked at Marseille from 30 September 1914 onwards, and shortly afterwards were sent to northern France. They were moved to Egypt in the following year.

Hindus in France. A Gurkha with his terrible combat knife.
Gurkhas are professional soldiers from Nepal who have been recruited into the British Army since 1817. In 1914 the Brigade of Gurkhas was part of the Indian Army. Gurkhas fought on the Western Front, in the Middle East, at Thessaloniki and Gallipoli among other places, and their enemies feared them for their valour and their skill with the *Kukri* (the 'terrible combat knife'). It is interesting that Indians and Nepalese were at first addressed as 'Hindus' on this and several other cards.

Apart from the forces sent to Europe, the Indian Army also sent the Indian Expeditionary Force B of 8,000 soldiers to Tanga in German East Africa, the I.E.F. C of 4,000 soldiers to Mombasa, the I.E.F. E and F, formed by the transfer of the four divisions from Europe to Palestine, to the Sinai peninsula and the Suez Canal, and the brigade sized I.E.F. G to Gallipoli.

The largest Indian force abroad, however, was the Indian Expeditionary Force D, in Mesopotamia (Iraq), of which the first division landed near Basra in November 1914. Another seven Indian Brigades were to follow. Also part of the Indian Army was the 'Brigade of Gurkhas', which consisted of ten regiments with twenty battalions at the beginning of the war and would grow to up to thirty-three battalions. The Gurkhas served on the Western Front, in the Middle East, at Thessaloniki and at Gallipoli.

Russia

In 1914 Tsar Nicholas II's Russia had a population of roughly 160 million. Even without general mobilisation, Russia could raise the world's largest army in 1914, comprising ninety-eight infantry divisions and thirty-seven cavalry divisions. The headquarters of the command of the commander-in-chief (Stavka), was led by Grand Duke Nicholas Nicholaievitch Romanov, an uncle of the tsar. His most important military leaders during the campaign against Germany were Rennenkampf and Samsonov, who had both seen action in the Russo-Japanese War.

Only a few of the high-ranking Russian officers

Infanterie russe s'élançant hors de ses tranchées.   d'après l'Illustration.
"GEO" 179.-1915.

Russian infantry storms out of its trenches.

While the fighting was quickly bogged down in the west and turned static, warfare in the east stayed mobile, not least due to the far larger combat areas. Although positions with main trenches and connecting trenches were also built on the Eastern Front, these were mostly not as complex and extensively fortified as the ones in the west. This trench is an unfortified natural feature of the landscape.

Captured machine guns.

This German picture postcard shows a large number of captured machine guns. Among them are not only Russian Maxim MGs, but also Austrian Schwarzloses, which Russia had captured in the early days of the war. It was common to deploy captured equipment against its former owners, especially when important weapons were concerned. The German Army gave official prize money for captured equipment, regularly publishing the amounts handed out in the *Armee-Verordnungsblatt*, the official medium for military announcements in Germany.

ERBEUTETE MASCHINENGEWEHRE   PHOT. E. BENNINGHOVEN

DEBARQUEMENT DES TROUPES RUSSES EN FRANCE

Russian troops disembarking in France.

The first units of a Russian brigade reached the port of Marseille in April 1916. Answering a French request, Russia sent around 45,000 soldiers (the request had been for several hundred thousand) to serve on the Western Front. After the October Revolution in November 1917 in Russia and the Armistice with Germany, the Russian troops separated into two groups; one refused to take any further part in the action whereas the other fought on the Allied side until the end of the war.

had seen combat and were well trained, unlike the majority of the officers leading the troops. This was even more true for most common soldiers, who were hardly trained and, as they were usually recruited from the rural population, were often illiterate. On the other hand, these men were used to hardships, showed courage and, as orthodox Christians and Russian peasants, had learned to obey the tsar, the church and their officers.

Although their enemies feared the Russian Army for its sheer size, the overall conviction was that it would take quite a while to mobilise these forces. In fact, Russia was able to come to the aid of its western allies rather quickly, and immediately started to attack. This was a practice it would repeat several times during the war. The German and Austro-Hungarian high commands saw Russia at a disadvantage, as the poorly developed railway networks made it difficult to move troops and bring up supplies.

The personal equipment of the Russian soldier was no worse than that of most nations, and his green field dress was actually more modern than most. Steel helmets were never introduced, and so the Russian soldier only wore his peaked cap up until the end of the war.

His equipment consisted of a belt with two ammunition pouches containing sixty rounds of

A German picture postcard from the 'Russian Type' series, showing one of the millions of tsarist soldiers in his greatcoat. Most soldiers were poorly trained, could neither read nor write and had never before left their native village in the expanses of rural Russia. But these men were used to hardships and knew only obedience to the church, the tsar and their officers. In combination with their comparatively good armament and equipment, this made them an enemy to be reckoned with.

ammunition, a spade and a haversack. Over his shoulder he carried his coat with spare clothes and a piece of canvas rolled into it.

The most important infantry weapons were the Mosin-Nagant Model 1891 rifle and the Russian version of the Maxim machine gun, both of outstanding quality and available in large numbers. At the outbreak of the war, Russia had more machine guns at its disposal than the German Empire. The artillery counted roughly 8,000 modern field guns, with around 7,000 76.2mm calibre. In addition there were 500 modern 122mm howitzers as well as 170 152mm

LE CONFLIT EUROPÉEN EN 1914
L'Armée Russe - Artillerie Russe partant prendre position

E. LE DELEY, Imprimeur, Paris.

The European conflict in 1914. The Russian Army. Russian artillery takes up position. This card shows parts of an artillery battery with 76.2mm field guns. The Russian Army commanded around 7,000 of these modern guns. At the beginning of the war, many picture postcards showing the Russian Army were published in France, as the country was regarded as a very important ally.

Cliché Chusseau, Flaviens

E. LE DELEY, Imprimeur, Paris

LE CONFLIT EUROPÉEN EN 1914

Sentinelle russe

The European conflict in 1914. A Russian guard.
A Russian marine wrapped up in a rain cape on guard duty. Although the majority of Russian soldiers were poorly trained, their personal equipment was state of the art. This also holds true for his rifle, the Mosin-Nagant. Introduced in 1891, it was very reliable and fired a powerful cartridge. The weapon came with a cruciform bayonet.

Ahead for the Home Country!
A fighter on horseback in front of the white, blue and red flag with the double-headed eagle. Compared to the western and central European states, Russia had a large, albeit poor population, most of whom were illiterate. The picture postcard business therefore, had little importance. Nevertheless, Russia also published many cards with military motifs during the war. This card promotes a war bond.

howitzers, followed by a large number of outdated types of guns. For each gun there were roughly 1,000 rounds of ammunition available, which was the international average. After a short start-up period, the Russian defence industry was able to ramp up production numbers substantially and satisfy the increased demand from 1915 onwards. The tsar's air force could already muster 244 aircraft in autumn 1914, which made it the second largest worldwide. The navy was far less important and with its twelve

battleships, was roughly on par with that of Austria-Hungary.

America

In 1914 the President of the United States, Woodrow Wilson, maintained that his country would remain neutral in the war. This was a view shared by the majority of around 100 million Americans. But over time, not only did the moral support for the Allies increase, but also the material aid. Exports to France and Britain were on the rise, whereas trade with Germany went down. German misconduct in Belgium and the so-called 'Zimmermann Telegram', which offered

Our American allies in France. Their presence is a big support from a military standpoint and their influence on morale will be considerable. Long live America!

In the spring of 1917 France was suffering from submarine warfare, while unrest grew in both the population and the army and in March 1917, Nicholas II abdicated the Russian throne. Therefore, the American declaration of war against the German Empire on 6 April 1917 was very welcome news.

military support for Mexico should it declare war against its northern neighbour, also played their part.

When Germany reintroduced unrestricted submarine warfare (targeting neutral (passenger) vessels without warning), the USA finally declared war against Germany on 6 April 1917. In June, a symbolic first advance force of the US Marine Corps disembarked in France, but they were to be followed by almost 2 million more soldiers. In the summer of 1917, the US Army could not exactly boast about having any special strength; including the National Guard and Marine Corps it numbered roughly 250,000 ill-armed and ill-equipped soldiers. Immediately after the declaration of war, the USA began to

War 1914-1917. American soldiers in France. New friends having a talk.

Young, healthy, well fed, well equipped and with a substantial measure of self-esteem, the American soldiers were especially favourites of the younger female members of the local population. The Frenchmen were most likely not as happy, but the publishers, whose postcards were supposed to demonstrate the new cordial relationship, were certainly grateful for these motifs.

A **private real** photo card showing American soldiers having breakfast under the watchful eye of French children. The picture was taken in Autumn 1917 or Spring 1918 in a camp behind the lines. The soldiers look well groomed and rested. The boys certainly hope to share in the meal.

expand its forces and initially President Wilson hoped he would only have to send volunteers into battle. However, these hopes were soon shattered. During the first phase, the army was supposed to grow by 1 million men, but six weeks after the declaration of war, only 73,000 volunteers had reported for duty. Compulsory service was therefore introduced and 2 million recruits were drafted.

In Spring 1918, the presence of the American forces finally became noticeable on the Western Front. Each week another 60,000 soldiers landed on French soil, which compared roughly to three German divisions. At the beginning of 1918 the first four US divisions (each around 27,000 men strong) were deployed alongside British and French troops in order to gain experience in combat. However, General Pershing wanted to unite all US units under a single command. In June 1918, his forces stopped the German spring offensive, and in September of that year, he led the First Army to victory in the Battle of Saint-Mihiel. Shortly afterwards, the strongest US

L'Armée Américaine en France
45 - Embarquement d'un train de combat pour le front
We use to act quickly and well
Visé, Nantes

The American Army in France. A military train for the front is loaded. We use to act quickly and well.
From Spring 1918 onwards, more than 60,000 Americans, the equivalent of three German divisions, reached France weekly. The majority of their armaments and equipment was provided by the British and French defence industries, whose production lines were at peak performance by this time. The European allies did not suffer from any lack of material, but were short on soldiers – a gap the Americans could fill perfectly.

Guerre 1914-1917. — LES AMERICAINS EN FRANCE. — AMERICAN SOLDIERS IN FRANCE.
Un campement bien aménagé. — A well organised en campment.

War 1914-1917. American soldiers in France. A well-organised camp.

American soldiers in their camp somewhere in a French village. The picture most likely shows a field kitchen; the rack in the foreground carries two water-skins. The area behind it is covered with a tarpaulin with branches on top, to camouflage it against views from the air; a telling sign that military aircraft had already become a serious threat.

American unit formed part of the Allied offensive that assaulted the Hindenburg Line, which eventually heralded the end of the war. Out of almost 2 million US soldiers, 116,000 lost their lives and 204,000 were wounded, while 25,000 soldiers died of the Spanish Influenza in autumn 1918.

Due to insufficient arms production in the USA, the American soldiers mainly relied on French and also limited British assistance. The standard field gun of the US Army was therefore the French 75mm field gun, of which 2,000 were procured in France and another 1,000 built under license in the US, although the latter only became available after the armistice. The 155mm howitzers, as well as the Hotchkiss and Chauchat machine guns, were also of French origin. The first machine gun designed and produced in the USA, the Browning machine gun, only became available shortly before the armistice. The basic

small arms used were the Springfield Model 1903 and Enfield M1917 rifles, the latter specially produced for the increasing demand of a growing army. Similar to the olive green uniforms and several other pieces of equipment, these small arms were produced in the USA. However, 400,000 steel helmets were procured in the UK at first, before local production came up to speed. Aircraft and tanks also had to be obtained from the French defence industry.

The US soldier was initially nicknamed 'Sammy' by the French press, modelled on the British 'Tommy' and derived from the designation 'Uncle Sam', but this was soon replaced by 'doughboy'. The true origin of this nickname is unclear, but it had already been mentioned in the Mexican-American War of 1846-48. The American soldier was described as being always covered with a thin white coating of dust, from the dry and loamy Mexican soil, giving him an appearance of unbaked dough.

Austria-Hungary

In 1914, the dual monarchy of Austria-Hungary (personal union between the Empire of Austria and the Kingdom of Hungary) numbered a population of around 53 million. In the course of mobilisation, 3.3 million men were called to arms and seventy divisions were formed,

A watercolour by Emile Dupuis from the *Leurs Caboches* (their heads) series. It shows an infantry officer of the Austro-Hungarian Army. Although the colourful picture postcards with Dupuis' illustrations were quite popular at the time, while the date and locations he added to each picture gave them an air of seriousness, the details of uniforms and headgear are often only rough approximations of reality.

Hungarians, there were also soldiers from Bosnia, Italy, Croatia, Poland, Romania, Serbia, Slovenia, Slovakia, Tyrol and Bohemia. Head of state was the 84 year-old Emperor Franz Joseph I, who made Arch Duke Friedrich his Commander-in-Chief in 1914, promoting him to Field Marshal at the same time. In reality,

including eleven cavalry divisions. The reliability and combat strength of the Austro-Hungarian Army units were quite diverse, as they were made from a combination of widely differing ethnicities that were only united by a central government. Apart from Austrians and

The four pictures on this real photo card show the Imperial and Royal Austro-Hungarian Army executing two men in civilian clothing by hanging. After they have had the sentence read to them, they are hanged one after the other. They had perhaps been accused of espionage, sabotage, desertion or treason. During the war a high number of death sentences based on these charges were passed and carried out against civilians and military personnel in multi-ethnic Austria-Hungary.

A proud group of Austro-Hungarian soldiers poses for the camera with their machine gun. The weapon was developed by the German, Andreas Schwarzlose, and produced at the Steyr factories from 1905 onwards. In 1908 it was introduced to the Netherlands' Army and from 1915 onwards, was also produced at the Artillerie-Inrichtingen in Zaandam. It would remain in service up to the Second World War, used by Czechoslovakia, Greece, Yugoslavia and the Netherlands.

however, the army was led by General Conrad von Hötzendorf. After Franz Joseph died in 1916, Emperor Karl I, who succeeded him to the throne, made himself Commander-in-Chief and von Hötzendorf had to hand over his post as Chief of the General Staff to General Arz von Straussenburg.

Although the army of the dual monarchy matched those of Germany or France on paper, in reality it was much weaker. The equipment was mostly outdated; there were only a few artillery pieces and machine guns and the units from outside Austria or Hungary were hardly motivated to fight for a country they effectively did not want to belong to. Desertion was a continuous problem and often whole units not only surrendered without firing a shot, but actually joined forces with the enemy.

The majority of the Austro-Hungarian Army was formed by the infantry, which went to war in a modern uniform in a colour called '*hechtgrau*', literally 'pike grey'. This colour soon turned out to be too light and was changed to field grey on 13 September 1915. At first the headgear used

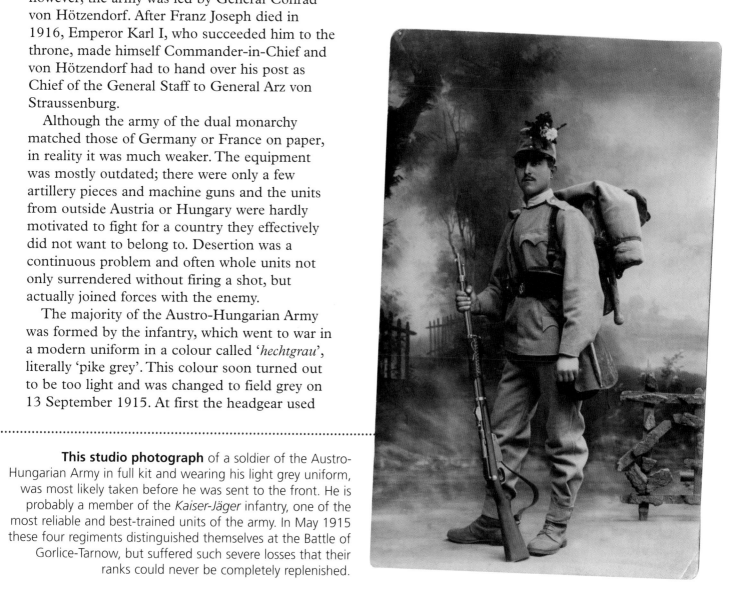

This studio photograph of a soldier of the Austro-Hungarian Army in full kit and wearing his light grey uniform, was most likely taken before he was sent to the front. He is probably a member of the *Kaiser-Jäger* infantry, one of the most reliable and best-trained units of the army. In May 1915 these four regiments distinguished themselves at the Battle of Gorlice-Tarnow, but suffered such severe losses that their ranks could never be completely replenished.

„Bereit zum letzten Hieb"

Ready for the last stroke.
A picture postcard with an illustration by Karl Alexander Wilke (1879-1954), a painter and illustrator from Leipzig. He worked in Austria from 1903 onwards, joined the NSDAP after the First World War and rose to a leading position in the *Österreichischer Landesverlag* publishing house. The illustration shows two Austro-Hungarian soldiers, followed by allies from Turkey, Germany and Bulgaria. As far as fighting strength was concerned, the Imperial and Royal Army was not on par with the German Army, repeatedly needing military assistance, and as the war carried on, the German high command also increasingly steered the Austrian campaigns.

....

was a shako, or a peaked cap, but from 1917 onwards, the German example was followed and a steel helmet introduced.

The army's standard weapons were the Mannlicher rifle M.95 and the Schwarzlose machine gun, both built by the Steyr weapons factory. The artillery commanded about 1,200 76.5mm calibre field guns as well as a 90mm field gun, 105mm and 150mm howitzers and a couple of heavy 30.5cm and 42cm mortars. The

42cm mortar was used by the Germans in 1914 to bring down the fortifications around Liège.

Germany

In 1914 Germany numbered roughly 65 million inhabitants, who lived in twenty-five federal states. The army was formed from contingents from these states, and its leader was His Majesty Emperor and King Wilhelm II, although at the outbreak of the war he transferred his command to the Chief of the General Staff, Erich von

Soldat d'infanterie (landsturm bavarois)

Infantryman (Bavarian Landsturm).
For a wartime picture, this card by Emile Dupuis is quite a friendly depiction of an enemy combatant, an older Landsturm militiaman from Bavaria smoking his pipe. Note the *Ersatz-Seitengewehr* bayonet mounted to his rifle. These 'substitute bayonets', as the term literally translates were roughly made steel bayonets, which could be produced faster and cheaper than the standard version. During the war the range of equipment made from substitute materials increased steadily.

Ein deutscher Soldat gibt einem armen Kinde Zuckerwerk.

A German soldier gives sweets to a poor child.
To counter Allied propaganda decrying real or alleged German atrocities, a number of picture postcards were published that supposedly proved the opposite. They showed civilians receiving aid, children being handed food or sweet treats, or prisoners of war being fed and medically cared for.

A German soldier takes up a threatening position for the camera. His Pickelhaube, or 'Lederhelm mit Spitze' (spiked leather helmet), as it was officially called, has been covered with grey cloth to hide the flashing metal decorations. Note the 'rifle', which is an Exerzier-Gewehr 98 training rifle that was produced for only a short time and had all metal parts made from cast iron. It had no mechanical functions whatsoever, could not be fired and was only used for training. The idea being to spare the real weapons.

Falkenhayn. The largest contingent of the army was provided by the Kingdom of Prussia, while the other three large kingdoms, Bavaria, Saxony and Württemberg, each provided their own army corps and claimed wide-ranging military autonomy. The troops of the smaller princedoms and duchies were incorporated into the Prussian corps. Due to this military autonomy, the army was not called the 'Imperial' German Army, unlike the Imperial German Navy.

In 1914 there was a total of twenty-five army corps, nineteen of them Prussian, three Bavarian, two Saxon and one from Württemberg. The largest branch was the infantry, who could muster 217 regiments, each with three battalions of four companies. A battalion numbered 26

officers and 1,056 NCOs and enlisted men. In addition, each regiment already commanded a machine gun company.

The light infantry consisted of eighteen Jäger (light infantry) battalions, with four combat companies, one machine gun company and one bicycle company each. The cavalry consisted of 110 regiments of 5 squadrons, whereas the artillery was structured into 101 *Feldartillerie* (field artillery) and 25 *Fußartillerie* (heavy artillery) regiments. Thirty-five engineer battalions built positions, temporary fortifications and bridges among other tasks and twenty-five

German Guard.
The front line trenches also contained reinforced
dugouts to give protection from artillery fire. This
example apparently housed medics operating a
casualty collection point under difficult and unhygienic
conditions, giving first aid and deciding whether to
send a casualty down the line to a dressing station.
The bell on the left side of the entrance was for gas
alarms. On the right the guard has prepared a couple
of stick grenades to repel enemy attacks.

···

Train-Bataillone (logistics battalions) were in
charge of supplies. Another thirty battalions were
united under the heading 'transport forces',
among them eight railway battalions, five airship
battalions and four air force battalions. The army
was 794,000 soldiers strong in 1914 and
structured into around fifty divisions.

Mobilisation brought substantial
reinforcements in large numbers, so that the so-
called reserve regiments, recruited from
experienced reservists, were raised alongside the
active regiments and followed them into the field.
New recruits and conscripts were trained at the
garrisons by the *Ersatz* (replacement) battalions.
13.25 million men served in the army until the
end of the war, 2 million of them were killed.

In 1914 the active troops still went to war in
the field grey uniform that had been introduced
in 1907. The tunics, attilas and kollets were
impractical and their production laborious, so in
1915, the simpler field blouse was introduced.
This was identical for all branches of the army
and more suited to the requirements of trench
warfare. The typical German *Pickelhaube*,
officially called *Lederhelm mit Spitze*, meaning
spiked leather helmet, was worn with a
camouflage cover. Although the spike was made
removable in 1915 to make the helmet less
conspicuous, the lack of protection and resulting
severe head wounds demanded the introduction
of a steel helmet, which was finally rolled out to
the troops at the front from mid-1916.

By now the cavalry, armed with lances, swords,
sabres and carbines, was an anachronism on the
modern battlefield and had lost its original role
in all the state armies. It no longer decided the
outcome of a battle and was subject to the
conditions of trench warfare and modern
military technology. In the best case, it still
carried out a reconnaissance role, especially on
the eastern and Balkan fronts, as long distances
could easily be covered on horseback. In many
places cavalrymen only served without horses,

Königl. Reserve = Infanterie = Regiment Nr. 239

Uns treibt nicht Eroberungslust, uns beseelt der unbeugsame
Wille, den Platz zu bewahren, auf den Gott uns gestellt.

4. August 1914

Wilhelm II.

We are not driven by a desire to conquer, we are filled with the unbreakable will to preserve the place we were given by God.
This card quotes Emperor Wilhelm II, who spoke these words on 4 August 1914, the day Germany invaded neutral Belgium. The card was posted on 17 June 1915. Almost all regiments had their own postcards. This one belonged to the *Königliches Reserve-Infanterie-Regiment* Nr. 239, a reserve infantry regiment, raised during the war.

and from 1916 onwards, so-called *Kavallerie-Schützen-Regimenter* (dismounted cavalry regiments) were formed, who served in an infantry capacity. The horses freed up by this were assigned to the artillery and supply trains, as the high losses among draft horses had brought the remount service (the service procuring replacement horses) to its limits.

At the same time, technical developments resulted in the creation of new branches of the army, such as the *Kraftfahrtruppe* motorised forces, who commanded a multitude of motorbikes, cars and lorries, some of civilian origin. The rather new air force underwent a special development in both technology and numbers. At the beginning of the war it numbered only four battalions, but by 1918 it had almost 48,000 aircraft at its disposal, half of which were lost in action, scrapped or taken out of commission. At first the pilots flew reconnaissance missions and gave directions for the artillery to fire on, but soon bombers and specially armed fighter aircraft were developed, the latter supposedly to engage enemy aircraft. Many cavalry officers found a new line of action as fighter pilots, as the one on one combat in the air promised a certain form of 'chivalry'.

The infantry, armed with the Gewehr 98 rifle

This Bavarian dragoon, who was photographed in 1915, is armed with a steel tube lance. Before the war cavalry was expected to play an important role on the battlefield, but this view was soon abandoned. Not only did the static warfare with its trenches and bunkers leave no opportunity for cavalry to operate, a soldier on a horse was a perfect target for machine guns and rapid-fire artillery.

FELDBÄCKEREI

Field Bakery.
Feeding and supplying an army on the move is a logistical masterpiece. This photo card shows a field bakery with horse-drawn mobile ovens to produce the typical *Kommißbrot* pan-baked rye loafs. These were nourishing bread loaves that kept well and were therefore popular with the soldiers, which explains why there is an armed guard to the right of the picture. The wood to fire the ovens could be logged on site meaning an important food staple could be produced right where the troops were at any given time.

in the 8x57 IS calibre, bore the brunt of the fighting. A shortened version, the Karabiner 98 AZ carbine, was in service for the cavalry and the artillery. As there was a continuous shortage of weapons that could be used in front line service, many units were still equipped with its predecessor, the Gewehr 88 rifle, and its carbine versions. Sometimes whole units even carried weapons conquered from the enemy, such as the Russian Mosin-Nagant M91. At times even Gewehr 71 and Gewehr 71/84 rifles were used to train the replacements at home.

The predominant standard machine gun became the MG 08 machine gun, mounted on a sled mount. The water-cooled machine gun weighed more than 50kg and fired fabric belted ammunition, fed from ammunition boxes that were first made of wood and later of metal. A slightly lighter version with a bipod and pistol

Im Schützengraben

In the trenches.
German soldiers manning an MG 08 in a trench. The machine gun has been fitted with an armoured shield, which protects the crew but also makes the machine gun heavier and less mobile. The two soldiers manning the machine gun wear slings that are used to drag the heavy weapon across the ground on its sled mount. In 1914 the German Army could muster about as many machine guns as its enemies, but was more efficient in using them tactically.

Motif No. 1 from the *Kriegspostkarten von B. Wennerberg* (wartime postcards by B. Wennerberg) series. All of Wennerberg's cards show a slender young woman; in this case she is apparently a mother and wife saying goodbye to her husband, who is following his Uhlan regiment into the field. He is armed with a steel tube lance and a carbine, fixed to the saddle in a case. Uhlans are light cavalry and were supposed to serve as reconnaissance forces and dispatch riders and carry out surprise attacks. They served on both the Western and Eastern Fronts, but during the course of the war they increasingly fought dismounted in an infantry capacity.

German engineers load an *Erdmörser* (literally: ground mortar). This improvised indirect fire weapon carried a heavy explosive charge across a short distance. The barrel containing the propelling charge was dug into the ground. The canister with the explosive charge received a certain amount of guidance by the rail leaning against the wall of the trench. As the opposing front line trenches were often very close to each other, this simple method was sufficient to carry charges across no-man's-land and into enemy positions.

grip was the MG 08/15 machine gun, which was in use from 1916 onwards. It was still water-cooled, but could be carried in a sling by a single soldier and fired from a simple bipod, making it an important weapon for assault troops. These highly mobile and lightly armed soldiers were specially trained to enter enemy trenches, knock out key positions and bring in prisoners. Apart

from rifles and hand grenades, the arsenals of these elite forces also contained flame throwers, knives, clubs and light grenade launchers for this purpose. Regular units formed assault companies, in addition to the dedicated assault battalions.

The backbone of the field artillery was formed by the 77mm Feldkanone 96n/A field gun (short FK 96) and the 105mm Feldhaubitze 98/09 howitzer. The FK 96, of which roughly 5,000

A group of German soldiers in their quarters, somewhere behind the front line, perhaps a barn on a farmyard. Their faces clearly show the hardships and experiences of their life at the front.

were built, was lighter and more mobile than its French counterpart, but had a smaller range and a lower rate of fire. With 1,250 105mm howitzers, Germany was superior to France in terms of mid-sized artillery. A multitude of mortars and guns of different calibres were also fielded.

During the war, developers mainly focused on guns with high-arching ballistic trajectories that were needed for the short distances of trench warfare. A prototype grenade launcher had already been invented in 1910 and was based on experiences and observations made during the Russo-Japanese War. Unlike 'normal' guns, this projectile did not have to be fired at the highest possible velocity, so the pressure on the barrel was much lower and the whole construction could be lighter. Even the walls of the grenades were rather thin to carry a maximum of explosives towards the target. More than 18,000 grenade launchers were produced up until 1918.

Engineers demonstrating the use of a flamethrower. The German Army fielded several versions, this picture shows the *kleiner Flammenwerfer* 1912 (small model). The flamethrower party consisted of two soldiers, one carrying the fuel tank, the other wielding the lance tube. The other soldiers provided cover, as the two flamethrower operators were a preferred target for enemy snipers and machine guns.

Group picture of an assault troop of the
103. *Infanterie-Regiment* (infantry regiment).
Beginning with a few assault battalions, more
and more assault units developed in the
regular regiments during the last phase of the
war. Assault troops were specially trained
soldiers equipped with a multitude of light
weapons and were considered an elite force.
Their task was to breach enemy defences,
advance swiftly and as far as possible and by
this open up a way for the main forces.
During the 1918 spring offensive, the
Sturmtruppen assault forces created important
breaches that allowed the German forces an
advance in a way that was difficult to stop.

The *schwerer Minenwerfer* heavy grenade launcher in
a position dug deeply into the ground. This 25cm calibre
indirect fire weapon was perfectly suited to the
requirements of trench warfare. It fired very heavy
grenades at short distances (ca. 600m maximum), which
hit the enemy positions almost vertically. At the beginning
of the war Germany had forty-four of these grenade
launchers at its disposal; in 1918 it was 1,300. The
grenade launcher, of which there was also a medium and
light version, was based on lessons the German high
command had learned from the siege of Port Arthur
during the Russo-Japanese War.

A German machine-gun model 1908 (MG 08) on its sled mount. The barrel was contained in a sheet metal jacket filled with cooling water. Therefore, each machine gun had a separate water container that was connected to it with a hose. In this picture the container is missing. On the other hand, the jacket for the barrel is fitted with an add-on armour to protect it from damage. The soldier on the left feeds the woven ammunition belt into the gun to prevents stoppages.

Chapter 5
The Western Front

1914

The first phase of the war in the west was shaped by the Schlieffen Plan, named after Alfred Graf von Schlieffen, who had died in 1913. Germany planned to avoid a war on two fronts by attacking along the northern flank through neutral Belgium, conquering the French capital, Paris, and gaining victory over France as a whole within six weeks. Afterwards, troops would then be free to move east for a war against Russia.

But the German advance through Belgium was opposed by the strong fortifications on the Meuse river in Liège and Namur. The fortresses here were strong enough to resist the strongest guns that were in use at the end of the nineteenth century. Germany hoped that neutral Belgium would put up a symbolic resistance at

This posed picture shows Belgian soldiers in an imaginary fire fight against German attackers. In August 1914 Belgium could muster an army of 200,000 soldiers, who despite their mediocre equipment and training, put up an unexpectedly strong defence. The men wear leather hats that were later exchanged for French steel helmets. They carry the Belgian standard infantry weapon, the Mauser Model 1889 rifle.

Armée belge   Mitrailleuse Maxim attelée.

Belgian Army. Dog-drawn Maxim machine gun.
In the late nineteenth and early twentieth century, the machine gun entered the arsenals of almost all armies. The basic model was developed by the American Hiram Maxim in 1886 and played an important role in the First World War. The roughly 25kg weapon was transported on pack horses or horse-drawn carts, but in Belgium (and for a short while in the Netherlands as well), dogs were also used as draft animals.

most, and gave them an ultimatum on 2 August 1914. The ultimatum claimed that France was planning an attack against Germany across Belgian territory, and demanded Belgium must not hinder Germany's defence. The king of Belgium denied this request and on 4 August, forces of the 2nd German Army entered Belgium.

Belgium mobilised an army of more than 200,000 soldiers. The army command, with the king at its head, had six infantry divisions and one cavalry division at its disposal, forming a field army of around 115,000 men. Approximately another 90,000 men manned the fortresses and fortifications, including those at Liège, Namur and Antwerp. Immediately after the German invasion, 20,000 volunteers reported for duty.

The standard weapon of the army was the Mauser Model 1889 bolt action rifle. The stores also held roughly 120 machine guns, mostly Maxim Model 1912, but also some older French Hotchkiss. The artillery fielded 75mm rapid-fire guns built by Krupp, but also licensed by the Belgian company, Cockerill. In 1914 Belgium

VAILLANT BELGE....MERCi!
84   Gloria

Valiant Belgium... Thank you!
The resistance put up by the Belgian troops against the invading German Army on its way to Paris, gave France and the UK almost two weeks of extra time. In this period the British Expeditionary Force crossed the Channel and the defence was organised. Belgium is symbolised here by a common, wounded soldier carrying a flag decorated with the place names of the heaviest fighting against the Germans: Liège, Namur and Antwerp.

The war. The exodus.
Many Belgian citizens fled directly after the German invasion. Some went south in the direction of France, while others, especially after the fall of Antwerp, fled north towards the border with the Netherlands. This retouched and coloured photograph shows Belgians with a dog-drawn cart and cavalry passing in the background.

EN GUERRE – L'EXODE.
THE WAR – THE EXODUS.

could muster around eighty-six batteries of four guns each. In addition there were a couple of dozen French Saint-Chamond 120mm howitzers and a multitude of mostly outdated mortars, howitzers and guns set up in the fortifications. During the war, replacements and spare parts were mainly received from France.

After the unexpectedly strong resistance by the Belgian Army, who had also blown up several bridges, the invading troops took extremely harsh action against the civilian population. Although acts of resistance by civilians were rare, there were several punitive strikes, even against women, children and members of the clergy. The victims were driven together and shot by firing squads, while survivors were bayoneted. Six people were murdered in Warsage, 211 in Andenne, 384 in Tamines, 612 in Dinant and 209 in Leuven, which was also pillaged and torched. This brutal behaviour served no military purpose, only causing popular outrage everywhere and damaging German reputation,

Franzose

Belgier

Engländer

Unsere Feinde im Westen.

Our enemies in the West.
This German card was published shortly after the beginning of the war and shows three members of the enemy forces, from the left to right; a French, Belgian and British soldier. Only the British soldier with his khaki uniform is suited for the requirements of modern warfare, and it would not take long for other forces to also change to less conspicuous colours.

August – Global war 1914-15. An attack by franc-tireurs at Leuven on 25 August.

Six days after the Germans had occupied Leuven (or Löwen, in German), shots were fired at the occupational forces, perhaps by other German units who mistook them for Belgian forces. The subsequent action by the German garrison cost more than 200 lives. The historic city centre, with the medieval cloth merchants' hall that housed a renowned collection of manuscripts and rare books went up in flames, causing international uproar and severe damage to Germany's reputation. This card was published in 1915 and tried to justify Germany's actions.

especially in the neutral states. Of course the atrocities were exploited by Allied propaganda and became the motifs of many picture postcards.

After a few days of very heavy fighting with substantial losses and only minor territorial gains, on 12 August the Krupp 42cm mortar nick-named 'Big Bertha' was brought into action against the fortifications at Liège. From a distance of 4km, heavy grenades weighing

1,000kg were lobbed against the fortifications, and once the gun was zeroed in, one fortress after the other fell and the garrisons had to surrender. About a week later, the fortresses at Namur suffered the same fate and on 24 August the last fortress fell at Namur. The Belgian Army then withdrew to the defensive lines behind the fortresses of Antwerp.

Ten days earlier on 14 August, France began to implement its Plan XVII, a major offensive

Original picture from the theatre of war.

This real photo card shows the armed cupola of Fort Loncin, one of twelve fortresses in the fortifications around Liège. Fort Loncin was destroyed on 15 August 1915 by a 42cm artillery shell that hit the ammunition bunker. The resulting explosion claimed 350 lives among the soldiers of the Belgian garrison. The remainders of the Liège fortresses decorated many German picture postcards and also attracted huge crowds of curious soldiers and civilians.

This Saxon uhlan wears the leather helmet called a *czapka* and his uniform tunic, which is also known as *ulanka*. During the invasion of Belgium the Uhlan regiments not only carried out countless reconnaissance missions but also several surprise attacks. They were highly mobile, could appear out of the blue and were consequently feared by their enemies. This soon gave rise to countless rumours about the cavalry.

during the night of 19-20 August, throwing the French forces back to their original positions. Further north in the Ardennes, the fighting had similar results. The French advance was stopped after a short time and pushed back by the Germans in coordinated counterattacks. By 24 August, Plan XVII had already been completely bogged down and had petered out between Givet and Verdun in a French retreat behind the Meuse. After three weeks of fighting, the French offensive had been beaten back and after the fall of Namur, the way was cleared for the Germans to bypass the French left flank through Belgium and march against Paris – as Schlieffen had planned. The French Army had suffered great losses during the Battle of Charleroi between 21 and 23 August, and so were unable to stop the subsequent German advance along the planned route.

against Lorraine, in the north-east, starting with the deployment of two armies to Sarrebourg. The Germans retreated for four days, before stopping and forming a well-organised counterattack

The British Expeditionary Force (B.E.F.) had

Bouclier humain

Human shield.
This motif is part of a series that also included titles like *L'Orgie* and *L'Achèvement des Blessés*. They were intended to show (alleged) atrocities committed by the German invaders of Belgium. Here, German soldiers led by an officer carrying a sword, use their bayonets to force bound civilians, including half-naked women, to march in front of them as a human shield.

Portraits of generals Joffre and d'Amade against a backdrop of the Franco-German border in 1914. On 14 August 1914, the French General Staff began implementing 'Plan XVII', which mainly consisted of advancing in a northern and north-easterly direction. The advance was halted after only a short time and the French forces were pushed back. Consequently, General d'Amade, who was in command of the territorial forces between Dunkirk and Maubeuge, was relieved of his command on 17 September 1914, as he allegedly withdrew too fast. His new command led him to take part in the Gallipoli operations.

arrived on the French left on 22 August. It had disembarked in France eleven days before and consisted of four infantry divisions and one cavalry division. The experienced and well-trained soldiers immediately dug in behind the Bergen-Condé-Canal, in well planned and deeply staggered trench systems. The Germans mounted a large scale attack against these

positions on 23 August and were repelled with heavy losses. Despite this, the British forces were commanded to retreat on the following evening. The German victory in Charleroi along with the French retreat had made it necessary to pull back the whole front line.

The retreat of the British and French forces took a fortnight, and were continually disrupted

Troupes Anglaises arrivant en France.
English troops arriving in France.
Англійскія войска, прибывающія во Францію.

English troops arriving in France.
The text on this card is printed in the languages of the Triple Entente: French, English and Russian. It is supposed to show the loyalty among the Allies, but also documents the commercial intentions of the publisher. The soldiers belong to the British Expeditionary Force (BEF) that disembarked in Boulogne and other ports from 11 August onwards. Initially the BEF consisted of four infantry divisions and one cavalry division, formed exclusively from professional soldiers.

English officers have tea on the way.
A Frenchman and four Brits enjoy their tea. The arrival of British forces was very welcome to the French and therefore large numbers of cards were published that showed soldiers of both nations together. This card also pokes fun at the British peculiarity of having afternoon tea, whether there is a war going on or not.

by skirmishes with German advance forces, before ending roughly 400km south and only 35km north of Paris. The French capital was put on the defensive and preparations were even made to blow up the Eiffel Tower. The majority of the Allied forces had escaped being surrounded by the Germans, and on the whole the retreat was carried out in an organised fashion. As the front line had stabilised in Alsace-Lorraine, larger parts of the forces no longer needed there could be moved to Paris by railway. By doing this, the French Commander-in-Chief, Joffre, managed to draw together thirty-six divisions between Paris and the Marne, with which he launched a counterattack on 5 September.

Roughly 2.5 million soldiers took part in this battle of the Marne from 6-8 September. The French and British forces quickly thrust into the gap between two German armies on the western

Marching Orders.

Volunteering. Marching Orders.
At the outbreak of the war the UK had a professional army. The necessary expansion of the forces immediately led to a marketing campaign using various manners of seduction, persuasion and social pressure to convince men of suitable age to join the armed forces. After all means had been exhausted, and the stream of volunteers threatened to dry out completely in early 1916, compulsory service was introduced.

Englische Schnelläufer
bei St. Quentin.

Unsere englische Armee zeigte prächtige Leistungen. Im Laufen war sie der deutschen Infanterie glatt überlegen, u. nur mit Mühe gelang es deutscher Kavallerie unsere Truppen zu erreichen. Die Verluste sind nicht gross, nur gab es viele verlorene Absätze. "Frei nach Kitchener."

TR. DRUCKEREI-GES. THIER.

English sprinters at St Quentin.
German cards could also contain well-made satirical motifs, like here: 'Our British Army showed splendid efforts. They were vastly superior runners to the German infantry and the German cavalry had trouble reaching them. There were few losses except for numerous lost heels. "Paraphrased after Kitchener"' The text was, however, hardly based on reality, as the engagement of 29 August 1914 was fought between the Germans and the French, and is considered a tactical victory for the latter.

flank. To avoid being surrounded themselves, the German forces now had to retreat and reached the northern banks of the river Aisne a couple of days later, on 14 September, where they immediately began to dig in. The French called this victory 'the miracle on the Marne' and Joffre received perpetual glory and gratefulness for it, but he had sacrificed almost 500,000 soldiers in the process.

In Belgium, the army still held the fortifications around Antwerp and even made three large sorties (on 24 August, 9 September and 27 September). But from late September onwards, the reinforced German forces began to slowly take the town. Soldiers of the British Royal Naval division were brought in as reinforcements, but the town fell on 10 October. The so-called 'Race to the Sea', in which both

10. Bataille de la Marne
6 au 12 Septembre 1914
Maurupt (Marne)
Champ de bataille à l'est du chemin
de Pargny-sur-Saulx

**Battle of the Marne
6 to 12 September 1914.**
This picture from the battlefield was taken in Maurupt, east of Bar le Duc, at the Chemin de Pargny-sur-Saulex, where tens of thousands of the hundred thousand casualties of the Battle of the Marne lost their lives. Over the course of the war the large publishing houses printed fewer and fewer cards showing casualties and if they did, they showed only dead enemies. Private photo cards with pictures of casualties were, however, printed during the whole war. It is unusual that in this picture, German casualties on the left and French casualties on the right lie so close to each other.

Cliché Chusseau-Flaviens
1914.. Troupes Belges dans les tranchées
à Lierre prés Anvers
1914... Belgian troops in the trenches
16me Série   at Lierre near Antwerp   (ELD)

1914... Belgian troops in the trenches at Lierre near Antwerp.

The village of Lier was part of the south-western defensive cordon around Antwerp. The Belgian king and his General Staff had accommodations here from 9 to 26 September. From 4 October onwards, German soldiers broke into defensive positions. The text of this card contains two errors. First the soldiers are not in a trench but taking cover along a road running along a small dam. Moreover, their weapons and uniforms indicate that they are British, not Belgian soldiers.

sides advanced towards the coast and tried to outflank the enemy, now began. The remaining Belgian troops withdrew behind the River Yser, near Ypres, in southwest Flanders and flooded large areas. They were reinforced by parts of the BEF and by French Marines. For almost two months, counteroffensive followed counteroffensive and despite heavy losses, neither side could break the enemy's lines. The German plan to gain a swift victory in the west and deal with Russia afterwards was thus rendered practically impossible.

After the advance of the German Army had been halted in northern France, the war on the Western Front lost its momentum. A frontline almost 800km long ran from the Belgian coast, through northern France and down to the Swiss border. Following orders from their high command, the Germans dug in even deeper, going on the defensive for the time being while it moved a number of divisions to the Eastern Front.

After storming a French village.

This motif was created after a painting by Max Rabes (1862-1944), a painter and sculptor from Berlin who was among the first official German war painters that followed the troops across the battlefield. Positions as 'war painters' were coveted, as there were far more applicants than available positions. Altogether, fifteen to twenty official war painters went to work, mainly on the Western Front. They could move around quite freely but had to be accompanied by an officer.

Belgium – death notice.

This cynical card was published after the fall of Antwerp. It reads:

'Death notice. Signed band of robbers, known as the Triple Entente, hereby makes public the deeply sorrowful news of the passing of their dearly beloved foster sister, or daughter and sister in law, Belgium, who after the fall of Antwerp caused by 42cm mortars and motorised batteries departed the landscape after short suffering.

The earthly debris will be put to eternal rest by the brothers in arms Germany and Austria. Europe, October 1914. In deep sorrow Russia, England, France. We ask for your silent sympathies. In lieu of flowers mourners are requested to make a donation to Japan.'

The siege was carried out by the Beseler Army Group, which in addition to German troops also had Austro-Hungarian artillery under its command. The 120,000 troops of the siege force were opposed by roughly 150,000 defenders, mostly Belgians, supported by around 2,000 British Marines. After long-lasting bombardments with the heaviest artillery, the defenders withdrew more and more, and Antwerp surrendered on 10 October 1914.

....

The British and French forces could not break the German lines, although at Christmas, there were several occasions where German and British forces fraternised.

1915

In 1915 there was little movement on the front. The Germans were mainly concerned with reinforcing their defensive positions, which the Allies tried unsuccessfully to break. The number of divisions in the foremost positions fell continuously, while more and more soldiers assembled behind the lines, waiting for the one

1914… Defence of Antwerp. Marines and their trophies.

The French marines who are posing with captured German weapons, Pickelhaube helmets and bugles, can be easily identified by their characteristic berets with the typical pompons. The *Brigade Fusiliers Marines* (brigade of marines) was first sent to Antwerp, but when the city fell they were moved to Gent. In the engagements at Melle (9/10 of October) they were able to beat the German forces and were afterwards deployed in the defence of the Yser line. The brigade was 6,400 soldiers strong at the outbreak of the war – it was almost completely annihilated in November 1915.

....

decisive attack. This was the particular wish of the Belgians and French, as the war in the west was being fought on their territory. Belgium was almost completely occupied, and 12,000km² of French terrain containing important industrial and mining areas, were in the hands of the enemy. In February France began a large attack in the Champagne, which after initial successes, soon became stuck. The British fought their

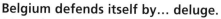

LA BELGIQUE SE DÉFEND PAR.... L'INONDATION
. BELGIUM DEFENDS ITSELF BY.... DELUGE

La Guerre Sociale

WE GAINED A GOOD BIT: OUR CEMETERIES STRETCH AS FAR AS THE SEA ALREADY

..NOUS PROGRESSONS TOUJOURS! NOS CIMETIÈRES VONT JUSQU'A LA MER!....

Belgium defends itself by... deluge.

Manneken Pis, the emblem of Brussels, wearing a bearskin and a sword, urinates on a German soldier. To halt the German advance in south-western Belgium, the floodgates at Nieuwpoort were opened in late October 1914, flooding wide parts of the Yser estuary. The Allies could hold their positions behind the flooded areas and Germany abandoned the offensive at the end of November. In the meantime, both sides had lost about 200,000 lives and the city of Ypres had suffered substantially. During the course of the war only the area behind the Yser remained unoccupied.

We gained a good bit: our cemeteries stretch as far as the sea already.

A postcard with an illustration by the Dutchman, Louis Raemaekers. Not only was he a very gifted painter, but he was also very shocked by the German invasion of Belgium. During the war he created a large number of anti-German prints that were published in their millions worldwide, as picture postcards, cigarette pictures and in journals and magazines. In this way, Raemaekers, more than any other private person, influenced the public perception of the war in general and especially that of the Germans.

second battle of Ypres in April, but gained no worthwhile ground. Their engineers had undermined the German positions on Hill 60 and filled the tunnels with high explosives so that during the battle, six large mines were detonated. Only five days later, German forces were the first to use poison gas on the Western Front, releasing a chlorine gas from canisters. The wind drove the gas cloud into the British positions where it caused substantial losses, although the Germans did not have sufficient manpower to take advantage of this breach in the British lines.

Large scale Allied offensives at Artois and Loos, and in the Champagne in May and September, once more resulted in hardly any gains in territory, even though France alone had committed thirty-five divisions. Hundreds of thousands of French soldiers lost their lives,

584. La Grande Guerre 1914-15 · En CHAMPAGNE.
FORTIN DE BEAUSÉJOUR · Poste d'écoute à 15 m. des allemands.
Un soldat tient une grenade, l'autre une bombe de crapouillaud.
Visé Paris 584   « PHOT-EXPRESS »

The Great War 1914-15. In Champagne. Fortin de Beauséjour. A listening post 15m in front of the Germans. One soldier carries a hand grenade, the other a mortar grenade.
Fortin de Beauséjour was originally an estate. The buildings were located on strategically important ground and changed hands seven times in the early months of 1915. From the end of 1915 onwards, the estate was held continuously by the French and was located at the rear of the French trench system.

whereas the defenders counted substantially fewer losses.

The British reinforced their army several times during the summer of 1915. Only a few soldiers had remained from the original five divisions of the BEF, but they were reinforced by the Territorial Army and the volunteers that had followed Kitchener's appeal. This meant that by the autumn, 100 French and 6 Belgian divisions held the lines on the Western Front, along with sixty divisions from the British Empire. In December 1915, Douglas Haig was made commander-in-chief, with the Allies agreeing to begin a large combined offensive in late spring or early summer of the following year. However, the Germans would beat them to it at Verdun.

1916

Verdun held a strategically important position on the Meuse river, and controlled the northern access to the lowlands of the Champagne, as well as the access route to Paris. The city was

LA BATAILLE SOUS VERDUN, 1916 | THE BATTLE AROUND VERDUN, 1916
Convoi de ravitaillement sur la route | Transports on the road   Visé, Paris

The Battle around Verdun. 1916. Transports on the road.
The French Army held Verdun through great effort and in spite of very heavy losses. The troops were resupplied by a never-ending stream of trucks and carriages via *La voie sacrée*, the Holy Road, from Bar le Duc to Verdun. This card shows a column of carriages bringing troops and supplies to the front.

The fight for Fortress de Vaux (June 1916). Positioned on top of the fortress, the German machine guns control all exits.

Vaux was one of the fifteen fortresses in the defensive ring around Verdun. It was completely surrounded during the German offensive, but tenaciously defended by the garrison under the command of *Capitaine* Raynal. Even after the guns of the fortress had been taken out by 42cm shells, the 600 strong garrison put up a fierce resistance for several more days.

157 LES COMBATS DU FORT DE VAUX (JUIN 1916)
POSTÉES SUR LE DESSUS DU FORT. LES MITRAILLEUSES ALLEMANDES
EN COMMANDENT TOUTES LES ISSUES.

surrounded by several fortresses and was able to resist the heavy German attacks in 1914. Consequently, and for other historical reasons, Verdun was an important national symbol, which France was determined to defend at all costs. This is exactly why General von Falkenhayn, the German commander-in-chief, decided to attack Verdun. In the most literal sense, he wanted to bleed the French Army to death and break the French morale.

But the German plan failed, as the French, led by General Pétain and later General Nivelle, managed to resist. Along the *voie sacrée*, the sacred road, a steady stream of trucks brought supplies into the city. The Germans ended their attacks on 12 July and by the end of the year had to yield all the ground they had initially gained. Altogether, 260,000 soldiers lost their lives at Verdun and more than half a million were wounded.

On 1 July, in order to take the pressure off Verdun, eighteen British divisions attacked along the Somme. After a heavy bombardment from 1,400 guns of all calibres, they attacked the enemy lines with three times the strength of the defenders. However, since 1914, the German

I.R. 53. Vauxstormers!

An NCO sent this card to his family at Mülheim a.d. Ruhr on 17 August 1916, and tells them that 'Uncle Ernst wants you to know that he is very well!' The text on the reverse reads 'Excerpt from the corps orders 8.6.1916: the honour of entering the fortress first with parts of its 1st battalion belongs to regiment 53.' Initially the regiment was part of the 14th infantry division and became part of the newly formed 50th infantry division on 10 March 1915.

J.R. 53. VAUXSTÜRMER!

La Guerre en Lorraine en 1914-15-16
GERBÉVILLER incendié par les Allemands
Rue Gambetta

The war in Lorraine 1914-15-16. Gerbéviller. Torched by the Germans.
Whether the Germans really burned down this village in Lorraine or whether the damage was caused by combat, remains unknown. But the war certainly caused great damage in Belgium and France, and so the number of picture postcards showing destroyed villages is quite high. Usually the text on the cards claimed that the damage was done by the Germans.

forces had enhanced and fortified their positions, and so most soldiers survived the preparatory artillery barrage unscathed. The subsequent attack ended in a fiasco, with British forces suffering the heaviest losses in its military history. When the offensive officially ended on 19 November, the Allies had gained just 11km of ground at the cost of 420,000 British lives. In September, tanks had been used in the field for

the first time in history, but their effects were rather small, as many of the armoured vehicles broke down with technical problems.

The winter of 1916-17 was very hard, and the warring factions needed time to recover from the losses sustained at Verdun and the Somme. While the high commands drew up plans for new offensives, for a few months, life on the front was rather quiet.

Guerre 1914-1917. — LES AMERICAINS EN FRANCE. — AMERICAN SOLDIERS IN FRANCE.
On fait vite connaissance — A french girl forming acquaintance with a soldier.

American soldiers in France. A French girl forming acquaintance with a soldier.
By the standards of 1917 this picture went pretty far to demonstrate how well the connection between France and its new allies had developed. A French girl has climbed onto a wall to kiss an American soldier, with her younger brother and sister watching on.

ALL GOOD LUCK SURROUND YOU.

Que la chance t'accompagne !

In the trench. The sentry.
The soldiers were subject to high physical demands not only in the trenches. Sentry duty, where the enemy trenches had to be watched constantly to recognise movements or surprise attacks in time, was also extremely tiring. Foul weather could actually be an advantage here: the winter of 1916/17 was so cold that there was little combat activity on the Western Front.

All good luck surround you.
Cards wishing soldiers good luck in surviving the war were quite popular. Good luck dolls, four-leaved clovers, horseshoes and a host of other symbols were well-known good luck charms. This card by Fred Spurgin shows a Commonwealth soldier and also a swastika, which is considered a symbol of luck, especially throughout Asia.

1917

The first months of 1917 were icy cold and the soldiers in the trenches suffered from the extreme temperatures. Larger engagements were therefore rare, which is also mirrored in the numbers of casualties. France lost roughly 4,000 soldiers per month during this time; a very low number by First World War standards. In February, Germany declared unrestricted submarine warfare in the hopes of blockading supply routes to England. In reply the USA declared war on Germany in April, although at the time it was yet to have an influence on what took place on the battlefields.

At the end of February, the Allies noticed that the enemy trenches between Arras and Soissons had been vacated. The Germans had straightened and shortened their front line and withdrawn up to 30km in places. The new defensive positions, which they had worked on for almost six months, were skilfully designed and perfectly executed. The Germans called it the Siegfried line, while the Allies referred to it as the Hindenburg line.

In April 1917, British and Canadian troops executed a costly but successful attack near Arras, which ended in the taking of Vimy Ridge. The almost simultaneous French attack on the Chemin des Dames was beaten back and resulted in a German victory. The victory at Arras was caused by both the element of surprise and the Germans having little reserves, whereas

A vous cette gerbe fleurie.
Aux trois couleurs de la Patrie.

Éditeur. PARIS
539

Visé Paris N° 7839 Dt.   ND. PHOT.

Salons de Paris

Pastel de Mᵐᵉ DE BOSREDON. — *Généralissime Nivelle.*

Commander in chief Nivelle.

For you this bouquet of flowers. In the three colours of the motherland.

Another means of cheering up the soldiers were cards with pictures of pretty young women. This card also has a patriotic element, as it mirrors the colours of the French flag. In 1917 the French Army could use every kind of positive motivation, as the morale of the troops had hit an all-time low.

....

the offensive at the Chemin des Dames had been expected and reserves were available in sufficient numbers. This caused heavy losses for the French, for which Nivelle was relieved of his command and succeeded by Pétain.

The failed offensive caused a mutiny in the French Army. Many soldiers refused to take part in further attacks, demanded more leave and better provisions and expressed their dissatisfaction with a number of societal injustices. This unrest was also fuelled by a rising discontent among the civilian population, who answered the rising prices, profiteering and hopeless military situation with strikes and protests. Step by step, Pétain managed to gain control of the situation,

Commander-in-Chief Nivelle.

Not least due to his successful defence of Verdun, Robert Nivelle (1856-1924) was made Commander-in-Chief of the French Army in December 1916. In April and May a large scale British-French offensive took place on his initiative. The French troops were quickly stopped at the German defensive lines, but despite heavy losses, Nivelle sent in reinforcements again and again. Resentment about the way the high command treated soldiers' lives grew in the French Army, and whole units refused to serve at the front. In the end, Nivelle had to step down and he was replaced by Pétain.

....

for example, by introducing more favourable rules for leave, but also by a more defensive demeanour. By now, France was grieving for a million casualties, and the will to fight had shrunk substantially. In Russia, the interior situation was even more serious. In early March, the tsar abdicated the throne and at the end of June, the Bolshevists were agreeing a truce with the Germans. The only good news for the Allies came from the USA, who declared war in April, but still had to raise an army fit for war.

Grand départ pour les tranchées boches.
A Joy Ride round the trenches to visit old Fritz.

A Joy Ride round the trenches to visit old Fritz.
The new British tank had seen its first action on 15 September 1916, but was not reliable enough to cause a quick change in the outcome of the war. Thirteen months later, however, a force of 476 tanks went into action and conquered the Hindenburg Line, which up until that moment was considered impregnable. Due to tactical mistakes by the British and determined resistance by the Germans, the breach was taken back only a couple of days later, although the massed use of tanks had left a lasting impression.

On the Allied left flank, the British were facing the German positions in and around Ypres and it was here that Haig began a large offensive to take the Belgian ports and deny the German submarines their operational base. After several enormous mines were exploded near Messines – it had taken eighteen months to dig the tunnels where the explosives were placed – the area south of Ypres was taken in early June. But the following advance was slowed down by heavy rain and flooded trenches, before being quite literally bogged down near Passchendaele, on 10 November 1917. So as not to be forced onto the defensive even more, Haig ordered a tank attack near Cambrai shortly afterwards. After a preparatory artillery attack, 476 tanks broke the Hindenburg line, but the advance petered out due to lack of reinforcements and too much distance between the tanks and the infantry. After ten days, the Germans managed to push the attackers back and to close the gap in their lines.

Nos Alliés Américains en France
Ayons confiance !
Ces vaillants ne sont que l'avant-garde qui va nous aider à châtier les auteurs de la guerre

Our American Allies in France. Be confident! These brave ones are but the advance force that will help us punish the instigators of the war.
In the spring of 1917 things were looking bleak for the Allies. Nivelle's offensive had failed and the Bolshevist government in Russia was working towards a truce with Germany. There could be no better moment for the USA to declare war than April 1917.

752 *MONTS DE CHAMPAGNE* — *Blockhaus sur le Moronvilliers.*
Blockhaus sobre el Moronvilliers. — *LL.*

The hills of Champagne. A blockhouse near Moronvilliers.

This German bunker on a ridge near Moronvilliers was taken by French troops in May 1917. The original German term, *Blockhaus*, meaning a small fortified position made from wood, stone or concrete was adopted by the French. The Hindenburg Line especially comprised of a multitude of these armoured positions in various sizes.

....

As large contingents of troops had been freed when Russia left the Entente, they could now be moved to the west by railway and in the winter of 1917/18, the German Army quickly grew stronger on the Western Front. They were preparing a superior force (197 German divisions against 178 Allied ones) for a spring offensive that was supposed to end the war before the USA could send enough troops that would make a difference to the outcome.

....

This real photo card shows two German soldiers working on a tunnel. They may be constructing a new dugout or undermining enemy positions. Some sections of the front saw a real mine war – both sides tried to dig tunnels under the enemy trenches without being noticed, in order to then fill them with enormous amounts of explosives and blow them up.

1918

On 21 March 1918, the German Army began 'Operation Michael', a large scale attack against the Allied lines with 76 divisions and 10,000 artillery pieces, whose supposed aim was to drive the British forces back to the coast.

The offensive started favourably and the Germans succeeded where the British and French forces had failed in the last three years. Even without the use of tanks, they broke through the enemy lines and were able to actually enlarge the gap.

The German divisions not only attacked on the right flank at the Somme, where weak British troops held partially unfinished trenches, but also used a new tactic which they had perfected in the east shortly before. This mainly consisted of a short but extremely intense artillery barrage in which the guns and mortars fired a mixture of all kinds of grenades, immediately followed by a massive infantry attack led by specially trained assault troops. These elite units, armed with hand grenades, light machine guns and flamethrowers amongst other weapons, entered the enemy trenches directly after the barrage stopped and created approach corridors for the regular forces who followed behind. There was no concern for what happened on their flanks, as potentially remaining pockets of enemy resistance could be surrounded and neutralised later on.

Ein britischer Löwe

A British lion.
A German soldier kneeling in the background aims his gun at a fleeing British cavalryman in parade dress. The Germans managed to break through on the Somme, in the section with the weakest British forces and partially unfinished trenches. This was a remarkable achievement, as the French and British had been unsuccessfully trying to do exactly this for three years.

This drawing by an unknown French artist is an impressive record of the hell of the battlefield. Drawings sometimes mirror reality better than photographs, which were usually carefully posed and often only showed an idealised reality. The drawing shows two French tanks, one of them stuck in a bomb crater, and infantry advancing with shells hitting all around. Several casualties lie in the left foreground of the picture.

The German offensive. French and English awaiting the enemy together.

A mixed unit of French and British soldiers waiting for the German attack in hastily dug defensive positions. The German breakthrough in the spring of 1918 finally caused the Allies to agree on a combined high command to better organise their defence. The French commander, Pétain, and the British Commander-in-Chief, Haig, were therefore subordinated to Marshall Foch, who managed to stop the German troops at the last minute.

L'offensive allemande.—Français et Anglais attendent l'ennemi ensemble.

German Sturmtruppen assault troops pose for a picture on 2 September 1918. A flamethrower can be seen on the far left. After a short preparatory artillery attack, the specially trained and lightly armed assault troops were to break into the enemy positions swiftly and deeply, creating breaches for the infantry following behind. This new tactic, which was published in the *Ausbildungsvorschrift für die Fußtruppen im Kriege* infantry training manual from 1917 onwards, would prove very effective during the German Spring Offensive.

A German long range artillery piece in firing position, in the woods at Gercourt, firing at Mort Homme and Côte 304.
This German 13cm L/35 gun was captured by the French, 20km north-west of Verdun. The gun has been painted in camouflage to be less visible from the air – hinting at the ever increasing role of the air force.

The German troops created a massive breach in the British lines and advanced nearly 80km to the south, almost reaching Amiens. To improve the coordination of the defence, the French Marshall Foch was made Commander-in-Chief of the Allied Forces and as the resistance put up by the defenders increased, the momentum of the German advance slowly dwindled. This was because the attack followed several directions, and so any initial pressure could not be maintained permanently. In addition, the exhausted German troops were facing temptations behind the British lines they could not resist, leading to widespread looting, mainly of things that were difficult to get or plainly unavailable in Germany due to the blockade. Food and drink were hoarded and the advance of many units substantially delayed.

Finally, just like the German offensives that followed it, Operation Michael slowly ground to a halt at the Allied defensive lines, not least caused by the American troops who were brought into action in steadily increasing numbers. From Spring 1918 onwards, 60,000

American advance, wounded and dying Germans spread along the road. Belleau Wood-France

American advance, wounded and dying Germans spread along the road. Belleau Wood, France.
Published by the *Chicago Daily News* this card shows an actual scene pictured shortly after the battle. Belleau Wood is located roughly 10km north of Chateau-Thierry and became famous by the fierce battle between US Marines and German forces that took place there, as well as by a US officer telling a Frenchman who was urging him to withdraw: 'Retreat? Hell, we just got here.'

One of the reasons why the Allies finally manage to break through the Siegfried and Hindenburg lines was the mass use of tanks. This new weapon had received little recognition by the German high command, and Germany produced hardly any tanks of its own. On the other hand, the German Army had a couple of specialised anti-tank weapons, among them this enlarged variant of the standard infantry rifle that fired 13mm ammunition and weighed 16kg. Here, British officers pose for the camera with a captured Mauser Tankgewehr M1918 anti-tank rifle.

soldiers reached France each week, roughly measuring up to three German divisions.

It was the Americans who primarily stopped the German advance in June, and on 18 July the French and American forces started a large counterattack that halted the German offensive, just as it had on the Marne in 1914. Both sides had suffered roughly equal numbers of casualties in the previous months, but whereas between mid-June and mid-July around 8,000 American soldiers reached France daily, Germany was hardly able to compensate its losses.

Moreover, Germany had failed to develop and produce a usable tank. The Allies could command several hundred tanks of different models by now, and Germany still had to make

TOUT ÇA POUR UN SAUCISSE !...

All this for a sausage!

The French cartoonist Mass'beuf created two series of postcards with satirical motifs during the First World War. Here a German soldier wants to exchange his rifle, bayonet and Pickelhaube leather helmet for a sausage, by which the card refers to the critical supply situation of the German forces. In Summer 1918, food supplies were so short that sometimes mass looting ensued once the British lines were breached, even delaying the advance of the German offensive.

do with fielding captured tanks, as there were hardly any German-made tanks available.

This new branch of arms, the tank force, was used more and more often towards the end of the war, and with good results. At the beginning of August, for example, a force of 600 French and British tanks supported by Canadian and Australian infantry attacked the Germans near Amiens and struck them heavily. The Germans had to retreat and could only gain a hold again behind the initial positions of their spring offensive.

On 26 September, the Allies began their attack against the Hindenburg line; the last German defensive line. Americans, Belgians, French and British began their move, with 123 divisions in all. After three days the result was clear and a breach was forced near St Quentin. In answer to this, the German high command began to negotiate an armistice, which six weeks later, at 11 am on 11 November 1918, became a reality on the Western Front.

After long years of an especially bloody war, the end is near. A German negotiator with a white flag fixed to his car makes contact with the French.

LONGWY, 12 Novembre 1918. - Le départ des Boches

Au Souvenir Lorrain, Longwy

Longwy, 12 November 1918. The *Boches* depart. On 11 November 1918 at about 05:15 in the morning, the German and Allied negotiators put their signatures to an agreement that defined the terms and conditions of an armistice, which was supposed to start at 11am the same day. This picture was taken on the next day, when endless columns of German soldiers on their way north passed through the small French town of Longwy, near the Belgian and Luxembourg borders.

Chapter 6
The Other Theatres of War

The Eastern Front

Russia mobilised its gigantic army faster than many in the west had expected. This was a nasty surprise for the German Empire, which from the beginning was caught in a war on two fronts, as Russia immediately attacked Prussian territories.

On 15 August, only twelve days after Germany had declared war on France, the 1st Russian Army under General von Rennenkampf crossed the border into East Prussia. Five days later, the 2nd Russian Army under Samsonov, invaded Germany from the south-east.

At first, the Russians were successful and advanced fast. The local German commander, General Prittwitz, panicked and reported his intent to withdraw behind the river Vistula to the high command. Consequently, Chief of General Staff, Helmuth Johannes Ludwig von Moltke, relieved him of his command and gave command of the armies in the east to Generals von Hindenburg and von Ludendorff.

Samsonov's troops continued their advance in a north-westerly direction, and the distance to von Rennenkampf's forces, from which they were only separated by the Masurian Lake District, increased continuously. Therefore, the Germans moved the majority of their army to the south by rail, a plan conceived by Colonel Hoffmann, although Ludendorff would receive the praise. In doing so, a strong German Army was able to score a decisive victory against the 2nd Russian Army at Tannenberg in late August. After heavy engagements in the first half of September, von Rennenkampf also had to withdraw his forces to the east.

Le général de RENNENKAMPF

E. LE DELEY, Imprimeur, Paris.

General Rennenkampf.
Descended from a German Baltic family, Paul Georg von Rennenkampf (1854-1918) commanded the Russian 1st Army that invaded East Prussia. After the defeat at Tannenberg and massive criticism against his style of leadership, he resigned his commission in 1915. During the October Revolution he was shortly incarcerated, but then set free again. The Bolsheviks asked von Rennenkampf to lead a unit in the Red Army and when he refused, he was executed on 1 April 1918.

Wo bleibt denn die russische Hilfsarmee?

Now, where's the supporting Russian Army?

This German card must have been printed in the very first weeks of the war. It shows an officer of the French Army, who is on the lookout for his ally from the east at a crossroads between London and Berlin. In fact the Russians surprised friend and foe alike, as they mobilised their army unexpectedly swiftly, and only eleven days after the Germans had attacked Belgium, the Russian 1st Army under Paul von Rennenkampf invaded East Prussia.

From the end of August onwards, the Russian Army also fought in engagements with Austro-Hungarian troops under the command of Conrad von Hötzendorf. His operational plans, like those of his allies, were based on the assumption that it would take Russia some time to mobilise its troops. After a short-lived advance by von Hötzendorf's troops, Russia started its counter-attack by invading Galicia and after victory at Lviv, carried on into the Carpathian Mountains. The Austrians suffered 500,000 casualties, more than twice as many as the Russians.

This caused Germany to come to the aid of its ally and to start an eastward attack at the beginning of October. In the last months of 1914, German troops took large parts of Poland and what would later become the Baltic States. In December, the Austro-Hungarian Army also managed to halt the Russian advance in the south-west.

Germany tried to eliminate its Russian opponant in 1915 by starting a large scale

Wie die Russen in Ostpreussen hausten!
Die von den Russen zerstörte Stadt Gerdauen.

How the Russians behaved in East Prussia! The town of Gerdauen destroyed by the Russians.

Damage resulting from a fight between Russian attackers and German defenders. Gerdauen in East Prussia had roughly 5,000 inhabitants and was in Russian hands for a couple of weeks in August and September 1914. When the borders were moved around after the Second World War, Gerdauen, which had been a part of Königsberg county, became Soviet territory in 1946 and its name was changed to Zheleznodorozhny.

The Russians being pursued through East Prussia.
After the distance between the two invading Russian armies continually increased, the Prussian Colonel Hoffmann came up with the plan to move large parts of the German Army to the south, in order to attack the isolated Russian 2nd Army. The operation was successful; the Russians suffered 120,000 casualties at Tannenberg and General Samsonov committed suicide.

offensive in the Masurian Lake District. But despite causing heavy losses for Russia and achieving a great victory, Germany made hardly any territorial gains. On the South-Eastern Front, the Russians managed to take the important fortress of Przemysl, at the foot of the Carpathian Mountains, in March. However, the town was taken back by German troops led by General von Mackensen in June, during an Austro-German offensive in Galicia. In the summer German forces, reinforced by units from the Western Front, managed to gain a lot of ground in the north-east and until the end of the year, the front line had been moved roughly 500km towards the east, from Riga in the north to the river Dnieper in the south.

In Spring 1916 the Russian Army, led by General Brussilov, again mounted a large-scale attack in south-eastern direction. Russia had to

Fiery and strong Cossack, proud and loyal soldier, France is waiting over there; that is why we call you.
The Russian Army mostly impressed people by its immense size. Although not all able-bodied men were actually conscripted into service, it was still the largest army in the world. The Cossacks had a special position in the army and were considered the best Russian troops of all, feared by the enemy, admired by their friends – as proven by this French card.

SÉRIE HUMORISTIQUE DE LA GUERRE 1914

40

Comment on le traite !
A LA RUSSE — Bravo Cosaque ! continue.

Humorous series from the war of 1914. That's how to treat them! In the Russian way. Bravo, Cossack. Carry on.
A drawing by the French graphic artist, A. P. Jarry, who rose to some fame during the First World War with his *Série humoristique*, our picture shows No 40. The picture of a Cossack flogging Emperor Wilhelm II was a popular motif and printed in several variations.

start the operation earlier than planned, as Italy was under massive pressure by an Austrian-Hungarian offensive south of Trento and urgently asked for help. Nevertheless, the offensive was a success for Brussilov at first. He could gain a lot of territory and take about 350,000 soldiers of the Imperial and Royal Army prisoner. But in the end the offensive ground to a halt. Germany again came to the aid of its ally and Russia was forced to move troops to

Romania, which had joined the Allies in August and had immediately been attacked by a Bulgarian-German army. So the offensive petered out in Summer 1916.

The enormous losses and low morale of the troops, combined with a population suffering from hunger and cold, due to a growing lack of heating fuel and food, caused civil unrest to break out in Russia. Starting in the work force, the insurrection spread to the army, and in

Victory to our united arms.
During the second half of 1915, a large offensive by German and Austrian troops could gain substantial ground. The German Army, who in the meantime had moved large amounts of troops from the Western to the Eastern Front, managed to move the front line by about 500km, from Riga in the north to the Dniepr in the south.

Sieg unsern vereinigten Waffen!

Tzar Nicolas II

scale offensive in Galicia, but this too was stopped within a few weeks as the army started to crumble. Shortly afterwards, Germany occupied the Ukraine without meeting any resistance. In December, an armistice was proclaimed and on 3 March 1918, the Treaty of Brest-Litovsk was signed.

The Balkans

In 1914 Serbia's 4.5 million inhabitants were ruled by King Peter I. The Serbian Army was mobilised on 30 July 1914 and was commanded by the elderly and sick, but experienced, Marshall Radomir Putnik. The army numbered around 420,000 soldiers in total, including 250,000 front line troops structured into 11 infantry divisions and 1 cavalry division. The country was supported by its small ally, Montenegro, who mustered another 50,000 troops.

March 1917, the tsar was forced to abdicate the throne.

In early July the army started another large-

Im Szurduk Pass.

At the Surduc pass.
German and Austro-Hungarian soldiers have made a photograph of their shelter at the Surduc pass, in the Carpathian Mountains, into a postcard. On 27 August 1916, Romania entered the war on the side of the Allies and crossed the Austro-Hungarian border, but the advance was stopped after 80km. Under the commanders August von Mackensen and Falkenhayn, the Central Powers went on the counter-attack and on 17 November managed to break through the strategically important Szurduc pass. The Romanian capital fell on 6 December.

Over the course of the war unrest kept growing in the Russian Empire. Interior tensions in combination with severe losses in the army led to ever-decreasing circumstances for the population and finally to the tsar stepping down from the throne. After the October Revolution, the Bolshevists decided to withdraw from the war, and so a peace treaty was signed with the Central Powers on 3 March 1918. This real photo cards shows German soldiers celebrating shortly after the treaty was signed, the sign on the front left reads 'Peace with Russia'.

....

The Serbian Army had roughly 600 pieces of artillery at its disposal, of which two thirds was relatively modern, although ammunition, like everything else, was in very short supply. There were only about 180,000 modern Mauser rifles and 200 Maxim machine guns for the 250,000 combat soldiers, and again, ammunition supplies were low. Supporting troops had to be content with receiving a tunic, but shoes or boots were not issued. During the course of the war, military aid mainly came from France and Russia who contributed rifles, uniforms and ammunition.

At the end of 1914, Serbia managed to beat off an invasion by Austro-Hungarian forces. Although Belgrade was taken on 2 December, it was taken back on the 15th, marking the first Allied victory. The country finally fell to Germany and its new ally, Bulgaria, in October 1915. British and French troops tried to come to Serbia's aid via Greece (Thessaloniki) and Macedonia, but were repelled by the Bulgarians. The remainder of the Serbian Army withdrew to

....

The Austrian considers the little Serbian sufficiently punished.
Schadenfreude on account of Austria-Hungary. In Autumn 1914 the Serbs could repel the invasion by the Imperial and Royal Army, in which Belgrade was taken on 2 December but was already taken back by 15 December, marking the first victory for the Allies. Finally, Austria-Hungary managed to take the much smaller Serbia in Autumn 1915, with the help of German and Bulgarian troops.

l'autrichien estime que le petit serbe est suffisament châtié.

LA GUERRE

Le plus jeune soldat serbe âgé de 12 ans en action à Belgrade.

The youngest Serbian soldier, age twelve, in action in Belgrade.
With only 4.5 million inhabitants, Serbia mobilised a military force of almost 420,000 soldiers. However, this card gives rise to the suspicion that the standards for recruiting and accepting volunteers were different from those in western European countries. In December 1914 Belgrade saw heavy engagements between Serbian and Austro-Hungarian troops.

the Albanian coast and was ferried to Corfu from there.

No other country suffered losses comparable to those of Serbia. In this part of the world, the war was extraordinarily cruel and ethnic cleansing and massacres of prisoners of war or the local population were commonplace. Of 4.5 million inhabitants 275,000 died in action as soldiers, 120,000 were severely wounded and about 500,000 civilians died of hunger, diseases or as a result of the hostilities.

Serbia's neighbour and enemy, Bulgaria, numbered 5 million inhabitants at the beginning of the war and was ruled by Tsar Ferdinand I. Before the First World War, the country was already involved in two wars on the Balkans, where several countries fought for parts of the Ottoman Empire (Turkey).

After the Second Balkan War, Bulgaria had lost large parts of Macedonia in 1913, and in October 1915, German diplomats convinced the tsar to enter the war on the side of the Central Powers, by promising he would receive the territories he desired.

Em. Dupuis

Misch
Oct 1914

Infanterie serbe

Serbian Infantry.
Another card from the watercolour series *Nos Alliés* by Emile Dupuis. The First World War started with a declaration of war against Serbia by Austrio-Hungary, who assumed an involvement of the Serbian intelligence agency in the assassination of the heir to the Austrian throne, Archduke Franz-Ferdinand, and his wife, Sophie Chotek, Duchess of Hohenberg, during an official state visit to Sarajevo.

Servian Artillery Officers going off for the war.
As Serbia was a French ally, similar to Russia, many picture postcards with motifs from the Serbian Army were published in 1914. The Serbian artillery commanded roughly 600 artillery pieces, among them about two thirds of modern guns, but ammunition supplies were very limited.

Compared to the number of inhabitants, Bulgaria's army was quite large. After mobilisation it numbered 600,000 soldiers structured into 11 infantry divisions and 1 cavalry division. The artillery commanded 1,200 guns, two thirds of them modern models. The 250 Maxim machine guns they used were practically identical to the German machine guns and the standard weapon was the Mannlicher Gewehr 1885 rifle, built in Austria. The Bulgarian uniforms were modern and utilitarian,

with a cap being worn instead of a helmet. Almost all military goods, however, were in short supply, as raising and outfitting an army of that size was beyond the small country's capacity.

The forces were commanded by General Nikola Todorov Zhekov and from October 1915 onwards, they took part in the attack on Serbia as part of the Mackensen army group, side by side with German and Austro-Hungarian troops. In Autumn 1916, the Bulgarian forces managed to conquer parts of Macedonia, but were

War 1914-15... In the Balkans. Serbian Maxim-Gunners.
Like many other nations – including Germany, Russia, the UK, Turkey and Bulgaria – Serbia also fielded the Maxim machine gun. The model was based on the first fully automatic firearm, which had been developed by the British-American engineer, Hiram Maxim, in 1885.

Deutsche Einquartierung im serbischen Bauernhause

Germans being billeted in a Serbian farm.
This card was published in Leipzig by 'Verlag von Dr Trenkler & Co', one of the biggest publishers of military picture postcards. The shared meal is supposed to look relaxed and amicable, but it is doubtful whether the girl on the front-right really enjoyed it.

A group of Bulgarian soldiers posing for a picture. This card was posted on 18 July 1917 and shows two of the approximately 250 Maxim machine guns of the 600,000 soldiers of the Bulgarian Army. The soldier sitting at the table in the centre of the picture prepares ammunition belts. The device he is using for this takes single rounds through the funnel on top, and by turning the crank he inserts them into the woven ammunition belt. The Bulgarian soldiers' caps are quite similar to the ones used in the Russian Army.

The fowler 1915.
A special card, produced in Germany in 1915, but carrying a French text. It shows the UK as the evil spirit of the war, who having already captured the Russian bear and the French cock, is now trapping Romania, while Greece and Bulgaria are still sitting in the tree as free birds. In the background a Turkish soldier welcomes his German comrade with open arms.

afterwards mainly on the defensive.

In the meantime, the Allies had changed Thessaloniki into a giant army camp and were holding eight divisions there. The soldiers were ravaged by malaria and fought in several engagements with the Bulgarian troops, one of them near Monastir in Macedonia at the end of 1916. The long lasting stalemate in this theatre could only be broken in September 1918, when French, Serbian, Greek and British forces attacked Bulgaria, which then negotiated an armistice, beginning on 30 September 1918.

The Italian Front
Since 1882 Italy was part of the Triple Alliance with the German Empire and Austria-Hungary, who therefore expected it to fight on their side when war was declared. This did not happen, however, as Italy considered the alliance to be a purely defensive one and therefore decided to wait. The Allies finally managed to convince Italy to enter the war on their side, promising territorial gains at the expense of Austria-Hungary, who had a 650km long border with Italy. Consequently, Italy declared war against the Dual Monarchy on 23 May 1915.

At this time Italy could field about 36 divisions numbering 500,000 soldiers, but had only a couple of hundred modern field guns at

Montenegrin Infantry.
Card No 7 from Emil Dupuis' *Nos Alliés* series, shows an infantrymen from Montenegro. Since 1910 the small country had been a monarchy ruled by King Nicholas I. Its army consisted of about 50,000 soldiers and was led by Serbian officers. Montenegro was occupied by the Central Powers at the same time as Serbia, and became part of the Kingdom of Yugoslavia when the war ended in 1918.

SALONIQUE - Soldats français débarquents des marchandises

France et Italie

.... On revient toujours
A son premier amour

Thessaloniki. French soldiers unloading supplies.
A force of several hundred thousand men was assembled at Thessaloniki. The Allies had landed in Greece without asking the Greek government for consent, the environment was about as bad as it could be and malaria claimed many victims. The political situation was also complicated, as the head of the government supported the Allies, whereas the king sided more with the Germans. This card was sent home by a *poilu* on 25 October 1916, and begins with the words: 'Dear parents, I have a small hope of seeing France again, but do not count on it, as things change fast around here.'

France and Italy. You always return to your first love.
Italy, symbolised by a young woman, nestles up against a French soldier while a German scowls at the scene. Both the Entente and the Central Powers tried to draw Italy into the war. When this card was published, Italy's choice was clear. The first love is pointing back at the nineteenth century, when France supported the young nation of Italy and both countries worked against Austria-Hungary together.

its disposal. The army and its equipment were continually expanded, assisted especially by the UK and France, and so almost 1.5 million soldiers were already deployed at the front by the beginning of 1916. In the meantime, the artillery commanded roughly 2,000 guns.

General Luigi Cadorna, Chief of Staff of the Italian Army, was a mediocre tactician at best and was ruthless with his soldiers. If a unit failed

in his eyes, he was capable of having soldiers and officers picked out at random and executed.

The army mirrored the Italian society of its time, which had become a constitutional monarchy in 1861, after the era of Risorgimento and several wars had united the many independent Italian states. There were substantial differences between the infantrymen, who mainly came from rural areas in southern Italy, and the northern Italians, who were better educated, achieved higher ranks and usually served in artillery or cavalry units or with the air force or

Domandatevi:
Che cosa fece Egli per l'Italia?
Che cosa ho fatto io?
Sottoscrivete!

PILADE ROCCO - IMPRESSIONI D'ARTE - MILANO

Bersaglieri mountain infantry. Many nationalists regarded Italy entering the war as the last phase of the Risorgimento, bringing an end to

What did he do for Italy? What did you do? Sign for war bonds!

Cesare Battisti, born in Trento, campaigned to unify the Trentino region with the Kingdom of Italy. He was elected into the Austrian Imperial Council but fled to Italy when the war began and joined the Italian Army. In 1916 he was taken prisoner and was sentenced to death by strangulation for high treason, despite having parliamentary immunity. The manner and mode of his execution and the smiling crowd who posed for photographs with his body caused severe damage to the reputation of Austria-Hungary.

reunification, as Italy laid claim to the Italian-speaking parts of Tyrol and the area around Trieste.

Between 23 June 1915 and 18 August 1917, the Italian forces attacked the Austro-Hungarian defensive lines along the Isonzo river eleven times without breaking through. In October 1917, the Austro-Hungarian and German units started a combined counter-attack, breaking the Italian lines at Caporetto and advancing almost 150km up to the Piave, in eleven days. The Caporetto fiasco (today the city is Slovenian and named Kobarid) marked the end of Chief of Staff Cadorna's career.

Cadorna was not the only commander to lose

Soldiers of the Imperial and Royal Austro-Hungarian Army in their sandbagged position, north of San Giovanni, on the Isonzo front, in Autumn 1916. The postmark names the sender as being the *Infanterie-Regiment* Nr. 47. They operate a Schwarzlose machine gun positioned in front of their dugout, which has been carved out of the rock.

Taking a walk through his favourite fields.
This Italian caricature shows Emperor Franz Joseph I of Austria passing through his favourite field, a field of gallows. He already carries the next gallows with him. Austria-Hungary was a multi-ethnic state and many of its inhabitants worked for independence or wanted to join other countries – often leading to charges of high treason, which was punishable by hanging.

A machine-gun section.
On 10 June 1917 this card was cleared by a censor in the Italian town of Terni. It shows a machine gun section of the *Bersaglieri*, who can be identified by their hats which are decorated with a cock's plume. They are armed with Fiat machine guns that they have strapped to their backs by breaking down the parts and fixing them in special carrying racks. Roughly 210,000 men served in the 12 elite regiments during the First World War, 32,000 of them were killed in action and another 50,000 were wounded.

A group of Austrian soldiers pose for the camera with their tools. As the pneumatic drill used to bore holes for explosives shows, they are preparing positions and dugouts in the rocks. The soldier in the centre is holding the necessary dynamite. Two of the soldiers carry carbide lamps, which are also used in mining. The picture was most likely taken in the Alps, south of Trento, where fierce and bloody battles were fought in June 1916.

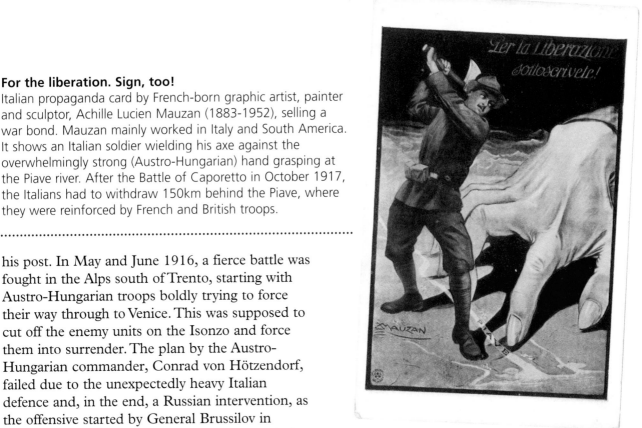

For the liberation. Sign, too!
Italian propaganda card by French-born graphic artist, painter and sculptor, Achille Lucien Mauzan (1883-1952), selling a war bond. Mauzan mainly worked in Italy and South America. It shows an Italian soldier wielding his axe against the overwhelmingly strong (Austro-Hungarian) hand grasping at the Piave river. After the Battle of Caporetto in October 1917, the Italians had to withdraw 150km behind the Piave, where they were reinforced by French and British troops.

his post. In May and June 1916, a fierce battle was fought in the Alps south of Trento, starting with Austro-Hungarian troops boldly trying to force their way through to Venice. This was supposed to cut off the enemy units on the Isonzo and force them into surrender. The plan by the Austro-Hungarian commander, Conrad von Hötzendorf, failed due to the unexpectedly heavy Italian defence and, in the end, a Russian intervention, as the offensive started by General Brussilov in Galicia, forced the Austrians to move the majority of their troops there. The Trentino Offensive cost around 150,000 lives and lost von Hötzendorf his post. At the urgent request of General von Falkenhayn, he was relieved of his command.

In Italy, Cadorna had by this time been replaced by General Armando Diaz. After the Italian Army, assisted by French and British troops, was able to repel a major attack by Austria-Hungary against its positions behind the Piave, Diaz went on the counterattack at the end of October 1918. They broke the Austro-Hungarian lines at Vittoro Veneto and the already demoralised Imperial and Royal Army suffered a crushing defeat from which it would not recover. On 4 November, an armistice was signed and Italy received the territories it desired. But the price had been high: around 700,000 Italians had died and roughly one million had been severely wounded.

Les Italiens à la Bataille du Carso. Août 1915

The Italians in the Battle of the Carso. August 1915. Austro-Hungarian troops (on the right) surrender to the Italians in great numbers.
This is supposed to have happened in August 1915 on the Carso, a high plateau on the Isonzo river, where both the Italians and their enemies suffered substantial losses in August without gaining any ground worth mentioning. As there was actually no single, outstanding event, this card was produced purely for propaganda purposes.

CROQUIS DE GUERRE 1915

302   Tirailleurs japonais dans une tranchée
à la prise de Tsing-Tao

Sketch of the war 1915. Japanese infantrymen in a trench during the capture of Tsingtao.
The former German colony around the port of Tsingtao (today's Qingdao) lies on the Yellow Sea and was captured in November 1915 by a Japanese infantry division, supported by around 1,500 British and Indian soldiers. The German garrison of 3,500 marines held out to an enemy eight times its size for a week, before the city finally fell.

....

L'ANGLAIS et le JAPONAIS
ou les deux extrêmes
se touchent

The English and the Japanese, where the two extremes meet each other.
A cartoon by Mass'beuf, whose French pun is difficult to translate. It shows Japan as England's little brother and takes reference to the 'Extreme-Orient', the Far East, where the British and the Japanese Empire met, but in fact the UK had to rely on the support of the Japanese Navy in these parts of the world. Among other places, Japan conquered the Caroline, Marshall and Mariana Islands, which was met with little enthusiasm in the USA and Australia.

....

The German Colonies: Africa, Asia and the Pacific Ocean

In 1914 the German Empire had colonies in Africa, Asia and the Pacific Ocean, all of which were attacked by the Allies in the first year of the war. The territories in the Pacific Ocean (Samoa and Kaiser-Wilhelms-Land in Papua New Guinea) were occupied by troops from Australia and New Zealand with little difficulty.

In November 1915 Japan, with British assistance, conquered the German colony around the coastal city of Tsingtao, after having already occupied the Carolina, Marshall and Mariana

Islands. The Americans and Australians were not exactly happy about the Japanese occupation of the islands and twenty-six years later, the world would know why. The UK, however, were willing to pay this price, as they needed the Japanese Navy to capture armed German merchant ships.

There were four German colonies in Africa: Togo, Cameroon, German East Africa (Tanzania) and German South-West Africa (Namibia). Togo was easily occupied in 1914 by a mixed force of British and French colonial troops, namely the West African Rifles and the *Tirailleurs Sénégalais*, whereas the last resisting forces in Cameroon only surrendered in February 1916. German South-West Africa was occupied by South African forces in the first half of 1915. Its capital, Windhoek, was taken in May and in July, the German *Schutztruppe* colonial armed forces surrendered unconditionally.

The struggle in German East Africa would take the longest. War started there on 6 August 1914, with the capital, Dar-es-Salaam, being bombarded by a British cruiser, and in November, British and Indian troops went ashore near Tanga. This enterprise turned into a fiasco and from 1916, a small German force, mainly comprised of local soldiers (*Askari*) and commanded by Paul von Lettow-Vorbeck, fought a guerilla war against a superior enemy, which only stoped after the armistice was signed in Europe.

Paul von Lettow-Vorbeck's *Schutztruppe* colonial force was vastly inferior in numbers to the attackers. He was continually on the move and so the growing Allied force could not pin the German-African troops down and force them into a decisive battle. They only lay down their arms (undefeated) on 25 November 1918, two weeks after the Armistice in Europe, after learning about the end of the war from the papers of a captured British officer.

The fights in this rather unimportant theatre, in which Portuguese and Belgian colonial troops also took part later on, cost the lives of hundreds of thousands, perhaps even millions. Hunger, exhaustion and diseases took a heavy toll, especially among the African troops and the inhabitants of the territories in which the war was fought.

Turkey and the Middle East

At the beginning of the war, the Ottoman Empire sided with Germany and against its old enemy, Russia. In 1914 Turkey numbered around 21 million inhabitants, and when it entered the war in late October, roughly 600,000 of them took up arms. The war against Italy in 1911-12 and the two Balkan wars of 1912 and 1913 had only resulted in defeats and heavy losses for Turkey, and therefore the army was not regarded highly. Although it underwent a phase of reorganisation by German military advisors, this was far from finished in the autumn of 1914.

Enver Pasha. Turkish Minister of War.
Enver Pasha (1881-1922) was one of the most important leaders of the Young Turk Revolution who tried to establish a modern Ottoman Empire. After a coup in 1913, the triumvirate of Enver Pasha, Talaat Pasha and Djemal Pasha practically became dictators of Turkey. In 1914 he was Minister of War and de facto Commander-in-Chief of the Turkish Army and was responsible for joining the Central Powers. After the war he and several other leading Young Turks had to flee, and for a short time he found asylum in Germany. Afterwards he joined the Basmachi movement in Central Asia and was killed in action in 1922, in an engagement with Russian forces near Dushanbe, the capital of Tadzhikistan, whilst fighting for the independence of the Muslim population.

Turkey would nevertheless play an active role in the war from October 1914 onwards, driven by pressure from Germany and the ambitions of its Minister of War, Enver Pasha.

The Turkish Army had around 1,000 relatively modern field guns of French, German and Austro-Hungarian origin at its disposal, mostly in the 75mm calibre, but with very little ammunition. Although the same model of Maxim machine gun as used in Germany was

The fable of the fox and the stork, with Turkey in the role of the stork and Germany in the role of the fox. In the fable the fox first makes a fool out of the stork, only to be fooled himself by the stork on the next day. Apparently the caricature wants to point out that both countries are unreliable allies. At the same time this card is a perfect example for the global business of the large postcard publishing houses. The London based company 'Raphael Tuck & Sons' produced this series with motifs taken from fables and drawn by Spanish artist, F. Sancha (1874-1936), with the respective texts on the reverse for England, Spain, Portugal and the Netherlands.

introduced in 1912, this was only available in small numbers until 1915. The standard weapon was a reliable bolt action rifle built by Mauser. Uniforms and equipment were well below average European levels, and supplies and logistics were especially poor. In addition, most Turkish soldiers were insufficiently trained and had little experience, but on the battlefield they were thoughtful and courageous.

On the initiative of Enver Pasha, Turkey started offensives on two fronts simultaneously. In the south-west they advanced along the Suez Canal and north Africa, and in the east against the Russian Caucasus. Mesopotamia (Iraq, which at that time was part of the Ottoman Empire) and the Dardanelles, a narrow strait separating Europe and Asia, also became theatres of war.

The Turkish attack on the vital Suez Canal petered out in Palestine in February 1915, but the Allies stayed on the defensive here until well

1914... Forces Anglaises préparant l'embarquement pour attaquer le port de Duala (Cameroun)
12ᵐᵉ Serie

English forces preparing embarkment to attack the port of Duala Cameroun) E.L.D

1914... English forces preparing embarkment to attack the port of Duala (Cameroon).
Duala, the capital of Cameroon, was bombarded by British and French warships on 26 September 1914. On the following day, troops landed to conquer the city and the last German units surrendered about half a year later. The colonial troops led by British officers pictured here, are among the soldiers who carried out the landing operation on 27 September 1914.

Colonial War Bond

As commander of the *Schutztruppe* colonial troops in German East Africa, Paul von Lettow-Vorbeck led an exceptionally successful guerilla war against the Allies, who up until the end of the war did not manage to defeat him decisively. He led his small army of German officers, volunteers and local *Askaris* against a superior force of Indian, British, South African, Portuguese and Belgian colonial troops. Estimates are that roughly 1 million people died in this strategically rather unimportant theatre of war. The majority of them were African porters and local civilians, who mostly died of exhaustion and hunger.

into 1916. Four Turkish armies supported by a couple of German units fought against troops from India, the UK, Australia, New Zealand and Arabia. The Allied spring offensive of 1917 ground to a halt near Gaza, but in October a new

attack with substantially increased numbers resulted in a breakthrough. Jerusalem was taken in December, and the advance north continued in 1918, until Damascus was taken on 1 October, before an armistice was signed on the 30th.

The second front in this theatre was the Russian Caucasus, where Turkey and Russia fought fierce battles in winter 1914/15. Despite a few Turkish victories, the large scale offensive operations mostly ended with no clear results.

The Allies wanted to support Russia by putting pressure on Germany's ally, Turkey, and so tried to force their way through the Dardanelles into the Black Sea. At the end of April 1915, they landed troops near Gallipoli, a

DOCUMENTATION DU MINISTERE DES COLONIES DE BELGIQUE

l'armement de la canonnière " Paul Renkin."

The arms of gunboat *Paul Renkin.*

This card was issued by the Belgian Ministry of Colonial Affairs and bears the mark 'cleared for publishing'. It shows a group of Belgians and local members of the Congolese forces. The weapons are a Colt machine gun and a 37mm Maxim machine cannon that was nicknamed 'Pom-Pom' due to its distinctive firing sound. The weapons come from the gunboat *Paul Renkin* which patrolled Lake Kivu. During the war they were also used inland against the Germans.

1914-15… In the Dardanelles – A charge.
To support the Russians and to put pressure on Germany by attacking its Turkish ally, the Allies tried to force their way into the Black Sea through the Dardanelles. To do this troops were landed near the coastal town of Gallipoli in late April 1915, but unexpectedly strong Turkish resistance prevented the expeditionary forces from Australia, New Zealand, the UK and India from leaving their landing zones.

The Great War 1914/15. The Holy War is declared.
In 1915 Germany tried to declare a holy war together with its Turkish ally, in the hope of encouraging an uprising amongst certain Islamic colonies of the British Empire. The attempt was unsuccessful and most of the Arab countries sided with the British in order to escape the Ottoman domination. The British officer, T. E. Lawrence, 'Lawrence of Arabia', would rise to international fame as their (self-appointed) leader.

War 1914-15-16… In Orient. On the right the Greek volunteers embarking for Sed-Dul-Bahr.
A Turkish fortress positioned at Sed Dul-Bahr on the Dardanelles, near Gallipoli, was captured by a force consisting of French troops and Greek volunteers in the spring of 1915. The picture shows the Greek volunteers embarking; the smaller ships will take them out to the large ships visible in the background. The port is most likely that of Thessaloniki.

ON DEMANDE
ASSOCIÉ

POUR
L'EXTENSION
DU
KULTUR

LA TURQUIE

Décidément, Guillaume deux, perd l'équilibre,
Et son immense empire est sur le point de choir,
Puisqu'il en est réduit à jeter le "mouchoir"
A cette vieille amie, en qui plus rien ne vibre.
ANDRÉ ROSS.

Wanted: employees to spread Kultur.

A French caricature mocking the affiliation of Turkey to Germany. In October 1914 the Turkish government and Enver Pasha in particular, decided that Turkey would go to war on the German side – against the old Russian enemy in the Caucasus, and the British presence in the Middle East. In French eyes, the culture (*Kultur* in German) that was supposed to be spread was the German double standard of considering itself a civilised nation on the one hand, but starting a war on the other.

Infantryman (Turkish).

In 1917 Emile Dupuis signed this card Number 32 of his *Leurs caboches* series. At the beginning of the war the Turkish Army consisted of about 600,000 soldiers, of which most were moderately equipped infantrymen with little experience. German military advisers commanded by General Otto Victor Carl von Sanders had been working in Turkey since June 1913. In 1915 he was given command of the 5th Turkish Army that defended the Dardanelles successfully.

coastal town close to the Dardanelles, but the soldiers from Australia, New Zealand, the UK and India were unable to leave their bridgehead due to an unexpectedly heavy resistance put up by the Turkish defenders. A second attempt in August did not change the situation, and so the remaining troops were withdrawn in early 1916. One of the two Turkish divisions that played an important role in the defence of the Dardanelles was commanded by Mustafa Kemal, who would later would rise to fame as Atatürk.

The Middle East was also an important source of petroleum in the Great War, and so the Allies

tried to conquer the oilfields. The first division of 'Indian Expeditionary Force D' landed near Basra, in southern Mesopotamia, in November 1914. It was to be followed later by another seven divisions, forming the largest Indian force outside India. But in April 1916, after a failed attempt to march from Basra to Baghdad, they were partially surrounded by the Turks at Kut Al Amara and had to surrender. The situation remained unchanged until the beginning of 1917, when the Allies grew stronger and could gain important victories. Baghdad was taken in March 1917 and they reached Mosul in 1918.

Inghilterra – England.
The sailing vessel on this propaganda card from Italy symbolises the UK with its mighty fleet. From the end of the eighteenth century onwards, the Royal Navy commanded the strongest fleet in the world. It formed the basis for the most influential means of Britain's foreign policy and was especially important in the protection of its overseas territories and trade connections with its Empire. Germany's bid for power on the continent, along with its fleet in other parts of the world, was a thorn in Britain's side, and the British reaction to it did not exactly improve European relations, either.

The Rt. Hon. Winston Churchill.
In 1914 Winston Churchill (1874-1965) was First Lord of the Admiralty and mobilised the Royal Navy even before the official declaration of war and without consulting the other members of the government. He was also among the instigators of the disastrous Gallipoli campaign, which led to his resignation. After a short interlude in the trenches of northern France, he was appointed Minister of Munitions in 1917 and became closely involved in the development of the tank force.

The War at Sea

Being completely surrounded by the sea, the UK could only afford to have a small regular army, although it needed a strong fleet to defend the home country and the sea routes to its colonies. In 1914 the Royal Navy could muster around 80 capital ships and 650 medium and light warships, making it the strongest navy in the world. The German Imperial Navy was second, with almost 50 capital ships and about 300 medium and light warships, although most of them were not very modern.

Immediately after the outbreak of the war, the UK declared a naval blockade against Germany and Austria-Hungary (thereby violating international law), the effects of which were soon felt. A few weeks later, the first naval battle ensued near Heligoland (28 August 1914), but like the following two naval engagements near the Falkland Islands (8 December 1914) and at Dogger Bank (24 January 1915), it had little effect on the course of the war.

On 1 February 1915, Germany started to use its submarines against merchant ships in order to

Guerre 1914-15... Débarquement d'une
44me Série   Escadrille à ALEXANDRIE
War 1914-15...   The landing of a Squadron
of aeros at Alexandria

War 1914-15... The landing of a Squadron of aeros at Alexandria.
To counter the Turkish pressure against the Suez Canal and the Middle East, strong forces were deployed to Egypt. The ground forces were supported in their efforts by aeroplanes that were especially useful for long distance reconnaissance. This picture postcard shows big wooden chests being unloaded in the port of Alexandria. They are marked with 'M.F. 464 Ailerons Aeroplanes M. Farman. Très Fragile' and contained disassembled planes.

cut supply routes to the UK, and even fired torpedoes against cargo ships from neutral states. From a military point of view, the operation was a great success, with Germany sinking 227 British freighters in 1915. But after the sinking of the British liners, Lusitania and Arabic, with the loss of more than 100 American lives, the outrage in the USA caused Germany to discontinue its unrestricted submarine warfare on 1 September.

The biggest naval battle in modern history took place on 31 May 1916, in the North Sea off Jutland, and involved more than 250 ships of the German Imperial Navy and the Royal Navy. In German it is called *Skagerrakschlacht*, while the British refer to it as the Battle of Jutland. The Germans tried to lure the British fleet into a trap, but this plan was doomed from the start, as

Battle of Tussum. From their trenches the Indian forces fire at the Turkish boats on the Suez Canal.
The Turkish Army attacked on two fronts: in the Caucasus and towards the Suez Canal in northern Africa. The Suez Canal was a vital supply route for the British Empire. In February 1915 the Turkish advance was halted there, but the Allies were tied down in defending their positions for a long time. Troops from India, the UK, Australia, New Zealand and Arabia fought against four Turkish armies, who were supported by some German units. D. Macpherson recorded the engagement in his drawing.

Bataille de Toussoum. (Egypte)
Dans leurs tranchées les indiens empêchent la mise à flot des bateaux turcs sur le canal de Suez.
D'après "The Sphere"   par D. Macpherson.

This photo card of a British military band in tropical uniform carries the writing 'The Drums, 2/10 Middlesex Regiment, Moascar, Egypt, November 1916' on the reverse. Moascar, a town in north-eastern Egypt roughly 10km south of Ismaila, was home to a quarantine camp. Troops coming from overseas were isolated here for two weeks before continuing to Alexandria or Europe to make sure that they did not suffer from any contagious diseases.

The British fleet sinks three German cruisers in Heligoland bay (28 August). This picture postcard in a rather naïve style – quite common at the time – shows the first sea battle of the war on 18 August 1914. During a rather chaotic engagement, the Imperial German Navy lost the light cruisers *Ariadne*, *Köln* and *Mainz* as well as a torpedo boat, and about 700 sailors were killed. On the British side the light cruiser HMS *Arethusa*, shown to the right of the drawing, was heavily damaged and fifty-five sailors lost their lives. The cruiser stayed afloat, however, and was able to be hauled to England.

Captured German *UC 5* Mine Laying Submarine.
UC 5 was one of fifteen German submarines especially constructed to lay sea mines. Their only armament consisted of twelve mines stored in six interior tubes. *UC 5* ran aground off the east coast of England on 1 April 1916 due to enemy action, and was raised by the British Navy shortly afterwards. In the preceding months, it had been instrumental in the loss of at least twenty-nine ships and was the first German submarine of its kind to enter the heavily guarded Channel.

Untergang des englischen Panzerkreuzers „Aboukir", der mit den Schwesterschiffen „Cressy" u. „Hogue" von dem deutschen Unterseebot „U 9" in Grund geschossen wurde

The British armoured cruiser *Aboukir* sinking.
The British armoured cruiser *Aboukir* and her sister-ships *Cressy* and *Hogue* were torpedoed and sunk by the German submarine *U-9* on 22 September 1914. 837 sailors were rescued, most of them by the Dutch merchant vessels *Flora* and *Titan*, but 1,459 British sailors drowned. The ships were too slow for their role, were not guarded by destroyers and did not zig-zag. The most important reason for the loss was most likely the underestimated danger posed by enemy submarines.

the British had already broken the German codes at the beginning of the war. Despite this, neither nation gained a clear victory in the battle; the UK lost more ships and lives, but the German fleet was trapped in the North Sea. In the further course of the war, the Imperial German Navy consequently relied increasingly on its submarine fleet, doubling its numbers from the initial 50 submarines, to about 80 in 1916 and topping out at 140 submarines by the end of 1917.

On 1 February 1917, Germany once more declared unrestricted submarine warfare. Its

hope was to force the UK and France into surrender within the next six months at most, by sinking enough ships and oil tankers in particular. It was accepted that this risked the USA declaring war on Germany, and it was common opinion that the war would have been won long before the US was ready to send its army to fight. The plan seemed to work. In only three months, 470 ships were sunk and both the UK and France suffered supply shortages. After five US American ships were sunk in a row, as expected, the US declared war on Germany on 6 April 1917. Although this had no immediate effect on the war, in the long run, American troops would play a substantial role in the Allied victory.

In an attempt to turn the tide, the British Prime Minister ordered the reintroduction of the traditional tactic of sailing in convoys, in May 1917. In the future, merchant ships were to sail in convoys of at least forty ships, guarded by destroyers armed with depth charges. The results were impressive; the number of ships lost fell drastically, whereas the number of submarines sunk continued to increase. In addition, transport capacities were growing as US

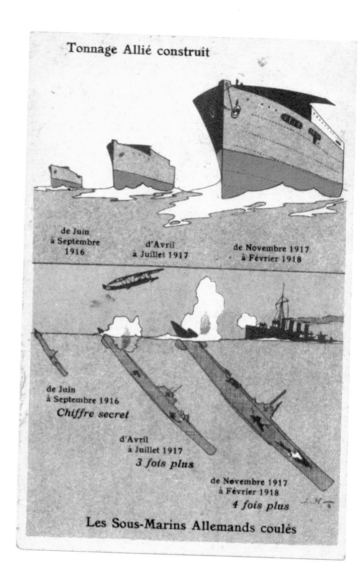

England's distress.

On 1 February 1917, Germany once more announced unrestricted submarine warfare and the number of torpedoed ships increased steadily. This German card shows the Allied losses between February 1917 and January 1918. April 1917 was the month with the heaviest losses. After that the British Navy began to sail only in convoy, which substantially reduced losses. Germany had risked a lot in this gamble, and lost. After Germany sank five American ships, the USA declared war against the German Empire on 6 April 1917.

....

shipyards were running at full speed and the whole of the merchant navy was now involved. In Spring 1918, it became obvious that the Allies had won the war at sea.

In the last days of October 1918, when it became clear that Germany had lost the war, the

Allied tonnage built. German submarines sunk.

Naval warfare reduced to the core: cut the enemy's supply lines. Here the success of the respective measures is portrayed by the number of newly built ships compared to the number of sunken submarines. This card dates the turnaround in April 1917, but in fact it came a month later with the introduction of convoys, the integration of the American merchant and armed fleets and the enormous shipbuilding capacities of the USA.

....

commander of the German High Seas Fleet, Admiral Hipper, ordered German ships to attack the British fleet. This suicidal decision caused open mutiny among the sailors in Kiel and Wilhelmshaven, which started the fall of the German Empire.

Chapter 7
Old and New Weapons

In 1914 the fighting power of an army was mainly measured by the number of soldiers it could muster. The common measure for this was the division, which on average consisted of 12,000 infantrymen armed with rifles, and formed the backbone of all European armies. The military doctrines of all general staffs saw victory being gained by a combination of the determined action of the strongest possible infantry units, and the rifle.

THE OUTPOST

A British "Tommy" watching the enemy through his periscope

Rifles and Carbines

In the last decades of the nineteenth century, the military rifle had seen a swift development, and in 1914 all forces were armed with a small calibre bolt action rifle.

On average, this kind of weapon weighed 4kg and was around 130cm long. It came with a magazine holding three to ten rounds, with a calibre between 6.5 and 8mm. The rifles had a cylindrical breech and the bolt was moved with a handle. With one single movement the soldier could eject the cartridge case of the spent round, insert a new cartridge into the chamber, and cock the firing pin – a well-trained soldier would fire ten to fifteen aimed shots per minute. Good riflemen would reliably hit a man-sized target at a range of 400m, but the bullets of an infantry rifle were lethal at substantially larger distances. A bayonet could also be fixed to the front end of the barrel for close quarter combat.

Military rifles changed little during the years 1914-1918, with only some parts that were difficult to manufacture being redesigned in order to speed up mass production. The enormous losses on the battlefields required a steady stream of new weapons, and some

The Outpost. A British 'Tommy' watching the enemy through his periscope.
This British soldier has his rifle with the bayonet fixed within reach. The weapon is a Lee Enfield Mk III bolt action rifle with a detachable 10-round magazine, introduced to the British Army in 1907. The periscope was a simple but much-used aid to observe over the top of the trench, without exposing one's head as a target for enemy snipers. It mainly consisted of two mirrors that were fixed in a housing at an angle of 45 degrees.

Campaign of 1914. British Army. A machine-gun section takes position.
The text on this card from the first months of the war is not completely correct. This is not a British machine-gun section but a Canadian one, as indicated by the uniforms and Ross rifles. The precision and reliability of the infantry rifles of the armies involved was quite similar, with the exception of the Canadian Ross rifle. This weapon featured a peculiar mechanism, engineered with small tolerances, which made the rifle sensitive to dirt and sand, and frequently caused stoppages. The Ross rifle was replaced before the end of the war.

375

CAMPAGNE DE 1914
ARMEE ANGLAISE
Section de mitrailleuse allant prendre position   ND. Phot.

Vue de Tranchée

J. Cateux, éditeur, Commercy

accessories were designed specifically for the demands of trench warfare.

Wire-cutters, for example, were fixed to the barrel in a similar way to a bayonet. Cup launchers for grenades were another innovation, as were covers that protected the breech and bolt assembly from mud and dirt, or plug-in trench magazines that allowed the availability of more rounds. Angled stocks, to which the whole weapon was fixed, allowed the use of a mirror to fire over the top of the trench without showing one's head.

A special piece of equipment that entered the modern armouries due to the static warfare was the scope. Optics originally developed for hunting made their appearance on the battlefield in late 1914, first on the German side and later with all nations.

View of a trench.
Four experienced French *poilus* in their dugout in a trench system. A variety of infantry weapons have been placed around them. The soldier on the left has a grenade launcher at his feet, his kneeling comrade holds a Lebel rifle, fitted a launcher for rifle grenades. With a special propelling cartridge this device was capable of firing a small explosive device over a distance of a couple of hundred metres. The French soldier started his message home with the words: 'I send you a picture from our pit...'

The troops are trained in using rifles with scopes.
German soldiers during sniper training. The picture dates from 1916 and according to the reverse, the officer in the foreground is Graf von Törring, the developer of the scope mount in use. The German Army was the first to field snipers issued with specially selected rifles and optical sights. Over the course of the war, however, the British Army would surpass them in this field, as it systematically enhanced the production of sniper rifles and the training of snipers.

A 'US doughboy' with the typical campaign or Montana hat. He carries an M1917 US Enfield rifle. When the US entered the war and mobilised their forces, weapons production also had to be increased to a maximum immediately. Although the American standard rifle was the Springfield M1903, the fastest way to increase production numbers was to expand existing production lines, and so the P14 that was already produced for the UK, became the P17 by changing it to the American infantry calibre. Between July 1917 and November 1918, three US factories produced around 2.2 million of these rifles.

The war 1914-1915. Northern France. Our warriors prepare for a bayonet attack.
In the front end of a sap, three *poilus*, with bayonets fixed to their rifles, wait for the signal to attack. The second man from the left is an NCO and carries a revolver. In 1915 several large scale French offensives succeeded in conquering some ground, but also claimed the lives of hundreds of thousands of soldiers.

La Guerre 1914-1915
Visé Paris 228

RÉGION DU NORD
Nos fantassins se préparant à une attaque à la baïonnette.
J. Courcier, 8, rue Simon-le-Franc, Paris

Im Schützengraben bei Gasalarm.

Specially trained snipers with precision rifles made life in the enemy trench very unpleasant and dangerous. They crouched in well-camouflaged positions, often for hours, and waited for an unguarded move in the enemy trench, which the soldier often paid for with his life. In this way, a single sniper could often pin down a whole section of the enemy trench. As a countermeasure, the areas where snipers were suspected to hide were hit with heavy artillery, which did not exactly make them popular, neither among the enemy nor among their own comrades.

Other Personal Weapons and Hand Grenades

Officers, medics, machine gunners and other specialised troops often carried either a pistol or a revolver in a holster on the belt. Many officers also carried a sabre or sword, which was really more a symbol of their rank than a weapon, and lost importance over the course of the war. So too did

In the trenches during a gas attack.
A German soldier sent this picture postcard home in Spring 1918. The photo shows a defensive position, most likely in the Vosges Mountains, secured with heavy tree trunks. All of the soldiers are wearing their gas masks, which they kept in tin cans such as the one visible on the back of the soldier in the foreground. He is standing in front of a box of ball hand grenades.

Clubs used by the Austro-Hungarian Army to finish up the wounded at the Italian front.
This Italian card with text printed in Italian, English, French and Spanish shows one of the many blunt instruments used in trench warfare. Coshes and clubs were often improvised at the front and there were only few regulation weapons of this type. Their use was the result of practical experience, as short and easy to wield cut and thrust weapons were of better use in the narrow trenches than a long rifle with a bayonet.

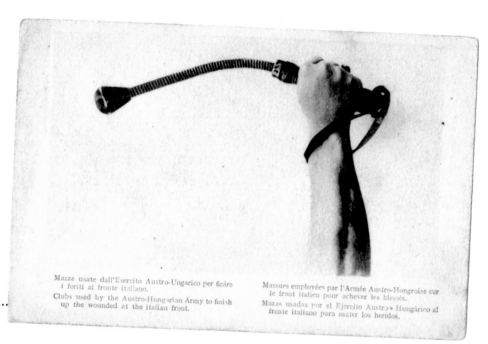

Mazze usate dall'Esercito Austro-Ungarico per finire i feriti al fronte italiano.
Clubs used by the Austro-Hungarian Army to finish up the wounded at the italian front.

Massues employées par l'Armée Austro-Hongroise sur le front italien pour achever les blessés.
Mazas usadas por el Ejercito Austro-Hungárico al frente italiano para mater los heridos.

the lances of the cavalry, which in the early parts of the war were actually used a couple of times.

Once the enemy trenches were entered, hand-to-hand combat ensued, during which the rifle with bayonet fixed often turned out to be too unwieldy and too long. Therefore a variety of implements were used in these situations, many of them bringing back images of medieval cut and thrust weapons. The German Army fielded various so-called 'trench knives' for close quarter combat. France simply shortened bayonets to the length of daggers, but spades with sharpened edges, clubs, coshes and pick axes were also used.

Although hand grenades had been in use for centuries, at the beginning of the war only the Germans had these explosive devices at their

Soldiers of the *Westfälisches Jägerbataillon* Nr. 7 light infantry battalion from Bückeburg in a carefully constructed trench. *Jäger* light infantry wore a leather shako instead of the Pickelhaube leather helmet. The soldier in the foreground, a *Gefreiter*, carries a stick grenade, which due to its wooden handle could be thrown better and further than a ball grenade. Two of the infantrymen also carry woven bandoliers around their necks. Each belt would hold fourteen strips of five rounds in small sewn pockets. This easy-to-produce piece of equipment was introduced in 1914. The soldier was to use the ammunition from his bandolier first, before starting on that in the ammunition pouches. Once the bandolier was empty, it was thrown away.

In a trench section showing the results of heavy fighting, a German sniper remembers fallen comrades. Their names are written on a board nailed to a simple wooden cross. Perhaps a whole section was buried in their dugout by a direct artillery hit and died this way. His weapon is a Gewehr 98 rifle with a scope and the front end of the scope is wrapped with cloth to hide it.

disposal. As they proved to be highly effective and lethal in trench warfare, soon all countries taking part in the war began to develop modern variants. Up to then the Allied forces made do with improvised models that were churned out by small workshops behind the front. In the end, Germany too had to align production numbers with real demand.

The best-known variants were the French Model 1915 and 1916 grenades, the British Mills bomb and the German ball and stick grenades. The wooden handle allowed a skilled user to throw the grenade up to 50m, whereas ball shaped grenades usually reached targets only 20m away. Special throwing devices, not unlike medieval trebuchets and catapults, were other ways to cover larger distances.

Machine Guns

Next to the standard issue rifle a new weapon appeared in the 1890s, which was vastly superior

A SCREENED MAXIM IN ACTION.

A screened Maxim in action. Three British soldiers man a Maxim machine gun. This model was replaced rather quickly by a modernised version called the Vickers machine gun, after its producer. A single machine gun matched the firepower of many riflemen, and so essential parts of infantry tactics had to be adapted to the new weapon. Not all military leaders implemented this insight at the same speed, however, especially the leading British officers, who for a long time were not convinced that the machine gun could decide a battle.

The Great War 1914-15. Mountain infantry using the new armoured fortress machine gun in the Nancy region.
During the First World War the French Army fielded two models of heavy machine guns in its infantry units, the St Etienne pictured here and the Hotchkiss. Unlike the Maxim models these two were not water-cooled, but featured thick barrels that could better dissipate the heat.

309. La Grande Guerre 1914-15 — La nouvelle Mitrailleuse blindée de forteresse employée par les Chasseurs Alpins dans la région de NANCY   A. R.

in fire power even to modern rifles: the fully automatic machine gun.

The mechanism of this weapon used the energy freed by firing a round. The gas that was produced when the charge exploded not only drove the projectile forward through the barrel but also pressed back towards the bottom of the cartridge. This recoil supported the mechanism that ejected the empty cartridge case and chambered the new round. The weapon therefore only had to be loaded manually once, afterwards it would fire as long as the trigger was pressed and ammunition was fed.

A standard machine gun of the era was manned by three to five soldiers and fired 500-600 shots a minute, matching the firepower of a couple of dozen rifles.

All European nations had introduced machine guns at the turn of the century. Most of them were based on the model developed by its American inventor, Hiram Maxim. More or less

modern variants of his design were fielded in Belgium, Bulgaria, Germany, the UK, Russia, Serbia and Turkey. France had the St. Etienne

Two German NCOs man a *Bosch Wurfmaschine*. This and other similar devices were developed to increase the range of hand grenades. Discus hand grenades could be thrown over a distance of 200m this way, ball hand grenades reached up to 155m. In trench warfare the hand grenade was a very effective weapon, as the distance between enemy lines didn't often span more than a few dozen metres. It could be used to attack, to take out enemy machine-gun positions, or even for defence if the enemy passed the wire obstacles in front of the defender's trenches.

The German Army also fielded a modernised variant of the Maxim machine gun. The weapon was named '08' after the year of its introduction, or 'Spandau' after the place where it was first produced. The photograph that underlies this hand-coloured postcard was taken during an exercise. The MG 08 machine gun has been fitted with a muzzle booster allowing it to fire blanks, which on their own would not create enough recoil to reload the gun.

and the Hotchkiss, while Austria-Hungary fielded the Schwarzlose machine gun.

As machine guns were not only expensive but also heavy and unwieldy, only a few were used at first, with around twenty-four machine guns per division. The state-owned rifle manufacturer, *Gewehrfabrik Spandau*, calculated the factory cost of an MG 08 at 1,035,- Marks, whereas private manufacturers such as DWM took as much as 2,335,- Marks. In comparison, a Gewehr 98 rifle from Spandau would sell for 54,- Marks. Including the mount, a machine gun weighed about 50kg, which made it a burden for the infantry, who were supposed to decide the battle

A German real photo card from the second half of the war. The soldiers wear the Stahlhelm steel helmet and the MG 08 machine gun is mounted on a small improvised mount. These mounts were often built on the spot to reduce the weight of the weapon and make it more mobile. The cooling jacket is fitted with an armour shield to protect it from damage by shrapnel or bullets. If the cooling water leaked out, the weapon would overheat and be rendered useless after a few hundred shots. Overheated barrels also wore out quickly, while the heat could cause the rounds to detonate prematurely.

by fast and determined attacks, at least according to contemporary military doctrine. So the new weapon hit resistance in many superior headquarters, as the staff officers either could not or did not want to acknowledge that technology had outpaced the human being, and that the firepower of a weapon might have more influence on the outcome than the courage and initiative of the individual soldier.

Shortly after the war began, the efficiency of

These British soldiers pose with a Lewis machine gun (left), a Vickers machine gun (centre) and a range finder (right) at their barracks. During the war almost all Allied forces fielded the Lewis and it was also used on aircraft. One of the first light machine guns, it was smaller and lighter than the mounted heavy machine guns such as the Maxim, Vickers, MG 08 or Hotchkiss. The light machine guns were more mobile and less conspicuous, but they also had a shorter range. The magazines usually carried fewer rounds and the weapons needed longer to cool down, so their firepower was smaller.

Front gondola of Zeppelin _L-49_, forced to land at Bourbonne-les-Bains on 20 October 1917.

Machine guns were not only used on the ground, but fitted to all kinds of military means of transportation. This card shows the MG 08 machine gun in the gondola of the German Navy airship _L-49_, which was forced to land by French pilots of Squadron 152 when returning from a bombing raid over England. At first the airship tried to escape by rising high and fast, but due to the lack of oxygen, the crew fell ill with altitude sickness and had to make an emergency landing on French ground. _L-49_ was only lightly damaged and became the model for British and American airships.

Poilus on a hillside in front of their dugout made from corrugated steel. They are standing behind a Hotchkiss machine gun, which could be considered the best French machine gun of the First World War and is easily recognisable by the rings around the barrel, which served as cooling fins and dissipated the heat. Usually the ammunition was fed into the Hotchkiss in strips of thirty rounds, but this weapon has been adapted for belted ammunition. The Hotchkiss was also used by the Belgians and was issued in large numbers to the American troops in France from 1917 onwards.

the machine gun had already become so obvious that even its most hardened opponents had to change their opinion, and the production numbers of this type of weapon increased rapidly. A new model, the 'light' machine gun, was also developed in this phase. It had a reduced weight and was fired not from a heavy mount, but a simple bipod. This made it more mobile and more difficult for the enemy to reconnoitre, as well as being easier, cheaper and faster to produce.

In the German Army the number of machine guns increased rapidly from 24 per division in 1914, to 72 in 1916 and finally 350 per division in 1918.

The tactics used to take enemy positions,

Aircraft being fired at with machine guns.

This hand-coloured photograph shows two German machine guns on special mounts that allowed them to be fired at enemy aircraft. A soldier is standing to the right of each machine gun and taking care that the ammunition belt is fed into the gun without any problems. Clouds of smoke from the so-called 'smokeless' powder emerge from the muzzles.

Beschießung von Fliegern durch Maschinengewehre.

La Guerre
Soldat belge fumant tranquillement
pendant le combat à Termonde

The war. A Belgian soldier calmly smoking during the fight for Termonde.
Termonde lies between Gent, Brussels and Antwerp and was heavily damaged by the German invasion. As the town was already taken shortly after the beginning of the war, the caption cannot be correct. The picture is obviously posed, as the Maxim Model 1912 machine gun has neither a mounted belt nor is it connected to a water-container. The Belgian Army could field about a hundred of these weapons.

however, changed more slowly, especially on the Allied side. After a preparatory artillery barrage, which basically announced the impending attack to the Germans, the infantry would storm the enemy trenches with bayonets fixed. Once the artillery had finished the bombardment, German machine guns would be brought back into their well-protected positions from underground bunkers, and nine out of ten times the attackers would be cut down without ever reaching their targets. The machine gun became the symbol of static warfare. It was everywhere and impressed attackers and defenders in equal measures by its destructive power, physical closeness and its characteristic sound.

Artillery

Most casualties, however, were not caused by machine-gun fire but by artillery, which dominated the battlefields of trench warfare. Roughly 60-70 per cent of soldiers fell due to artillery bombardment, which is not exactly surprising considering the number of grenades fired. According to reputable estimates, Germany

This German soldier had his picture taken with an unexploded artillery shell. The 305 painted onto the huge grenade names the calibre, which allows us to identify it as a projectile of a French 305mm Modèle 1893/96 railway gun. Originally these were naval artillery pieces, but during the First World War they were re-used on special railway carriages and were fielded on the Western Front. About 25 to 30 per cent of the artillery shells fired did not explode, and pictures with enemy duds, the larger the better, were popular motifs.

1914...

4me Série   Un groupe d'Artillerie attendant les ordres | A group of artillery awaiting orders

A group of artillery awaiting orders.
A French unit with 75mm field guns ready to move out. Four 75mm guns formed a battery, which numbered about 170 soldiers, 4 officers and 160 horses. Six horses each drew a gun on its limber, which also carried seventy-two rounds of ready ammunition. On this card three batteries have been brought up, which means more than 500 men and almost 500 horses.

and Austria-Hungary fired roughly 350 million grenades and the Allies roughly 420 million. The number of duds, i.e. grenades not exploding on impact, was substantial – with roughly 25-30 per cent failing for various reasons.

These enormous amounts were fired by a variety of artillery pieces, which can be roughly divided into guns, howitzers and mortars. The main difference between the three is the

A German NCO and two enlisted men present one of the most feared weapons of trench warfare; the *leichter Minenwerfer* light grenade launcher. The weapon had a weight of about 130kg and fired a 78.5mm calibre round at a distance of 160 to 1,300 metres. Due to the low production costs, the high mobility and the effectiveness of its grenades, the number of fielded weapons continually increased and in 1918, the German Army had more than 12,000 of these launchers at its disposal.

That's what you call an intense artillery preparation. Spent artillery shells accumulate in great heaps near the batteries.
This card clearly illustrates the enormous amount of ammunition used by the artillery, which all warring nations equally underestimated and caused dangerous supply shortages in 1915. Hundreds, if not thousands of guns were drawn together in advance of large offensives to prepare the infantry attack with tremendous barrages.

trajectory of the projectiles, which was flat for guns, arched for howitzers and high-angled for mortars.

The most famous artillery piece of the First World War, and the pride of the French Army, was the 75mm Model 1897 field gun. It was the first gun to feature a hydro-pneumatic recoil mechanism, allowing rapid and well-aimed fire. This meant the *soixante-quinze* was ahead of all other guns of its time, and Germany was forced to modernise its newly

introduced Feldkanone 96 field guns.

The 75 was not only an important player on the battlefield, but also played a role in public relations and as propaganda object. The gun, its ammunition and its inventor were the motifs of countless postcards.

Four guns formed a battery, which numbered about 170 soldiers and was led by four officers. It took 160 horses to draw the guns on their limbers as well as the ammunition and equipment carts. The most important field gun

A British heavy gun in action.
This photograph from the '*Daily Mail* War Pictures' series carries the following text on the reverse: 'This heavy gun on the British Western Front, seen in action, is a unit in the tremendous siege which we are making, "not on a place, but on the German Army".' To the left of the picture, a soldier is opening the transport cases for the grenades while another artilleryman adjusts and primes the fuses.

A BRITISH HEAVY GUN IN ACTION.

Two German soldiers had their picture taken next to a water-filled shell hole to demonstrate the force of the detonation. The handwritten text on the reverse claims the place to be the Hartmannsweilerkopf, a heavily fought over mountain in the Alsace, and the calibre of the grenade is given as 28cm.

Artillery going to the Front – War 1914-15. Compiègne. British artillery going into the fire.

The 18-pounder (84mm) field gun was the standard artillery piece of the British field artillery. The carriage rested on a two-wheeled limber that was drawn by six horses. Six guns formed a battery. In 1914 the British Army commanded about 1,200 of these guns, another 9,900 would be built until 1918.

GUERRE 1914-1915. — Compiègne. — L'Artillerie anglaise allant au feu.
Visé Paris n° 156
Artillery going to the front. — LL.

Plate 1: Various unexploded enemy mines.

Whereas the Germans preferred to use the grenade launcher in trench warfare, the British developed mortars and the French the so-called *crapouillot*. In this type of grenade launcher the projectile is not inserted into the barrel, but the grenade features tailfins and is put onto a peg with its hollow end. The projectiles were manufactured by many different companies and as a result, quite often refused to explode.

Tafel I: Verschiedene feindliche Minenblindgänger

Four *Granatwerfer 16* grenade launchers lined up. This German launcher was originally developed for the Austro-Hungarian forces by a Hungarian priest and was therefore also called a *Priesterwerfer*, i.e. priest launcher. It weighed 38kg and fired a 2kg heavy projectile over a maximum distance of 500 metres. Due to its low weight and compact construction, it could be carried along into the front line trench. The bell in the rear of the photograph was rung during gas alarms.

155mm howitzers, Germany was a leader in this category of weapons for a long time, both in quality and in quantity.

In the wake of large scale offensives, hundreds – later thousands – of guns were drawn together to kill the enemy in heavy bombardments and render his position ready for assault. This tactic had the disadvantage that the extensive artillery preparations gave the enemy ample warning of the imminent attack, meaning he was able to bring up reserves to the front. In addition, many German positions in northern France were dug so deeply into the ground and were so heavily fortified that they suffered nearly no damage during the barrages.

Towards the end of 1915, the French developed the new tactic of the creeping barrage, where the artillery fire advances at the speed of the infantry entering enemy territory. This pinned down the enemy and allowed the

of the German Empire was the 77mm 96 n/M field gun, the British had their 18-pounder (84mm) and the Russians the 76.2mm field gun.

The heavy calibre guns were positioned far behind the front line. With their 105mm and

This real photo card shows the early days of air defence. Searchlights helped to discover enemy aeroplanes, airships or balloons in the dark. In the background is an acoustic locator (barely visible behind the soldier on the field telephone), which was used to calculate bearing and elevation for firing enemy artillery, but the same principles also allowed it to locate aircraft. To add some dramatic elements to the picture, four of the soldiers are posing with their C 96 pistols. These had a wooden stock, which also served as holster. However, they were completely useless against airborne targets.

Artillery observation post Geitner battery.
At first, artillery fire was directed by observers, who watched the effects and the position on the target from advanced positions, and communicated necessary corrections for example by field telephone, light signals or semaphore messages. The observers used range finders, binoculars or, like here, trench binoculars.

advancing troops to take their objectives. Of course, the creeping barrage relied on the perfect coordination and timing of the artillery and the advancing infantry. These fine-tuned plans could not always be implemented exactly, and several times severe losses were caused by a side's own artillery fire.

The amount of ammunition spent was far larger than previously expected, and the warring nations struggled with increasing production

capacities – but we will speak of that later.

Many different variants of rounds were used, the most important certainly being the explosive shell and the shrapnel shell. The latter contained many steel or lead bullets, housed in a thin grenade shell. The shell would shatter on ignition, giving way to a conically shaped array of projectiles, which had a devastating effect against soft targets.

In addition to this, the artillery fired a

Loading a Trench Mortar.
The reverse of this '*Daily Mail* War Postcard' reads: '"Tommy's" nickname for a trench-mortar is a "flying pig" and this picture shows some of our men loading one of these useful weapons.' Actually, the nickname 'flying pig' referred to the projectile, not the weapon, the heavy 9.45 inch trench mortar, which had been introduced especially for trench warfare together with the 3 inch Stokes mortar. Like the German and French grenade launchers, the trench mortars were built for a high-angled trajectory and short distances.

LOADING A TRENCH MORTAR
OFFICIAL PHOTOGRAPH. CROWN COPYRIGHT RESERVED.

'Daily Mail' WAR POSTCARDS

Observateur d'artillerie. Par André Lynen.

combination of smoke, gas and incendiary shells and anti-tank rounds. The shells were exploded by a detonator or fuse, whose operation could follow different principles – there were impact fuses, timed fuses, delayed action fuses and mixed versions of all three. The impact fuse would detonate when the shell hit its target, the timed fuse at a pre-set time after being fired, ideally before or above the target, and the delayed action fuse some time after impact.

Over the course of the war, the number of artillery pieces increased constantly, with the majority of the acquisitions being light artillery pieces, such as motors and grenade launchers. These were shot at high trajectories in order to hit an enemy in a trench from dozens to hundreds of metres away. Another important new invention were anti-aircraft guns to counter the ever increasing threat from aircraft.

In early 1918, the Germans, who had destroyed the Belgian fortresses with their heavy 42cm mortars at the beginning of the war, opened fire on Paris with three specially built giant guns. Despite their effective range of 120km, which was quite a technical feat, the resulting damage was manageable. These extra heavy guns were very expensive to both build and maintain and were impractical to use due to being both easily spotted and difficult to move. Weapons of this kind were used more for their impact on morale and for propaganda.

The development of forward observation and fire direction would turn out to be far more effective, as artillery fire only makes sense if the objective is actually hit.

At first artillery observers were used, who would find the highest possible ground, observe the impacts with telescopes, trench binoculars or range finders, and report their observations back to the battery. Captive balloons and even aeroplanes to support long range guns, were also used for this purpose. The pilots could not only give corrections to the artillery, but also acquire and designate targets on their own initiative.

In the late stages of the war, guns were no longer visually zeroed in on their targets, but by detailed maps and measuring devices that allowed the precise calculation of the trajectory.

Poison Gas and Flamethrowers

Only an estimated 100,000 of the roughly 10 million soldiers who lost their lives in the First World War were victims of poisonous gas, which was used on countless occasions. Nevertheless, the use of poisonous gas has engraved itself into collective memory as one of the most important distinguishing marks of this war.

The gases used most often were tear gas, phosgene, mustard gas and chlorine, with their effects ranging from strong lacrimation and

34. LES RUSSES AU CAMP DE MAILLY — Masques contre les Gaz asphyxiants

Reprod. interd.   Русскія Войска въ лагерѣ Майльн. Испытаніе респираторовъ.   Visé Paris N° 570

vomiting to permanent eye damage and even death by pulmonary edema. At first, the gas was released from canisters and then driven towards the enemy lines by the wind, but in most cases it was delivered by means of special artillery shells.

The British Army fielded the Livens Projector, which was named after its developer. This mortar fired thin-walled drums that could deliver poisoned gas or flammable fluids. Captain Livens' invention was quite successful and therefore copied by other nations, Germany included.

The first gas attack occurred in August 1914, when France used tear gas against German troops attacking in Alsace. The German counter-attack followed in October, but both actions were of limited success.

The beginning of 1915 saw the first Phosgene shells used by Germans against Russian troops, in the battle of Bolimov. The most well-known gas attack happened on 22 April 1915 at Ypres. When the wind was blowing from a favourable direction, German troops opened dozens of cylinders filled

British machine gunners wearing gas helmets.
The development of suitable defensive measures started immediately after the first use of poison gas as a weapon of war. In 1915 Dr MacPherson of the Royal Newfoundland Regiment designed the so-called gas helmet, which is worn by the two Vickers machine gunners pictured here. It consisted of an airtight sack made from impregnated cloth, which was drawn over the head. The front side carried two pieces of glass to allow vision and a breathing opening with a tube connected to a container filled with chemicals that was supposed to neutralise the gas. More comfortable gas masks soon followed.

"Daily Mail" WAR PICTURES

62. BRITISH MACHINE GUNNERS WEARING GAS HELMETS.   OFFICIAL PHOTOGRAPH. CROWN COPYRIGHT RESERVED.

with chlorine and a big yellow cloud blew across the Allied positions. The exact number of casualties is unknown, but it must have been thousands.

The development of counter measures against gas attacks started immediately afterwards. At first, improvised methods such as cloths drenched in water or urine were pressed against the mouth and nose. Soon gas masks appeared, which protected the face and eyes and cleaned the inhaled air by filtration, but it was not complete protection. In July 1917, Germany used mustard gas for the first time, which could permeate textiles and was reabsorbed via the skin.

The French and British mainly used shells filled with chlorine-phosgene, and in the Battle of the Somme alone, their artillery fired roughly 1,200 tons of this agent during ninety-eight bombardments.

During the course of the war it became common practice to mix in gas shells with

Campaign 1914-1917. Noyon (Oise). Signal for asphyxiating gases. (March 1917).
Poison gas was usually fired in artillery shells. During the war it became common practice to mix explosive and gas shells during artillery raids, so as to hide the use of gas in the explosions. As soon as a gas attack was detected, the soldiers had to be alerted to put on their gas masks as soon as possible. On both sides at the front, bells were rung for this purpose, often using improvised shell cases.

A casualty is retrieved during a gas attack.
American soldiers wearing gas masks (most likely the British 'small box respirator') carry a casualty, who also wears a gas masks, from a contested trench. Although obviously posed, the motif was supposed to lessen the widespread fear of gas attacks. This picture postcard is one of the rarer specimens of propaganda cards published by official authorities, in this case the *Service Spécial de Propaganda Belge.*

Service Spécial de Propagande Belge.   Nº 17.   NOS ALLIÉS.
La relève d'un blessé pendant une attaque de gaz.

explosive shells during artillery raids, so that the gas clouds would be hidden by the normal explosions. The frequent gas attacks made life in the trenches even more uncomfortable, as gas masks had to be kept on hand at all times.

Flamethrowers had one thing in common with poison gas, as despite playing a rather minor role in the war, they were considered inhuman weapons by many.

The portable flamethrower is an invention of the twentieth century and the German Army had experimented with it since 1908, and was the only armed force to have devices fit for service in 1914.

Another three or four models differing in weight, size of the fuel tank and number of crew, were developed during the war. All in all, about 1,000 flamethrowers were built and the range of

German soldiers are training with a flamethrower. Germany developed several models during the war, which differed in weight, fuel capacity and number of crew. All in all about 1,000 flamethrowers were produced and used with varying success. Flamethrowers were also a danger to their crew, as the maximum range was about 50 metres and flamethrower parties were a preferred target for every enemy bearing arms.

The war. Belgian machine gun cars in action.
The earliest known picture of two armoured vehicles, which at the time were still called 'machine-gun cars'. Apparently their armament was more important than their armour. The picture was taken before 19 August 1914, i.e. shortly after the Germans invaded Belgium, and shows two regular passenger cars that have been modified by mounting a couple of armour plates. A Lewis machine gun is visible on the left vehicle, whereas the right one carries riflemen.

the largest one was around 50m. They were used on approximately 700 occasions during the war, the first successful use being in October 1914 in the Argonne forest.

The Allies also developed a number of models but produced only few of each, as they considered its disadvantages outweighed its advantages. Its main problem was its short effective range and also its short period of use; even the largest model would exhaust its fuel supply in 45 seconds.

The previously mentioned Captain Livens was also responsible for the development of a large-scale non-portable flamethrower, of which only five or six were built.

Tanks and Armoured Vehicles

Although several nations had been experimenting with armoured and armed vehicles since the beginning of the twentieth century, no country was actually able to field a tank when war broke out. However, this changed quickly when the Belgian Army sent improvised armoured passenger cars into action against the advancing Germans, in the second week of the war.

In Belgium. *Autos mitrailleuses* setting out for the front.
A detailed shot of a Minerva armoured car and its crew. Originally this was a large passenger car, which was armoured by the Cockerill company and carried a rotatable machine gun in an armoured shield. The crew has named this car *Lion of Flanders*.

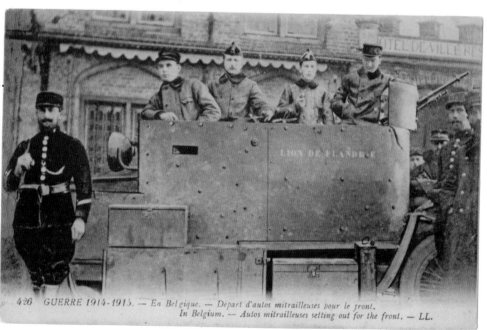

426 GUERRE 1914-1915. — En Belgique. — Départ d'autos mitrailleuses pour le front.
In Belgium. — Autos mitrailleuses setting out for the front. — LL.

The Great War 1914-15. Near Furnes. Belgian machine-gun car at the front.
A Belgian armoured car of the SAVA (*Sociéte Anversoise de la fabrication des Voitures Automobiles*) type that was introduced towards the end of 1914. The vehicle had a 7mm armour at the strongest part, was manned by three to four soldiers and was powered by a 35hp engine. The armament consisted of a Hotchkiss machine gun mounted in a half-open rotatable cupola.

The earliest known picture of two of the so-called *auto-mitrailleuses* dates to 19 August 1914. Shortly afterwards, production started on a small series of armoured vehicles based on Minerva passenger cars. In France, first Renault and later Peugeot began to build similar vehicles, while in Germay manufacturers included Daimler, Erhard and Büssing.

Although a focus lay on armoured vehicles at the beginning of the war, they soon lost importance once the war became static. As these armoured automobiles ran on wheels, they were restricted to hard ground and their weight was limited, which only allowed a relatively light armour and armament. Tanks did not suffer from these limitations, as they ran on tracks.

The first usable tank was a British Mark I. It was almost 10m long, 4m wide, had a 105hp

An armoured car used by the Belgians.
This picture from 1914 shows another SAVA armoured car, this time from the left side. The designation 'armoured car' is used instead of 'machine gun car'. Most likely the picture was taken far behind the lines, as the armoured car has drawn in a crowd of civilian spectators, while the driver is talking to another Belgian soldier.

"GEO." 30. - 1914.　　　　Auto blindée utilisée par les Belges.

BRITISH TANK IN ACTION
SMASHING GERMAN DEFENCES.

PASSED BY PRESS BUREAU
FOR PUBLICATION 24TH NOV. 1916.

VALENTINES SERIES
COPYRIGHT

British tank in action. Smashing German defences.
Although the first ever deployment of tanks in 1916 was not a big success, some vehicles at least managed to cross no-man's-land and break the German lines. This gave the British high command increased trust in the possibilities of the new weapon and led to an order of more than 1,000 vehicles of an improved model. Depictions of tanks had to be presented to a censor before publication, and so this drawing also carries the text 'Passed by Press Bureau for publication 24 November 1916'. It shows a Mark I tank.

engine and ran at a top off-road speed of about 3.5kph. Two variants were built: the 'male' carrying two six-pound cannons and three machine guns, and the 'female' carrying seven machine guns. Due to its large track running around the whole of the vehicle, its off-road capabilities were quite good and it could cross ditches up to 3.5m wide.

The crew of these heavy 28-tonne monsters numbered eight soldiers, who had an exceptionally dangerous and uncomfortable task. Not only was their tank a prime target for all enemy weapons, they also had to do their work immediately next to an unscreened six-cylinder engine. They had to cope with the heat, the stench, the noise, the exhaust fumes and even the smoke coming from their weapons. There was hardly any ventilation and communication was

British armoured vehicle (tank).
This British Tank Mark II (No. 799) was captured by German troops near Arras on 11 April 1917. The Mark II was a slightly improved version of the Mark I, of which only about fifty were built for training and exercise purposes. As the production of the new Mark IV model did not pick up speed fast enough, some of these training tanks were deployed to France after all. They were used in the Battle of Arras until they fell prey to German armour piercing ammunition. The pictured tank is a 'male' model with two cannons and three machine guns.

Nº 197 Engl. Panzerauto (Tank)

As one of the first light tanks with a fully rotatable turret, the Renault FT-17 could fire in all directions without turning the hull. Due to a steel shortage and limited production capacities, its production came up to speed slowly, but in May 1918 the first tanks were ready for action. Around 3,000 would be produced up to the end of the war.

very limited, both within the vehicle itself and with the outside. Carrier pigeons were therefore used to signal readiness and communicate its position to HQ.

On 15 September 1916, fifty-nine tanks were used for the first attack at Flers-Coulette. Almost two thirds of them became bogged down or were taken out by technical problems. The remaining tanks managed to cross no-man's-land and break into the enemy positions. Although the German

troops managed to close the gap rather quickly, the British high command was now convinced of the possibilities offered by the tank, and immediately ordered another 1,000 to be manufactured.

The first large scale attack with the improved Mark IV model took place at Cambrai, in November 1917. After a short artillery bombardment, a force of 476 tanks attacked and managed to breach the Hindenburg line.

French and British officers in front of a captured A7V *Sturmpanzerwagen* armoured assault car. Unlike the Allies, who designed tanks that could cross ditches and therefore could be used in almost all terrain, German engineers designed a sort of mobile fortress. With a crew of eighteen soldiers, the colossus was superior in almost every aspect to the British and French tanks on the roads, but when going cross-country it swiftly became bogged down. Only twenty A7V's were built until the end of the war, each one slightly different from the next.

It is still a mystery why the German high command did not see the potential of the tank. Especially as on many other occasions, they had shown their willingness to adopt or implement new ideas. Unlike the British and French, who developed a machine of war that would cross no-man's-land for the infantry, roll over wire obstacles and breach the enemy lines, Germany developed the *Sturmpanzerwagen A7V* armoured assault vehicle at the end of 1916 to support the infantry. The result was as could be expected.

The first A7V was handed over at roughly the same time 476 British tanks attacked at Cambrai. It was 7.3m long, about 3m wide and 3.3m high. It weighed 30 tonnes and was crewed by eighteen soldiers, who among other tasks would handle the 57mm main gun and the seven machine guns. The A7V had more weapons than the British tanks, was heavier armoured and much faster on roads, but due to its carriage and its small ground clearance, it was routinely bogged down when off road. As a result only

Champagne front. German defences against our tanks (Magenta south of Beine).
The Allied tanks had mainly been developed to cross no-man's-land, roll over and through wire obstacles and to enter the German trench systems. On realising that they could actually breach all defences, the Germans started to construct special anti-tank obstacles, among them were these tree trunks, which have been dug into the ground at an angle.

Apart from defences like anti-tank obstacles Germany also developed special weapons to stop the Allied tanks. Steel core armour-piercing ammunition was developed, the first specialised anti-tank gun was built and an anti-tank rifle with a 13mm calibre was fielded. This picture depicts British soldiers studying a captured anti-tank rifle.

twenty *Sturmpanzerwagen A7V* were built and most tanks used by the Germans were captured British and French vehicles.

The French tank development was parallel to that of the UK, except for the fact that three separate models were developed more or less simultaneously: the Schneider, the Saint-Chamond and the Renault FT-17. The first two were large and heavy tanks, 6.3m long with a crew of six, or 8.7m long with a crew of eight, respectively. They were similar to the British models in dimensions and armament, but due to their shorter chassis, their performance was far worse in difficult terrain.

At about the same time as the appearance of the British Whippet, the Renault FT-17 also hit the battlefields. This was a completely different model which could be called the first in a new type of vehicle; the light tank. The vehicle was 4m long, 1.74m wide and 2.14m high, weighed 7 tonnes and was crewed by only two men. In addition, it was the first tank to feature a fully

French soldiers have captured a German anti-tank rifle and demonstrate its enormous size next to a Berthier carbine. The Tankgewehr anti-tank rifle built by Mauser, of which around 15,000 were produced, was 170cm long and weighed 18kg. The weapon fired a 13.2mm calibre bullet at a maximum effective range of 500 metres. At 100 metres the bullet could pierce 26mm of armoured steel.

Sacred Alliance. We will continue until the end, we will defeat Germany. So we can finish this harsh campaign.
This card, published in the first half of 1915, evokes the 'sacred alliance' of France, the UK, Italy, Russia and Belgium (from left to right). The typical headgear of the early phases of the war would slowly give way to steel helmets from the end of 1915 onwards.

rotatable turret, allowing it to fire quickly in all directions, which still remains one of the main features of this type of weapon. By the end of the war, 3,000 FT-17 had been built.

The Allies invested a great deal of time and care into the formation of large tank units, in the hope of breaking the stalemate on the Western Front. On 8 August 1918, a large-scale combined arms attack took place near Amiens, when 600 tanks, artillery and Australian, Canadian and British infantry assaulted. The ground forces were supported by 600 planes of the Royal Air Force and later by 20,000

cavalrymen. In the course of a few days, they broke the main defensive line of the Germans and the German high command had to tell the emperor that the war was lost.

Defence and Protection

When the German soldiers faced the tank for the first time, their only logical response was to flee. The search for ways to stop and destroy the steel vehicles led to concrete blocks and tree trunks being dug in in places where tanks were expected to attack. Other successful defensive measures

CAMPAGNE DE 1914-1915
LE CASQUE ADRIAN
Nouvelle coiffure de campagne de l'Armée Française (1915).

Campaign of 1914-1915. The Adrian helmet. New campaign headgear of the French Army.
The French Adrian M15 was the first modern steel helmet produced in great numbers and introduced as standard headgear. Its name refers back to the officer August Louis Adrian, who was influential in its design and production. The helmet gave relative protection against smaller shrapnel, but due to its thin metal, could not resist bullets or larger shrapnel.

War Memorial Card. Our Enemies.
This hand-coloured German picture postcard was published shortly after the beginning of the war. It nicely illustrates that not all nations wore uniforms in camouflage colours at that time, and that the colourful uniforms of the nineteenth century were still in use. With the relatively short range of muzzle loading weapons and the resulting tactics this had not been a problem, unlike on a modern battlefield where far-reaching weapons were used.

were aiming small arms fire at the observation ports, placing hand grenades under the tracks or climbing the tank and throwing grenades into the ventilation ports. However, these three methods not only required a lot of courage, but also quite a bit of luck. Another reliable method was the use of armour-piercing ammunition with steel core projectiles, which was available for rifles and machine guns from 1916 onwards.

At the beginning of 1918, the German troops received a special weapon that could pierce 25mm of armoured steel at a distance of 100m.

The Mauser T-Gewehr anti-tank rifle, a substantially enlarged version of the standard Model 98 infantry rifle, was built for a 13.2mm ammunition with a hardened steel core. In addition, special light guns were developed or modified for anti-tank purposes. Rheinmetall, for example, changed the mount of the Leichter Minenwerfer light grenade launcher to allow firing directly at the approaching enemy armour up to a distance of 1,200m.

Apart from lighter versions of the Model 96 field gun, the so-called infantry support guns,

The European war 1914/16. Mobile field kitchen.
A rare early colour photograph shows rations being handed out from a mobile field kitchen. Apart from the field-grey uniforms, the soldiers also wear the popular dark leather jackets and leather trousers of the automotive corps, which were designed to protect the wearer from the weather in the often open cabins of the trucks.

FOURS - En attendant l'Embarquement pour le Front

Cliché Blondeau, à F[...]

Fours. Waiting for transport to the front.
There are several villages named Fours in France, most likely the one mentioned here is Fours in Burgundy, roughly 350km south of the front. The soldiers have probably finished their basic training and are now waiting for troop transport to the front. The picture must have been taken in 1917 or 1918, as all are wearing the blue-grey uniforms and steel helmets. Most *poilus* seem to be relaxed and well rested.

there were also the 20mm automatic cannons by Becker and Erhardt and the 37mm revolver cannon, as well as light guns made from supernumerary 37mm barrels. As armour technology advanced, the calibres of anti-tank guns also increased and special shells were developed to attack armoured targets. The last phase of the war also saw the use of the first anti-tank mines, which were improvised devices at first, but later produced industrially.

The many dangers a soldier faced at the front were countered by an equal number of defensive measures. The first aim was to be as invisible as possible and so uniforms were changed to inconspicuous colours. Camouflage became increasingly important and soon all factions raised units tasked with concealing soldiers and equipment from enemy view, and deceiving the enemy. With the rise of aerial surveillance, their

Gloire à la plus grande France
9387

Glory to great France.
A *Tirailleur Sénégalais* with two German Pickelhaube leather helmets. The Pickelhaube was introduced in Prussia in 1842 and was made from pressed and lacquered leather. Reed-green covers for the 'peaked leather helmet' were introduced in 1892 to be worn on exercise. As the Pickelhaube gave no protection against projectiles or shrapnel, the Stahlhelm steel helmet was introduced in 1916. Nevertheless, the characteristic headgear remained a symbol of the enemy army and was therefore the ultimate trophy.

A fag after a fight.
Three British soldiers light each others' cigarettes. The text on this card from the 'Daily Mail War Pictures' series reads: 'Before battle, in battle, and after battle, our "Tommies" are ready for a "fag". These men are lighting up after a scrap.' All three carry the characteristic shallow steel helmet designed by John Brodie and issued from the end of 1915, early 1916 onwards. Despite being made from thicker steel, this model was easier to produce than the French one, as it was pressed from a single piece of steel.

Hill 304. The front end of a sap.
Three German soldiers at the front end of a sap, a short trench dug forward from the main trench. Hill 304 was located in the vicinity of Verdun and saw heavy fighting in Spring 1916. The soldiers are armed with Gewehr 98 rifles and stick grenades and wear the Model 16 steel helmet, which was made from a single piece of steel. Its eye and neck protection gave the best protection of all steel helmets. A brow plate, called *Stirnschild*, could be fixed to the front and gave additional protection against frontal hits.

12 Les Masques Allemands Août 1917

Collection F. Flameng

German masks. August 1917.

A drawing of a German trench in August 1917. The soldiers wear gas masks, steel helmets and trench armours, as well as a roughly 10kg heavy and several mm thick piece of equipment consisting of a breast plate with two shoulder plates riveted to it. Three plates were flexibly fixed to the bottom with leather straps. This personal body armour was not exactly comfortable, but gave quite good protection and was therefore especially issued to soldiers in highly exposed positions.

work became more and more important.

When war broke out, soldiers wore leather helmets or caps in inconspicuous colours at best. However, men also went to war in shiny parade helmets that gave no protection at all but made them easy targets. Shortly after the beginning of the war, dressing stations were soon flooded with soldiers with head wounds. In three quarters of the cases, these were caused by shrapnel, fragments of stones or wooden splinters. Consequently, the steel helmet, which had been a standard piece of equipment in antiquity and all through the Middle Ages, but had disappeared during the seventeenth century was reintroduced.

At General August Louis Adrian's initiative, France took the lead and as early as the end of 1914, was experimenting with metal 'skull caps' to be worn underneath the kepi. In 1915, the first viable steel helmet of the war was produced and was modelled after the helmet worn by French fire fighters. It would later become famous as the 'Adrian helmet', named after its developer.

In late 1915, the UK decided to introduce a helmet designed by John Brodie. With its shallow crown and broad rim it could be produced from thick steel in a single pressing and was

introduced in great numbers in 1916.

The Stahlhelm steel helmet developed in Germany was also made from a single piece of steel and, with its neck and eye protection, gave the best protection of all models. In addition, a separate brow plate could be mounted to the front, giving protection against rifle fire even at short distances.

Except for Russia who did not introduce any steel helmets, almost all soldiers wore protective headgear in the second half of the war. Belgium and Italy introduced the French model, the US copied the British helmet and Austria-Hungary decided to use the German one.

Other developments were face masks and safety glasses to protect the eyes, and breast plates. The German Army procured about 500,000 *Grabenpanzer* cuirasses and equipped almost all frontline companies with them from 1916 onwards. This personal body armour was made from steel plates about 3mm thick, and consisted of a breast plate with a collar, two shoulder plates riveted to it and three bottom plates that were fixed to the breastplate with two leather strips. With a weight of about 10kg, it was not exactly comfortable, but offered good protection.

Chapter 8

The War in the Air

Captive Balloons

Shortly after the first manned balloon flight, balloons were already being used for military purposes. From the end of the eighteenth century onwards, they were used for reconnaissance and surveillance, as they had the ability to see approximately 100km when the air was clear. During the First World War, captive balloons were often fitted with field telephones, with the phone lines running down to the ground along the cables tying down the balloon. The observer could direct artillery fire in real time or relay information on troop movements and other important discoveries. On the other hand, this made balloons a favourite target for enemy airplanes. Therefore the crews, called 'Ballonatics' in England, carried arms and wore parachutes, unlike fighter pilots. Although balloons were still in service at the end of the war, their role had been gradually taken over by the air force, whose rapid development slowly made balloons redundant.

Airships

Another aircraft, the airship, was based on being lighter than air. Its cylindrical gas-filled hull was stretched across a frame, carrying one or more gondolas underneath and was powered by an engine with a propeller. In 1914, several armies had airships at their disposal, which at first only carried out reconnaissance and surveillance missions. The German Army and Navy were the first to use airships for bombing raids as well.

Two companies in Germany built airships: Zeppelin and Schütte-Lanz – and the name Zeppelin would become a synonym for airships

LES AEROSTIERS. Observation en Ballon Captif aux environs de Soissons

Balloonatics. Reconnaissance from a captive balloon near Soissons.

This card by Léon Hingre shows the work of observers in a captive balloon. They search the surroundings for enemy movements and positions and report their findings to the ground via telephone. A basket with carrier pigeons is fixed to the outside of the gondola and a rifle to provide at least some protection against enemy aircraft can be seen in the left corner.

FRIGHTFULNESS!

Mon Dieu, Herr Capitaine, cela ne leur fait plus peur.

Frightfulness! Dear Lord, Herr Captain, they are no longer afraid.
The German airships could carry a huge load of bombs, and both Liège and Antwerp were among the first targets for strategic bombing raids. Paris and London were also attacked later on, although the psychological effects were far larger than the actual physical damage. This especially well-made British card pokes fun at the Zeppelin attacks.

additionally armed with 2-3 machine guns.

Despite dozens of raids against England between January 1915 and August 1918, the damage was more of a psychological than physical nature, as navigating the ships and aiming the bombing drops turned out to be quite difficult. During the course of the war, airships became more and more vulnerable, as the Allies as a whole. As they were the first to carry out strategic bombing raids against civilian targets, they were soon famous in Germany and infamous outside of it. At the beginning of the war, they bombarded Liege and Antwerp, and would later bomb Paris, but mostly London. Depending on its type, a Zeppelin could carry between 1,000 and 3,000kg of bombs and was

THE END OF THE "BABY-KILLER."

The end of the 'Baby-Killer'.
A Zeppelin airship has been caught in the searchlights and set on fire by anti-aircraft artillery. About half of the Zeppelins lost during the war went down due to enemy action, the others were the victims of accidents. Airships were the first weapons that could carry the war far behind the actual front line. At the beginning of the war there was major outrage in the Entente states at the bombing raids by German Navy and Army airships against towns far away from the front, which indiscriminately targeted civilians.

Londoners afraid of the Zeppelins.
This satirical German picture postcard ridicules the fear the Zeppelins caused among the London population. The airships appear above Trafalgar square and people flee in panic or duck under their umbrellas. In 1916 the attacks against England reached their highest point, as 23 bombing raids claimed 293 lives. By 1917 fighter planes were so highly developed and anti-aircraft guns so widespread that the number of Zeppelin attacks decreased substantially.

developed incendiary and explosive ammunition for their airplane machine guns.

In answer to this, the German Empire began to develop Zeppelins that could fly at great heights (up to 6,000m) and outside the reach of enemy fighter planes – but this made aiming the bombs practically impossible. In the meantime, planes could climb higher and higher and so the Zeppelin went out of service as a bomber during 1918. Of about 115 German airships, 53 were destroyed and many more were deemed damaged beyond repair.

Aeroplanes

At the onset of the war, all major countries had air forces commanding a couple of dozen to a

War 1914-1917. Zeppelin L 44 shot down in flames by D.C.A. No 174 near St Clément in the Lunèville (Meurthe-et-Moselle) district on 20 October 1917 at 6:45 in the morning.
The wreck of L 44 with the mutilated body of a crew member. Pictures of fallen pilots of airships and aircraft were commonly used to illustrate that they were not invulnerable.

CAMPAGNE DE 1914-1915
Tir des Pièces de 75.

17   ND. Phot.

couple of hundred planes. These were mostly simple, all-round planes with a maximum speed of about 100km/h and a ceiling of 4,000 metres. They ran reconnaissance and surveillance missions and were unarmed. As the reconnaissance missions quickly grew more and more important, attempts were made to keep the enemy from gathering information. At first the pilots took along pistols, revolvers and rifles, but soon airplanes were fitted with machine guns. As

another armament, aerial bombs were already in use in the second week of the war. So in the shortest possible time, the all-round airplane developed into three different kinds of specialist vehicles: reconnaissance planes, fighters and bombers.

The field of aircraft armament had its own special problems, as the construction and engine power of early aeroplanes were not calculated for the extra weight of a machine gun and the

31 GUERRE DE 1914. — Aéro-mitrailleuse Deperdussin

Reproduction interdite

LL.

War of 1914. Deperdussin air machine gun.
An experimental French fighter aeroplane from the first year of the war. As it was still impossible to fire through the arc of the propeller, the machine gun has simply been mounted to fire over it. This had the disadvantage that the gunner had to stand upright in the plane at a speed of about 100 km/h. Over the course of the war, aeroplanes built by Deperdussin would play an important role under the name of SPAD (*Societé de Production des Aéroplanes Deperdussin*).

In Belgium, France, the Netherlands and other countries, the Farman biplane was one of the first ever military aeroplanes. However, as is common for early aircraft, the performance data of the Farman is not exactly impressive. It did feature a pusher configuration, which at least allowed the mounting of a machine gun and gave an unrestricted field of fire to the front. The pictured plane served with the Netherlands Air Force.

necessary ammunition. Further problems were the placement, mounting and handling of the weapon.

Two-seater aircraft with a pusher configuration allowed the machine gun to be fixed on a mount in the front cockpit, which gave the spotter a clear field of fire in all directions, except backwards. However, pusher planes were far less agile than aircraft with a tractor configuration, and when attacked from behind they were also completely defenceless.

After countless intermediate, improvised and experimental solutions, the ideal armament for a single-seater fighter aeroplane finally emerged. It consisted of one or more synchronised machine guns, which the pilot could fire with the control stick and which fired directly through the propeller. Two-seater reconnaissance planes were also fitted with machine guns mounted on a ring mount and operated by the spotter, who could fire to the rear and to the sides. Bombers

Guerre de 1914-1918

FÈRE-CHAMPENOISE — Avion allemand atterri à Fère-Champenoise le 21 Octobre 1917
Les deux aviateurs ont été faits prisonniers

War of 1914-1918. German aeroplane forced to land near Fère-Champenoise. The two crewmen were taken prisoners.
A German two-seater reconnaissance plane. The pilot sat in the front and operated a synchronised machine gun, the observer in the rear often operated an aerial camera and had a machine gun on a ring mount for defence.

EINST. JETZT.

Once. Now.
This picture postcard from Germany shows how the boy flying a kite grows up to be a member of the new air force. At the outbreak of the war the German Army had around 450 planes at its disposal, roughly 300 of them fit for service. Towards the end of the war approximately 80,000 soldiers served in the German Air Force, with around 15,000 planes on record.

received several machine guns too, in order to defend themselves against fighters.

Although the pilots of the First World War were spared the misery of ground warfare and the privations of the trenches, they were hardly better off, and in fact, fared rather worse. They always had the wind in their faces and suffered from extreme cold, deafening noise and total exhaustion. Pilots and spotters ran a far higher risk of becoming casualties than soldiers on the ground, as dangers such as technical problems and friendly – or enemy – fire were literally everywhere. This meant that on average, a pilot survived for fourteen weeks at the front.

Reconnaissance Planes

Before the outbreak of the war, military aviation experts had already predicted a role for the airplane in terms of reconnaissance and fire direction.

Even though the plane was later used for many other tasks, reconnaissance and surveillance

Campaign of 1914. A seaplane taking off.
The development of seaplanes started shortly after the first flight of a regular plane, and on 28 March 1910 the Frenchman, Henri Fabre, piloted the first successful take-off from water. At the onset of the war, most larger nations commanded a small number of seaplanes, which were usually under the command of the navy.

CAMPAGNE DE 1914
348   Départ d'un hydro-avion   ND...

Imp. Baudinière. Nanterre Visé Paris. Nᵒ 133

133. La Grande Guerre 1914.15 — Le repute Aviateur Anglais SAMSON à Amiens
English aviators at Amiens

The Great War 1914-1915. The renowned English pilot, Samson, at Amiens.

Charles Rumney Samson was a pioneer of naval aviation and one of the first four pilots of the 'Royal Navy Air Service', which in 1918 was amalgamated with the army's 'Royal Flying Corps', to form the 'Royal Air Force'. In the autumn of 1914 Samson fought in south-western Belgium with his unit, where he drove improvised armoured cars. Later on, units under Samson's command bombe the Zeppelin hangars at Cologne and Düsseldorf.

Rebouleq, libraire-éditeur - Reproduction interdite

Guerre 1914-1915

Cadavres des Aviateurs allemands

remained its most important tasks throughout the war. At first the observations were logged in notebooks and on sketchpads, but from late 1914 onwards, planes were fitted with increasingly better cameras, producing high quality aerial pictures. At the end of the war, Germany had cameras that could picture a footprint in the mud from a height of 500m.

Artillery observers played an essential role in directing the fire of long-distance heavy artillery. Planes were used to search out targets, communicate their positions to the artillery and correct the position on the target by observing the impacts. At first, optical signals helped with this and were written down by an observer on the ground, who followed the plane with his telescope. In addition to this, the plane could also drop containers with written messages over its own lines. As both of these methods were unsatisfactory, aeroplanes were soon fitted with transmitters, which allowed them to send messages by radio.

Unlike fighter pilots, the pilots and spotters in

War 1914-1915. Bodies of German pilots.

French soldiers look at the wreck of a German aeroplane, which has crashed into a forest. The photographer was apparently more interested in the bodies of the crew than in the remainders of the plane. The average life expectancy of a First World War pilot was around fourteen weeks.

AS FORÇAS BRITANNICAS D'AVIAÇÃO
Pilotos e observadores
marcando posições allemãs

„HOCH KULTUR"

LES BOMBES AÉRIENNES

With the British air forces. Pilots and observers mark German positions.
After Portugal reacted to the German declaration of war on 9 March 1916 by joining the Entente, a comprehensive series of picture postcards were published focusing on pictures of British forces. This motif shows a reconnaissance plane armed with a Lewis machine gun, as well as some pilots and observers studying maps.

'Hoch Kultur' Aerial bombs.
This card by graphic artist, Raemaekers, focuses on the outrage at the bombing of cities behind the lines, in this case Paris, and the victims among the civilian population. Like London, the French capital was first attacked with Zeppelins and later with heavy Gotha bombers.

the reconnaissance planes had a rather unspectacular task, and so were often denied public recognition. But in fact, their contributions and successes throughout the war were far more important than those of the fighter and bomber pilots.

Fighters

A fighter plane is basically no more than a flying firearm, specifically designed to shoot down enemy aircraft and gain air superiority. Its quality is determined by its engine power, agility and armament. Technical developments were fast in

these areas during the First World War, and so air superiority was constantly changing hands.

The Fokker E.1 was the first plane with a synchronised machine gun that provided the ability to fire through the turning propeller without damaging it. The synchronisation gear let the pilot control the plane and fire the machine gun at the same time. He only had to turn his plane towards the enemy and pull the trigger. The device was developed at the German Fokker aircraft factory in spring 1915, shortly after French fighter pilot Roland Garros had been forced to land behind German lines. Garros had been able to take down three German planes with his Morane-Saulnier monoplane aircraft,

A nice portrait of a German pilot, whose thick leather jacket shows the insignia of the *Flieger-Bataillon I* on his shoulder. He wears a woollen cap under his padded helmet for protection against the cold in the open cockpit. Conditions were harsh for the pilots of the First World War, as they were not only exposed to the weather, but also to the exhausts from the engines. Having to land due to a technical failure was as much of a danger as being shot down by enemy fire.

blades were armed with steel sheets to deflect projectiles to a safe direction, at the cost of a lesser engine performance. Fokker saw the synchronisation device and, less than two weeks later, presented a perfectly working interrupter gear which synchronised the firing of the machine gun with the turning of the propeller. Although the construction was actually devised by one of his technicians, it was Anthony Fokker who would become famous for it.

From August 1915 onwards, the Fokker E.III, an improved version of the E.I, dominated the skies. In spring 1916, the lead was taken over by the French Nieuport 17, as it outranked the Fokker in both engine power and agility. With the Sopwith Pup and the S.E. 5A, the UK also had excellent planes at their disposal.

using a statically mounted machine gun with an interrupter gear. As the synchronisation did not work reliably yet, the backs of his propeller

MACHINE GUN ON NIEUPORT 'CHASSE' PLANE.

Machine Gun on Nieuport 'Chasse' Plane.
Between 1914 and 1918 the French aeroplane manufacturer, Nieuport, developed a great number of different biplanes, amongst which the fighter plane Nieuport 17 was perhaps the most successful. The aeroplane was built in great numbers and fielded by several Allied air forces. This picture clearly shows the armament consisting of a synchronised Vickers machine gun and a Lewis machine gun in a Foster mount.

Anthony Fokker in front of a Fokker M5. The Dutch aeroplane manufacturer worked in Germany from 1912 to 1918 and built many planes for the new German Air Force. He poses in front of an aircraft with a clearly visible LMG 08. It was the first plane to feature a synchronised machine gun that could fire through the arc of the propeller, and was used successfully on the Western Front under its military designation, Fokker E I. Fokker, who was awarded German citizenship in 1915, is wearing the ribbon of an Iron Cross 2nd Class on the lapel of his suit jacket.

Unser erfolgreichster Kampf-Flieger
Freiherr von Richthofen.

In August 1917 Fokker delivered the famous Dr. I triplane, which could rise faster than the Allied planes and was even more agile. The 'Red Baron', Manfred von Richthofen, piloted this plane very successfully, but he also died in one on 21 April 1918. The best French plane of 1917 was said to be the Spad XIII, of which about 8,500 were built and was used by the USA, Belgium, France and Italy. Fokker's last, and

Our most successful fighter pilot, Freiherr von Richthofen.
With eighty confirmed victories, Manfred Albrecht Freiherr von Richthofen (1892-1918) was the most successful fighter pilot of the First World War. He was nicknamed 'The Red Baron', as he painted his planes, which included an Albatros and Fokker Dr.I, completely in red. As was common practice among flying officers, in this picture he continues to wear the uniform of his original unit, the *Ulanen-Regiment Nr. 1*. He died on 21 April 1918, most likely from a bullet fired from the ground. Next in line were the 'fighter aces' René Fonck (France, seventy-five victories), Billy Bishop (Canada, seventy-two), Ernst Udet (Germany, sixty-two), Edward Mannock (England, sixty-one) and Raymond Collishaw (Canada, sixty-one).

Schwester, Deine
Anna Engelhardt.

At the airfield.
In his motifs, Brynof Wennerberg worked on the idea that pilots led an exciting and glamorous lifestyle. Here they are driven out to the airfield by young socialites in a luxury car, and while the lieutenant slips into his heavy coat, she carries his helmet and scarf.

The Battle of Picardy. French machine gun against aircraft.
As a new weapon, the aeroplane immediately forced the development of counter measures such as anti-aircraft guns and special machine guns, for which (in addition to special mounts and aiming devices) new kinds of ammunition were also developed. Tracers allowed the observation of the projectiles' trajectory and improved the aim, while incendiary bullets were supposed to maximise the effects of a hit. This St Etienne machine gun has been mounted on a post using parts of the regular mount.

best, First World War plane, was the Fokker D. VII, which was flown from Spring 1918 onwards, and counted Hermann Göring as one of its first pilots.

Bombers

Similar to the fighter planes, the first bombers were also originally reconnaissance planes. On 14 August 1914, French Voisin 5 planes performed the first bombing raid of the war against a Zeppelin hangar near Metz. The damage cannot have been too heavy, as the low engine performance limited the amount of ordnance that could be carried to a little less than 60kg.

For this reason, planes often dropped flechettes during the first phase of the war. These were steel darts about 10cm long and weighing 60g, which could easily penetrate helmets and skullcaps. But things went beyond the improvisation state fast. Special aerial bombs were soon fielded, as well as matching launchers, which were the target optics necessary to aim the drop, and of course planes that could carry large amounts of bombs.

For a long time, Russia commanded the heaviest aeroplane in the four-engined Ilya Mourometz. A squadron of these bombers, the most modern version of which could carry 700kg of bombs, was used very successfully on the Eastern Front from the beginning of 1915 to the end of 1917, and flew more than 400 sorties.

The German Gotha G.IV went into service

LA BATAILLE DE PICARDIE. Mitrailleuse Française contre Avions.

The Handley Page O/400 was the best British bomber of the First World War. The huge biplane, almost 20m long, and with a wingspan of 30m, was powered by two 360hp engines. The maximum bomb load was 900kg at a range of 1,100km. The crew numbered five and could operate the same number of machine guns. As these large planes, with a maximum speed of 150km/h were an easy prey for German fighters, they mainly flew their missions at night. With the wings folded in for transport, this plane is being pulled across the field by a tractor.

at the beginning of 1917 and would become the best known bomber of the First World War. It was specially developed for long distance flights to England, and could carry 1,500kg of bombs. Between May 1917 and May 1918, Gotha formations consisting of twenty to thirty

Great torpedo bomb dropped by a German aircraft. Weight 300kg, height 2.72m, diameter 360mm.
The dimensions and weight of this German aerial bomb illustrate the rapid development that military aviation took in a short time. Whereas the aeroplanes of 1914 could only transport a payload of a few kilos, a few years later bombs of several hundred kilos in weight were being dropped. The British Handley Page bombers could even carry single bombs of 750kg.

Aerial war. A Shower of arrows. Gunners of a German battery decimated by our aeros.
At the onset of the war aerial bombs were still under development and the maximum payload of the planes was low. Consequently, enemy ground forces were attacked with so-called *flechettes*. These steel darts, about 10cm long and 60g in weight, were manually dropped by the pilots in bundles. Due to the high speed gained during their drop, their impact was deadly.

GUERRE AÉRIENNE — La Pluie de Fléchettes
Servants d'une batterie allemande
décimés par nos avions

AERIAL WAR — A Shower of arrows
Gunners of a German battery
decimated by our aeros

planes, flew about twenty-five attacks against the UK, which killed approximately 800 British citizens.

The most famous British bomber of the war was the Handley Page O/400. The two-engined biplane was used from Spring 1918 onwards, and could carry a bomb weighing up to 750kg.

In 1918 however, tactical inventions turned out to be far more important than all technical developments. The Entente especially relied increasingly on combined missions where ground forces were supported by aircraft.

For example, the great Allied offensive on 8 August 1918 was accompanied by a huge number of reconnaissance planes and fighters, who were in action above the German lines. At the same time, bombers attacked the railways behind the German lines to make bringing in reinforcements and supplies more difficult. This meant that the combined efforts of the different branches of the air service were the decisive factors in the success of the operation.

The two-engined German Gotha G V was a modified variant of the G IV, which was introduced at the beginning of 1917 and was specifically constructed for long-range bombing raids against England. Since the spring of 1917, the Gothas flew missions to London and Paris among others, and caused hundreds of casualties among the civilian population. The G IV still carried the fuel tanks in the engine nacelles, which led to dangerous fires, and so these were moved to the body of the plane on the G V.

Chapter 9

Transport and Communication

In terms of armament, the forces that went to war in 1914 were well equipped, as most states had built up extensive arsenals of modern weapons in the years leading up to the war. Thanks to bolt action rifles, machine guns and rapid-fire guns, the available fire power was immense. Using these weapons acurately – i.e. have the right fire at the right time and on the right target – required fast and reliable communications, which were usually inadequate.

Communication and Coordination

Most communication was run by word or written note, and was carried by a courier delivering the message. Semaphores, optical Morse transmitters and flag signals were also used, but their range was limited and the messages did not always reach the recipient intact.

Carrier pigeons turned out to be a fast and reliable means of transmitting messages, and at least 100,000 were used during the war. According to orders, a German division had 200 pigeons and 4 soldiers who looked after them at its disposal. In 1918 about 20,000 carrier pigeons served in the British Army, looked after by 380 soldiers. During the war several armies even developed special gas proof cages for their pigeons to keep the animals safe during gas attacks. The birds were also used in tanks, captive balloons, airships, aeroplanes and submarines.

Other means of communication were necessary to exchange information between the advancing infantry and the artillery, or to have the barrage moved forward, as questions and answers had to be addressed immediately. This was also true for the long-distance heavy artillery, as the gunners could not see the impact of their shells and therefore had to rely on the

The British Navy's pigeon post. A British Submarine Officer sending a message by a carrier-pigeon.

Warships, of course, had radio transmitters and receivers, as the generators needed to send the messages were easy to bring along. However, there was always a risk that the enemy would listen in on transmissions, and so a number of carrier pigeons were brought along nevertheless.

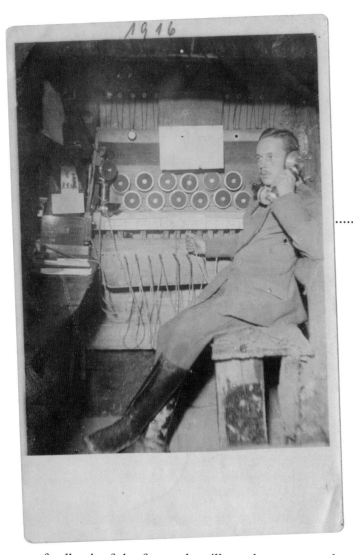

1916

Telephones, Radios and Telegraphs

The field telephone, which had been used by all larger armies for about ten years, was the best means of communication available. It worked perfectly in static warfare behind the lines, badly in mobile uses, and was highly unreliable in combat zones. Here the necessary phone lines, which could be run above ground behind the

feedback of the forward artillery observers on the ground or in the spotter planes. Real-time communications were similarly indispensable between the troops at the front and the battalion, regimental, brigade and divisional headquarters, some of which were positioned far behind the lines.

Swift and precise exchange of information was often a key factor in the success of an offensive, but as the technical means were unavailable, many missions failed.

132. Guerre 1914-15. — SUR LE FRONT. Cavaliers indiens.

"Ed. Pays de France"

War 1914-15. At the front. Indian cavalrymen.
Communications were often still sent by word of mouth in the most advanced lines, as telephone lines were prone to damage and radios were still in their infancy. Apart from optical Morse transmitters and signalling flags, the most important means of communication on the battlefield was the dispatch runner, who carried orders and situational reports between the positions and the headquarters. Dispatch riders were often used if larger distances had to be covered.

lines, had to be dug at least 2 metres into the ground to be even halfway safe from artillery hits. In reality this meant that repair squads had to be constantly in the field to keep the network of lines intact. Even so, the connection to those behind the lines was routinely severed during larger attacks.

Radio telegraphy, or spark-gap telegraphy, in which Morse messages were transmitted via electromagnetic waves, was an alternative to field telephones. At first this wireless technology seemed far more suitable than the telephone, but spark-gap transmission was not developed far enough to be a real option. Transmitting and receiving messages required electrically powered devices, which in turn required large and heavy generators and were therefore relatively immobile. The mobile German radio station

Field telephones were the most important means of connection in the trenches. Each unit commanded specially trained soldiers who had learned to run phone lines and set up connections. This picture shows a communications troop with its special equipment. The soldier on the left is holding a staff with a hook on its end, which was used to lift the cable up into trees or higher positions. The soldier on the right has fixed a wire drum to his belt and is reeling out the cable. The three wooden boxes in the centre are field telephones and the large leather pouches on the belts of the soldiers hold the necessary tools.

The War. Telephone military post.
Even though this picture only shows a small part of the apparatus, this seems to be one of the rare mobile radio stations. Almost all larger armies at the time had a number of 'portable' radio stations at their disposal – even though 'portable' meant several hundred kilograms of technical equipment were moved on horse-drawn carts.

needed two carts and at least ten porters. Also, all messages had to be encoded, as the enemy could listen in on the transmission.

Due to their exceptionally important role, reconnaissance and surveillance planes were fitted with transmitters from the end of 1914 onwards, to allow them to report their findings as quickly as possible. Communication was one-sided however, as due to weight reasons, there were no receivers on board the planes.

Before the war, the French officer, Ferrié, had already developed an alternative means of communication; the *Télégraphie par le sol* (TPS) or ground telegraphy. It made use of the fact that radio waves can pass through the ground for several hundred metres. The transmitter consisted of an electromagnetic relay that opened and closed an electrical circuit, transmitting Morse code signals that were received by a telephone receiver with a tube amplifier.

This method was useful for short range transmissions on the battlefield, as there were no

Greetings from the field. A military telephone exchange.
This picture shows the telephone exchange of a rear headquarters. It is located in an occupied French house and was apparently meant to be used for a longer period of time. Note the carefully run telephone lines on the rear wall leading up to the switchboards.

GUERRE 1914
Le Général Joffre inspectant le poste
de télégraphie sans fil d'un aéroplane

War of 1914. General Joffre inspects the wireless telegraph station of an aeroplane.
Due to their important role as artillery observers and reconnaissance positions, aeroplanes were already fitted with experimental transmitters shortly after the beginning of the war. This allowed them to report their findings to the headquarters on the ground immediately, without losing any time.

error-prone cables. Also, the users stayed mobile, as transmitters and receivers were connected to ground electrodes with cables. In addition the receivers could catch the signals transmitted by nearby enemy telegraphs and phone lines, so TPS was often used to intercept enemy communications. Roughly 10,000 TPS sets were manufactured during the war.

Railways

The railway was undoubtedly the primary means of transportation of the First World War. Without the railway network, the war would certainly have

taken a different turn or not begun at all, as mobilisation and deployment of troops to the front followed a detailed and fixed plan. If you failed to implement the meticulously planned scheme, the enemy might manage to bring up his troops to a strategically important starting position before you, and the battle might be lost before it had even begun. After the troop transports started rolling, war was basically unavoidable. In the first weeks of August 1914, countless goodbyes were said on European platforms, when more than 20,000 trains and almost a million railway carriages with soldiers,

Départ de Volontaires.   d'après l'Illustration.

I. — 1911.

Volunteers departing.
A train full of volunteers leaves a French station somewhere in 1914. The flags of Switzerland and the Netherlands, which are depicted in addition to the French flag, were most likely meant to suggest that there were foreigners among the volunteers. In reality, however, the flags were added to the propaganda picture later on. It is true, nevertheless, that the railway played a major role in both the mobilisation and transportation of troops and supplies to the front.

A German field railway takes ammunition up to the front. Each single heavy artillery shell was packed in a wicker basket during transportation. Once the shell was fired, the basket was supposed to be collected and sent to a special depot. Here they were checked for usability and then sent to the home country to be refilled.

horses and supplies started their way to the front.

But the railway would provide an important service to the war even after mobilisation was finished. When the war changed from mobile to static in the west, the railway network had an important influence on where the front line was drawn – the railway line from Metz to Lille ran closely behind the German front line and the one from Nancy to Arras via Paris, closely behind the Allied lines. After the Russians invaded East Prussia, the railway helped to move large bodies of troops from the Western to the Eastern Front in a short space of time. In this theatre of war the railway network was of special importance, as the armies were expected to be highly mobile and the front line was continually shifting. The German Empire and Austria-Hungary had a far better railway network at their disposal than Russia, which was certainly one reason for their victory on the eastern battlefields.

67. La Grande Guerre 1914-15 – *Blessés Français avec leur trophées* - French wounded with the trophys « Phot-Express »

French wounded with the trophys [sic] – The Great War 1914-15. French wounded with their trophies.
Lightly wounded French soldiers sit in the open door of a freight car and wait for the ride to a field hospital or recovery centre behind the lines. They proudly present the most coveted trophy of every ally – a German Pickelhaube.

Refreshment station.
German soldiers on their way to the front, in a railway carriage decorated with oak leaves. During a stop at a station the local Fräuleins provide them with coffee and give them flowers, which were traditionally handed out when soldiers went to war. The soldiers then put the flowers on their helmets or the front of their uniforms. This picture postcard is Number 2 of the *Kriegspostkarten* war postcards series by B. Wennerberg.

Trains were indispensable to move troops, but materials, supplies, provisions and ammunition could not be brought up without them either. On their return, the carriages would be filled with prisoners of war or wounded soldiers. If the latter were lucky, they travelled in special hospital trains, in which the carriages were fitted with beds with medical personnel taking care of the passengers, but often all they had was straw on the floor of freight carriages.

As some of the guns were too heavy to be moved on the roads, the artillery also used railways to move its equipment up to the front, mounting the guns on special carriages.

In addition to the standard gauge railways, a wide network of narrow gauge train lines was

GUERRE 1914

Anglais de la Croix-Rouge se dirigeant sur le front

British Red Cross members move towards the front.
The steady stream of troops and supply goods such as food and ammunition were brought to the front by railway. But trains also carried wounded soldiers away from the front line on their way home, or whole units destined for resting quarters where they would receive re-enforcements and be brought up to numbers again. The caption given here is incorrect, as the picture does not show civilian members of the Red Cross, but medics of the British Royal Army Medical Corps.

Eine Feldbahn, die in die vordersten Linien des heiß umstrittenen Kampffeldes führt.

A field railway leading to the front lines of the heavily contested combat zone.
The narrow gauge railway was developed by the Frenchman, Paul Decauville, in 1875. He owned a large estate and could not bring in the harvest by horse and cart due to heavy rainfall. The track elements with a gauge of 60 to 80cm are therefore named Decauville gauge after their developer. During the war both sides made good use of the narrow gauge railway, especially on the Western Front, as it was perfectly suited to transport soldiers and material between the front and the rear.

built behind the front. The narrow gauge railways would connect the regular railway stations and depots with the front, sometimes the tracks literally running right up to the trenches. The track elements weighed about 100kg apiece, which made them quick to install and easy to repair. The trains could carry far heavier loads than carts or lorries and ran a smaller risk of being bogged down in bad ground.

Horses and Donkeys

Horses played an important role on the Western Front as draft animals. After the front lines had settled into static warfare, the cavalry could not fulfil their tactical missions any more, meaning the cavalrymen now mainly fought in an infantry capacity next to regular foot soldiers. There were some automobiles and tractors, but in 1914 the transport of supplies and troops was impossible

War of 1914. French territorial soldiers provide something to drink for German prisoners of war.
Of course the trains bringing up troops or ammunition to the front did not return empty; they also took away wounded soldiers or prisoners of war. This photograph of German prisoners in a freight car, who are given drinks by members of the territorial forces, has most likely been staged for a propaganda picture, but the situation is quite realistic. On the Western Front at least, prisoners of war were usually treated quite well.

17. GUERRE DE 1914 — Territoriaux français donnant à boire à des prisonniers allemands   A. R.

AU FRONT

· RAVITAILLEMENT — LES ÂNONS ·
+ SUPPLIES BY DONKEYS +

Supplies by donkeys.
This illustration was created by Jean Kerhor, a pseudonym of André Dupuis (1876-1974). He combined a promising career in the French Ministry for Colonial Affairs with his successful work illustrating books, magazines, calendars, picture postcards and more. Dupuis was drafted in 1914 and made the leader of the topographical section of Army Group North. During the second half of the war, he published a series of twenty-six picture postcards showing everyday life at the front. Here, heavily loaded donkeys bring supplies to the front line trenches on an apparently rather quiet section of the front.

to manage without horsepower. Each infantry division therefore fielded about 5-6,000 horses that drew guns, ammunition carts, ambulances and wagons for provisions, personal packs and supplies and served as mounts for higher officers, usually from captain upwards.

To answer the demands of the mobilised troops, not only were recruits raised in the late summer of 1914, but large numbers of horses also entered service. These replacement horses, called 'remounts', were drawn together in special depots. There was about one horse for every four soldiers, and in Autumn 1914, 2.5 million horses were already serving with the armies. Keeping and feeding these animals created a high demand on the limited resources (a horse needs about ten times as much food as a soldier), but there was no alternative. Despite the animals being brought in, bought in and imported from everywhere, all forces suffered a permanent shortage. Sometimes

A French Army four-wheeled baggage cart loaded with supplies and drawn by three horses or mules. The end of the convoy cannot be seen in the picture. This must have been a common view on countless roads and lanes in northern France day in day out for years.

Visé à Paris Nº 401. — Guerre 1914-1915. — **MAILLY-MAILLET (Somme)**
Dans une ferme les poilus teignent les chevaux blancs en noir. — *Dyeing horses black in a farm*

Guerre 1914-1915
Les ravages du 75 - Un Cheval boche projeté sur un pommier

this caused serious problems, the field artillery, for example, could not move their guns without horses.

Estimates speak of around 6 million horses being used in the war, with most of them not surviving it. About 25 per cent died in combat, and a far larger number of diseases and exhaustion. Despite all of its care, the British Army alone lost almost 500,000 horses. The veterinarians of the Army Veterinary Corps treated 2.5 million cases, of which 80 per cent were fit for service again after treatment. This 'success' earned the corps the designation 'Royal', in August 1918.

Special gas masks were developed to protect horses from poison gas. White horses were even painted black to camouflage them, as supplies were often brought up to the front under cover of darkness. As well as horses, donkeys and mules were also used in large numbers, with the British and Indian armies alone using several hundred thousand of them.

War 1914-1915. The ravages of the 75mm. A boche horse has been flung into an apple tree.
The horrors of war included the ubiquitous presence of the cruelly mangled bodies of humans and animals, torn apart by exploding shells. According to the text on the card, this cadaver is the remains of a horse that was hit by a French 75mm grenade.

Cliché Marchand
1914... Type de Muletier Indien | Indian muleteer type
11ᵐᵉ Série

1914... Indian muleteer type.

The British Empire not only provided soldiers from all over the world, but also auxiliary forces and labourers, the last group mainly consisting of Chinese. Around 140,000 of them worked on the Western Front as part of the 'Chinese Labour Corps'. This muleteer from India belonged to the auxiliary forces of the Indian Army. At the onset of the war, India had 155,000 soldiers under arms, rising to 573,000 by the end of 1918. Almost 48,000 soldiers were killed or went missing in action, and 65,000 were wounded.

Motorised Transport

In Summer 1914 motorised vehicles were still rare in the armed forces. Mobilisation changed this, as governments of all European countries demanded automobiles and requisitioned the necessary passenger cars and trucks from private persons and companies. Civilian vehicles were mostly used for courier services and to transport soldiers and supplies. The British Army also established eight companies equipped with double-decker buses to transport troops in the UK and on the continent. Parisian taxis also lay claim to having played an important role in the battle of the Marne, in September 1914, by bringing soldiers up to the front. Although it is

A German cavalry patrol in a village in northern France. The soldier on the left is a Uhlan, while the others are members of a hussars regiment. They can be identified by their characteristic uniforms – the Uhlan wears an *ulanka* and a *czapka* for headgear, while the hussars wear the atilla decorated with loops and knots of braid and a busby, which is hidden here under a field grey cover.

Photo-Press, Agency
1914... Autobus de Londres avec des blessés
d'Anvers arrivant a Gand
1914... London motor-buses with wounded
from Antwerp arrive at Ghent
16me Série

1914... London motor buses with wounded from Antwerp arrive at Ghent.

With the mobilisation of armies consisting of millions of men, the demand for transport capacities grew massively. Auto-buses were ideally suited for troop transport and so many London double-deckers were drawn into service. This bus must be among the first vehicles to be deployed on the continent. As Antwerp has apparently not yet been taken by the Germans (or at least had been very recently), this picture must have been taken around 10 October 1914.

true that the taxis did in fact transport soldiers, it was only a couple of dozen at most, and it certainly didn't make a difference in the outcome of this enormous battle.

Throughout the war, the number of motorised military vehicles grew swiftly. In 1914 the British Army fielded only a few Holt gun tractors, the drive train of which would later leave its mark on the development of the tank and tens of thousands of them were used as gun tractors in all Allied armies in 1918. The transport of supplies and soldiers was also mechanised more and more. The French Army procured about 25,000 Berliet CBA trucks and in 1916 alone fielded 3,500

This drawing gives an impression of the nightly traffic on the *Voie Sacré*, the 'holy road' from Bar le Duc to Verdun. Supplies were brought into the besieged fortress following the system of an uninterrupted supply line developed by Pétain. More than 3,500 trucks took part in the action, as well as other vehicles.

20. Guerre de 1914 — Dans la forêt de Compiègne
les Autobus Parisiens employés pour le ravitaillement

trucks, 500 gun tractors, 200 buses, 800 ambulances and 2,000 more transport and liaison vehicles in the Battle for Verdun. But still, compared to railways and horse-drawn carts, motorised transport was certainly of less importance in the First World War.

The war of 1914. In the Compiègne forest, Parisian auto-buses are used to bring in supplies.
The town of Compiègne lies 80km north-east of Paris, where the river Aisne meets the river Oise. The Armistice was signed here in 1918. In 1914 the town was taken for a short time when the German advance was at its furthest point. After the First Battle of the Marne in September 1914, Compiègne was 15km behind the front again. There is no way to determine whether this picture was taken before or after the Battle of the Marne.

A German driver in front of his truck, which has been fitted with special front wheels. Due to the Allied blockade, Germany suffered various supply shortages, including a lack of rubber for tyres. But as the number of motorised vehicles grew, several experimental alternative solutions were devised. Here, for example, the rim has been fitted with springs holding a steel hoop as a running surface. Travelling comfort and rolling capacities were most likely rather 'robust'.

Chapter 10

In the Trenches and Behind the Lines

After the offensives in the west had ground to a halt, the soldiers at first began to build hastily thrown up parapets and simple trenches that gave protection against rifle and machine-gun fire. When it became obvious that the front would not be moving again in the near future, orders were given to deepen and fortify the temporary positions. In the end this resulted in an almost 800km long front line reaching from the Belgian coast, across northern France and down to the border with Switzerland.

The German Army especially, who had been forced to withdraw several divisions from the Western Front and move them to East Prussia after the Russian advance, built strong defensive positions until the attack in the east could be subdued.

The British and French also built trench systems, but at first these were designed as a point of departure for further attacks, rather than for any defensive measures, especially since the Allied high commands wanted to get back on the offensive as soon as possible. The Germans were at an advantage, however, as they had withdrawn to positions mostly on higher and drier ground that had a good view over the enemy lines, and so were easier to defend.

Hunting in the trenches.
A group of German soldiers in a machine-gun position reinforced with sandbags. The sign *Gefahrzone* (danger zone) means they are within reach of enemy fire and should not stick their heads out above the parapet. The men are hunting for lice, a permanent scourge in the trenches. Jokingly one of the soldiers tries to counter the threat with his Pistole 08, the standard service pistol of the German army.

CAMPAGNE DE 1914-1916
A travers les boyaux de Champagne.

The Trenches

If the ground was dry enough, trenches were dug approximately 1.5m deep. On the parapet (the side facing the enemy), they put up breastworks and reinforced them with sandbags, stones or fascines. On the parados (the back of the trench), similar but lower defence mechanisms protected the soldiers against the splinters of

Campaign of 1914-1916. Through the underbelly of the Champagne.
After the Battle of the Marne, the German armies withdrew to higher and drier ground and the Allies were forced to dig in opposite them. Here, the high water table made life very uncomfortable, as this picture illustrates. Note that a portion of the miles of telephone cables which ran across the battlefield can be seen along the side of the wet trench.

grenades coming in behind the lines.

To improve protection, trenches were dug deeper and deeper and gained a fire-step, which the soldiers stood on when firing over the top of the trench. What's more, the builders had to prevent the enemy from firing down along the

Machine-gun position.
Well-fortified machine-gun positions were spread out across the whole trench system. They were placed so as to be almost invisible to the enemy and to give the crews the best protection against small arms fire and shrapnel. During artillery attacks, the soldiers were supposed to seek shelter in an underground bunker, along with their weapons, and then return to their positions once the barrage had finished.

Maschinengewehr-Unterstand

A German position on the Western Front. After the advance ground to a halt in the west and Russia invaded East Prussia, the Germans set up strong defensive positions to allow them to move units from the western to the eastern theatre. This picture was most likely taken in 1915, before the Stahlhelm steel helmet was introduced. It shows a wide trench system finished with strong beams and looks almost comfortable. The soldier on the right is a picket watching the fore-field through an embrasure.

trench, should they manage to get through the lines. Therefore trenches never went in a straight line but featured bends or curves in regular intervals, which also gave additional protection if a grenade hit the trench directly.

If the ground was loose, the walls of the trenches might be reinforced with planks or wickerwork, or additional holes could be dug to give the soldiers protection against barrages and the weather. If possible, these holes grew into

subterranean bunkers where the ceilings were reinforced with tree trunks. These protective structures could lie more than ten metres under the ground and gave reasonably comfortable accommodation for the soldiers, as well as providing suitable housing for dressing stations, command posts and depots.

The Allied soldiers posted on the north-western section of the Western Front, i.e. in the southwest corner of Belgium, probably faced the

In the dugout. This German dugout was made for a longer duration of stay. Two rows of straw-lined beds, one above the other and with tables and benches in front, run along the wall. The rifle rack on the facing side holds two dozen rifles and the same number of soldiers lived in this confined underground space.

Guerre 1914-18 - Belgique   Un petit poste retranché.
Oorlog 1914-18 - België   Een versterkte kleine post.

Photo Musée de l'Armée, Bruxelles.

War 1914-18, Belgium. A small fortified position.
Some areas in south-western Belgium were flooded on purpose, whereas in other places, the ground water table was so high that it was impossible to dig trenches anyway. The small fortified position in this picture is therefore more of a reinforced 'hill', which could only be reached by wooden runways. Of course an exposed location like this is an easy target for enemy artillery, so the position was most likely far behind the front line trench.

worst conditions of all. The ground water level here was very close to the surface, and even shallow trenches quickly filled with water, meaning pumps often had to be used to remove it. In this terrain positions were built from sandbags and reinforced with planks and beams. The bottom of the trench was covered with duckboards and these log walkways kept the feet at least marginally dry.

However, all these measures could not prevent the whole area from turning into a desert of mud in wet weather, covering anything and making any movement more difficult.

The Trench System

A carefully prepared defensive position not only consisted of a single trench, but usually a whole system of three parallel lines, named 'front line trench', 'support trench' and 'reserve trench' from the front to the rear. The distances between the lines were about 100-300m and were connected with communication and connecting trenches, so that the front line could be reached under cover.

COMMENT ON SE DÉFEND CONTRE L'EAU
Le " Caillebotis "

How we try to defend ourselves against the water. The 'gratings.'
Another card showing *poilus* in the water and mud of north-western France. To keep feet even partially dry, log walkways were installed at the bottom of the trenches. As the soldiers are wearing the Adrian helmet, this picture must have been taken in the second half of 1915 or later.

The **Hartmansweilerkopf, as** the Germans called it, known as *Vieil Armand* to the French, is a peak in the southern Vosges Mountains where tenacious engagements took place in 1915 and almost 30,000 soldiers died. This German real photo card, with its collection of dugouts, tunnel entries and huts, is a good example of the ways in which soldiers tried to protect themselves from the effects of enemy weapons and the elements. The reverse reads '*Reserve-Lager Juni 1916*' – 'reserve camp, June 1916'.

Communication trenches could even have narrow-gauge railway lines running along them. These were sometimes even covered so they could not be spotted by the enemy. Saps (forward trenches) ran forward from the front line trench in the direction of the enemy, and listening and observation posts were placed at their forward ends, watching the enemy day and night to catch hints of an imminent attack in time.

Fallen Russians trying to crawl through a wire obstacle.
These two Russian soldiers were killed trying to crawl underneath a wire obstacle. The roughly 5 metres wide obstacle was placed on the open ground in front of the defender's trench, and whoever was spotted in it was helplessly exposed to the enemy. Wire obstacles on the Western Front could be several times as wide.

NECKEREI MIT PUPPE

Teasing with a dummy.
A German soldier pushes a dummy clad in a coat and peaked cap over the edge of the parapet to check whether the enemy is paying attention. This was not meant as a joke, because if the dummy was shot at it was used as a means to spot where the enemy was positioned or to check for the presence of snipers.

In front of and between the lines were well-camouflaged bunkers called blockhouses, holding machine gun and grenade launcher positions. The machine guns were positioned so that they could catch an advancing enemy in the flank with so-called flanking fire.

At first the trench systems were laid out quite clearly, but permanent additions, improvements, gains and losses slowly formed a labyrinth where not only single soldiers but whole units could get lost. Consequently, sign posts and name plates were placed everywhere, as well as guards who helped with orientation. The length of the complete trench system on the Western Front was estimated to be about 40,000km – the same as the circumference of the earth.

In the first months of 1915, positions began to be defended with wire obstacles. At first these were narrow barriers, but soon they reached depths of several dozen metres. Gaps at certain points or moveable obstacles allowed troops to

Christmas service in the trench. A memory of Christmas 1914 in the field.
German infantrymen celebrate Christmas 1914 in a trench on the Eastern Front, instead of at home. However, they do have a Christmas tree, an accordion and letters and parcels from home. The trench is neither very deep nor reinforced, but secured in front with wire obstacles. As the Eastern Front line was not very static, trench systems were rarely as elaborate and fortified as in the west.

Weihnachtsandacht im Schützengraben

Zur Erinnerung an das Weihnachtsfest 1914 im Felde

Kr. 219 b
Verlag von
GUSTAV LIERSCH & C.º
BERLIN S.W.

A. Kühlewindt
offic. Kriegsphotograph
Königsberg i. Pr.

D'après l'illustration.   G SCOTT

LES CONSEILS DE L'ANCIEN.   A.N
                                                        PARIS
288

Advice from an old one.
A drawing by Georges Scott from 1915, showing an older and experienced soldier giving advice to a young recruit. These tips were really important, especially as newcomers did not know the dangers, or how to react correspondingly, and were often among the first victims on the front. A soldier who survived the first few weeks stood a good chance of surviving for a longer period of time.

pass through and in some cases, the trenches were even protected with electrical fences.

In 1916 the first casemates made from reinforced concrete were built by the Germans. Variations on the standard model, with walls between 30 and 80cm thick, were created for different purposes. In the completely waterlogged soil of south-west Belgium, the Allies also adopted this building method and created these small bunkers both between the trench lines and behind them. The Germans built 2,000 casemates, bunkers and blockhouses in the Ypres area alone, creating an almost impenetrable line. The best known and strongest position was definitely the Hindenburg line (the Siegfried line to the Germans.)

After the severe losses from the Battle of the Somme in 1916, the German high command decided on a strategic withdrawal to free soldiers

405. La Grande Guerre 1914-15. — *Bataille de l'Aisne - Chargement de fils de fer barbelé pour être conduit aux tranchées.*   « Phot-Express »

The Great War 1914-15. Battle of the Aisne. Rolls of barbed wire are loaded to be transported to the trenches.
In 1873 the American, Joseph F. Glidden, requested a patent for barbed wire to fence in pastures for cattle. However, it was also well suited to prevent humans from entering or leaving certain places. In 1914 barbed wire was used rather haphazardly, but from 1915 onwards, it was systematically used in more and more places and in growing amounts.

"Daily Mail"
Official Photograph

A wiring party going to the trenches.
This card from the 'Daily Mail Official War Pictures' series carries the following text on the reverse: 'Every British trench is its own post office, with telephone and telegram wires. A wiring party is here going forward to its special work.' In fact, the picture shows men on their way to construct wire obstacles as they are carrying screw piles, which were fixed in the ground and held the wire.

and material for other sectors, by shortening the front line. In February 1917, they finally withdrew to the new defensive line, which they had been working on for some time.

Creating new positions not only required lots of energy and labour from the troops, but the civilian population also paid a high price. All buildings and civilian infrastructure were destroyed in a large strip of land, and about 125,000 people had to leave their homes. The line was approximately 7km wide and consisted of various staggered trench systems with a

multitude of bunkers, machine gun positions and artillery positions between them.

Although considered impregnable, the position could not hold up to the Allies' new weapons and tactics, and so in late September, the tanks and infantry finally managed to break through the Hindenburg line with the support of the air force and the artillery. Four weeks later, the war was over.

Front Line Service

Duties in the front line trenches started with reveille shortly before sunrise and the order to

Night work of British engineers in 'no-man's-land': fixing barbed wire in front of the trenches.
Fortuniono Matania (1881-1963) was born in Italy and was an official war painter for the British Army, becoming famous for his realistic portrayals of trench warfare. This can be seen in the way he depicts this mission: the men feel their way through the darkness, fall down, get up again, and are always afraid of being spotted by the enemy whilst doing their dangerous work.

Travail de nuit du Génie Anglais au "Pays de Personne" : Pose de Fil de Fer barbelé devant les tranchées   F. MATANIA

The coffee.
Ernest Gabard (1879-1957) was a French artist who served as a sergeant in the French 270th Infantry Regiment. He created a total of forty-two water colours of life at the front, which were published as picture postcards. Here he portrays a common misfortune: one of the soldiers fetching coffee has slipped and the precious juice (coffee) is dripping away into the snow. The soldiers at the front of their dugout are visibly horrified.

stand to in the trench, with rifle and bayonet fixed waiting for a possible attack.

This safety measure, which would be repeated at sunset, was taken by both sides and was based on the experience that most attacks took place at dawn or dusk. After about an hour the greatest danger had passed, and in the morning, breakfast would follow. Even though the quality and quantity were not always the same, all leaders tried to ensure good provisions were given to their soldiers, as a full stomach was good for

morale. Mobile field kitchens were of particular importance in this matter (soldiers' slang called them *La roulante* or *Goulash kanone*).

After breakfast came an inspection by the company commander, lieutenant, captain or perhaps a sergeant. If no special duties were required, most men spent the day maintaining and repairing the trenches (deepening, filling sandbags, reinforcing or stabilising walls etc.), repairing telephone and telegraph lines, or cleaning their weapons. Some were on camp

War 1914. A German field kitchen captured by the French in the Battle of Vic sur Aisne.
In September 1914 engagements took place near Vic sur Aisne, north of Soisson, as part of the Battle of the Marne that would halt the German advance. This Goulash cannon was captured there, along with other items, and would have been a welcome trophy as the German Army could muster more and better field kitchens than the French.

Food and mail being transported into the front line trench.
These two soldiers carry a canteen and some comforts from home to the front line trench. Connecting trenches were dug for this purpose and allowed the men to move out of sight of the enemy between the front lines and the rear, which was where the headquarters, dressing stations and kitchens were located.

duty, which included both digging and cleaning latrines as well as fetching water and provisions from behind the lines. No one was allowed to leave their position in the trench without an order, and soldiers in the front line trenches wore their complete battle kit throughout the day.

On quiet days the most important task was manning the observation and listening posts, from where no-man's-land and the enemy lines were continually observed. As snipers were a constant danger, the observers used a multitude of officially introduced or improvised periscopes and trench binoculars to look out over the top of the trench. After dark the listening posts took up their duty. Small groups of soldiers continually left the trenches in the dark to patrol no-man's-land, bring in prisoners, spy on the enemy and repair and enlarge the wire obstacles.

Time off was spent reading and writing letters or picture postcards, sleeping, playing cards and hunting lice, fleas and rats. These pests were a permanent scourge, and lice especially caused

The listening post.
At night soldiers were posted at forward listening posts at all times, tasked with immediately reporting all suspect noises so that no surprise attacks could take place. These men had to stay completely quiet in their positions and listen into the darkness – an unnerving but vital mission. A watercolour by Gabard.

The patrol.
French soldiers lie in no-man's-land, close to the German wire obstacles. Patrols were sent out at night to discover what the enemy was up to, bring in prisoners, or control and repair their own defences. Silence was extremely important here, as the enemy also had listening posts set up. Flares were fired at irregular intervals to illuminate the foreground and find enemy patrols. This watercolour was also created by Gabard.

terrible itching and carried diseases such as trench fever, which could result in several weeks of illness. Although there were mobile devices to clean and disinfect uniforms, as well as delousing stations for the soldiers, about 95 per cent of all soldiers suffered from lice.

The trenches were also a perfect breeding ground for rats, which made soldiers' lives even more difficult. They grew especially big and aggressive due to the surplus of food in most areas, mostly in the form of corpses and body parts in different stages of decomposition. Although soldiers quickly became used to seeing such sights, the stench must have been unbearable.

A soldier would be on duty at the front for around half a month, spending four to five of

Two French soldiers with their improvised bunk beds, most likely in a farmer's barn. The location is named as Berry-au-Bac on the reverse, a village about 10 kilometres south-east of the Chemin des Dames. This is where General Nivelle tried to continue his failed advance in April and May 1917 against all resistance, leading to mutinies within the French Army. The men are in a resting area behind the front, where each month they would spend a couple of days or even up to two weeks to recover from front line service. The soldier in the foreground is cleaning his gun; the latch is lying on the table.

Visé Paris

Nos Poilus en chasse.

Our *poilus* hunting.
Apart from rats, flies, fleas and lice were also an everlasting scourge. Lice not only caused permanent itching, but were also considered as carriers of bacteria that caused the so-called trench fever, which spread epidemically and infected more than a million soldiers. There is no heroism in this picture; the soldiers look tired and dirty and were most likely staying in a ruined building just behind the front lines. The man on the far right has his face bandaged.

these days in the front line trench, followed by the same time in the support trench and about eight days in the reserve trench. This relief schedule did, however, vary widely between the countries. British units, for example, rotated much more swiftly between the front line trench and the reserve trench than French or German troops. Sometimes the fighting was so heavy that no relief was possible, and units had to stay in their positions for a longer time. But in general, two weeks at the front were followed by two weeks behind the lines.

Behind the front soldiers were quartered in either tent camps, abandoned or unoccupied buildings or huts that they built themselves, or were billeted with citizens of the occupied areas. Although a time of relative quiet, there were regular exercises, weapons and equipment had to be repaired and replacements from home had to be integrated. Time behind the lines also offered

German Soldiers resting in roughly made bunk beds in their quarters behind the front lines. The postmark identifies them as members of the 12th company of *Infanterie-Regiment* 371 infantry regiment. The unit was raised by the XI Army Corps on 13 July 1915 near Thiaucourt, and served on the Western Front until the end of the war as part of the 43rd Infantry Brigade of the 10th Reserve Infantry Division.

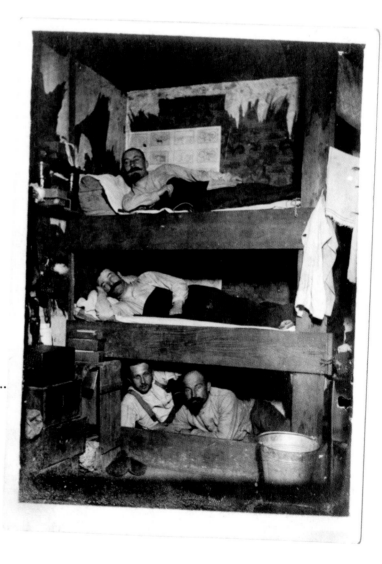

'The bag of the rat hunt' A night in the forest of Argonne.

The rats in the trenches were large, aggressive and plentiful, mainly because the many unrecovered bodies of fallen soldiers meant there was an abundance of food. Although the beasts were constantly hunted, keeping the population down was a hopeless endeavour. This picture alone shows around forty dead rats.

some variety in the form of mess halls, cafés and brothels.

As far as the latter are concerned, France was far more liberal than Germany and the UK, much to the delight of the soldiers stationed there. In 1917 there were 137 registered and approved brothels in 35 towns behind the Allied lines. The standard of these troop entertainment establishments was quite diverse, with big differences between those for officers and those for enlisted men.

Discipline was strict, more so in the British and German armies than in the French, and violations and offences were heavily punished. A British company commander could either have a culprit arrested for a maximum of twenty-eight days or have him officially shackled-up and left out under the open sky for the same amount of time.

Severe violations were handled by a court martial, as happened to about 6,000 officers and 300,000 NCOs and enlisted men of the British Army. Mostly the charges were absence without leave, drunkenness and desertion. About 3,000

Bathing and delousing station.

To keep on top of the pests, special sanitary facilities were set up behind the lines. Here the uniforms were cleaned and disinfected, while the soldiers could bath and see to their personal hygiene. There were also mobile delousing stations that went from unit to unit, but their success was usually short-lived and the lice soon returned.

47. La Grande Guerre 1914-15 — Exécution d'un espion par les soldats Anglais   A. R.

death sentences were passed, of which 350 were carried out. Soldiers were mainly sentenced to death for desertion, cowardice in the face of the enemy, leaving their posts and sleeping whilst on guard duty. The firing squad would usually await the delinquent at dawn, but being the member of a firing squad was one of the few orders a British soldier was allowed to disobey.

The best gift for a soldier at the front was the permission to go on a leave, allowing him to escape hell for a couple of days and reconnect with family and friends.

Officers were granted short leaves regularly, but things were far worse for the rank and file, as they only received about five to ten days of leave per year. After the unrests in 1917, French regulations were relaxed.

The officers' advantages regarding provisions, accommodations, brothels and leaves were outweighed by substantial dangers to life and limb. The percentage of officers killed and wounded was higher than that of the NCOs and

GABARD   LE RETOUR DU PERMISSIONNAIRE

Returning from leave.
This watercolour by Gabard shows a soldier on his way to rejoin his unit after home leave. His body language clearly shows his reluctance; his head hangs down and his thoughts are most likely still with loved ones at home, as he walks towards an uncertain future. He carries a parcel with some comforts from home under his arm to make life at the front more bearable, perhaps including thermal underwear, food, tobacco and alcohol.

„Auf Urlaub" Stürmische Begrüßung

enlisted men. Captains and lieutenants were especially at risk, but also many staff officers and even around eighty generals died in combat.

Attack and Defence

The permanent scourges of the men in the trenches were pests, boredom and the weather. But sooner or later the ghastly routine was interrupted by an even more severe assault on their physical and psychological integrity; an artillery barrage. The enemy artillery would fire shrapnel or gas shells at them, or a mixture of different shells. Often this long-range engagement would turn into hand-to-hand combat in or between the trenches, where all kind of weapons were used to disable the enemy and survive.

In the first phase of the war an enemy attack was always foreshadowed by an artillery barrage that could last for hours or even the whole day. Once the realisation grew that this allowed the

The German photographer
who took this picture managed to catch a heavy artillery shell at the very moment it exploded – not an easy task with the technological means of the era. Infantry attacks were usually foreshadowed by an artillery barrage. The numbers and calibres of the shells fired varied widely, but such a barrage was certainly a frightening experience. Artillery fire caused far more casualties than the damage done by the bullets of rifles and machine guns.

War 1914-15-16. In the Somme. British offensive. German trenches upset by the bombardment.
However well set up and reinforced positions and trenches might have been, they did not offer protection from a direct hit by heavy artillery. Relative safety from artillery shells was only available in the dugouts, which were often built more than 10 metres below ground. But of course, the entrance to the dug out could collapse, leaving the soldiers inside buried alive.

defenders to know the exact location of the impending attack, the barrages became shorter, but no less intense.

It would start with a wave of thundering, whistling and howling noises, swiftly growing louder and coming ever closer, until the ground suddenly exploded and fountains of dirt, stones, wood, metal and human remains were thrown up. The sky would darken, the ground would shake and heave, and the air would fill with the hissing and whirring of shrapnel. Explosives, dust and chemical agents were everywhere, making breathing difficult and irritating the mucous membranes.

Deafening explosions would be mixed up with the screams of the wounded and dying. The survivors would duck as far down into the trenches as possible or hide in dugouts and bunkers, waiting for the attack to pass, dazed and stunned by the noise of the explosions and the blasts. They lost track of the time and minutes seemed like hours. They feared for their lives and waited for the end, and even non-believers would start to pray and weep and beg to be spared.

Onwards with a 'hurrah!'
With his sword drawn the commander heads the attack of his unit. The soldiers follow with bayonets fixed and shouts of 'hurrah'. Perhaps this really is an original picture from the battlefield, as the German text claims, but if it is, it was not taken during real combat but posed for the camera. In June 1915 the Prussians had already ordered officers commanding combat troops to exchange their swords for standard issue rifles, as they were too easily identified by snipers.

Kampfgraben nach Trommelfeuer.

Trenches after an artillery barrage.
This real photo card really drives home that no trench, however well fortified with sandbags, beams and planks, could withstand an artillery barrage or give shelter from shells. The ground has been basically turned over and the location of the original trench is hardly identifiable. Soldiers who stayed here must have stood little chance of survival.

A battlefield after an artillery barrage. Tree stumps are visible in places, but apart from that, the terrain has been completely destroyed. If you look closely you can identify some torn up wire obstacles. Across this hellish result of the artillery barrage, the infantry would then set out to attack and be met with strong fire by the surviving defenders.

War of 1914. A bayonet charge by the French infantry.
This picture seems to have been taken during an exercise. Although the soldiers would approach the enemy trenches with bayonets fixed, there were rarely larger bayonet fights, as the defenders could fire their rifles from under cover. If the enemy trench was reached, a rifle with bayonet fixed was rather a hindrance in the narrow confines of a trench system, as it was almost 2 metres long.

92. GUERRE DE 1914. — Infanterie Française "Charge à la baïonnette"
A "CHARGE A LA BAIONNETTE" of the French infantry
reproduction interdite
LL.

The attack.
After the artillery barrage, the attack was ordered and the soldiers climbed over the tops of their trenches to storm towards the enemy positions across no-man's-land. They would hope that the barrage had destroyed the enemy's defensive positions and as many wire obstacles as possible. This was often not true and the attackers were met with devastating defensive fire and they usually suffered more casualties than the defenders without gaining any ground. Here, E. Gabard has caught the beginning of the attack in his picture.

Silence would set in within an instant and most men would regain their senses. Now the screams and whimpers of the wounded and maimed were audible again, but drowned out by commands from officers and NCOs, who ordered their soldiers to man the defensive positions. Machine guns were swiftly fetched from their underground shelters, and were set up, loaded and cocked. Ammunition was laid out and cooling water prepared, whilst hand grenades were placed within reach and rifles were aimed. Enemy soldiers were visible through the dust and gunpowder smoke, quickly crossing the torn-up no-man's-land and the destroyed wire obstacles.

These men had been brought into assembly areas behind the front line trench while their artillery fired at the enemy across their own lines. They received a sip of alcohol whilst they waited in the densely crowded trenches. They were often smoking, stiff from fear and praying that the seemingly unending barrage would never actually stop.

Finally, orders were given to fix bayonets, followed by the signal to attack. Slowly they would climb out of their foxholes and trenches, hindered by their heavy equipment and rifles, and run

Französischer Graben nach dem Sturm.

A French trench after the assault.
This repulsive sight of an overrun trench with bodies, weapons and equipment scattered all around, shows the intensity of the fighting. As the trench is hastily dug and not fortified, and the soldiers are all wearing helmets, the picture may have been taken during the German Spring Offensive of 1918.

In the Trenches and Behind the Lines 213

Battle near Fromelles, 19 August 1916.
In July 1916 a badly planned Allied attack, during which 5,500 Australians lost their lives, happened near Fromelles, south of Armentières. This German real photo card was taken in the same region about a month later and shows dead British or Australian soldiers behind a trench wall. There is still a Lewis machine gun standing among the bodies; it has not yet been picked up by German troops.

towards the enemy lines through gaps in their own wire obstacles. From a distance the positions looked completely destroyed, but the closer they came, the more obvious it was that the wire obstacles were almost completely intact.

The first soldiers had just reached the first wire obstacles when a hidden machine gun began to fire into their flank. Those that were not immediately hit tried to duck into the shell holes where they were met with a barrage from the grenade launchers. There was no way ahead and none back, and more and more comrades fell prey to the machine guns or the grenade launchers firing indirectly. Helplessly, they pressed against the ground whilst around them more and more were wounded or killed. The screams and moans of the wounded set their teeth on edge and only rarely would they be able to help their comrades.

Obviously this only was a minor attack, meant to divert from more important actions in other sections of the front line or to measure the strength of the enemy defences, as only a couple of companies had been sent into the no-man's-land.

In the trench. The chaplain is listening to the last will of a dying soldier.
Chaplains of various denominations served in all armies. As well as field services, they also held funeral services and gave comfort and spiritual care to the wounded and dying. This card shows an idealised farewell; most men died alone, in miserable conditions and often after long suffering.

German bodies in a trench near lake Blanckaert.
The Blanckaert is a wetland in south-west Belgium and lies between the Yser and Diksmuide rivers. These German soldiers were photographed shortly after they had fallen.

Slowly the fire died down, all officers and NCOs had been taken out and the soldiers would just stay down, hoping they could get back to their own lines under the cover of darkness. A good many of them managed, but they had to leave the wounded behind, although their screams and whimpers would be heard for another two days and nights.

The attack had been repelled before the enemy had even crossed the wire obstacles. Therefore there had been no hand-to-hand combat in the trenches, where soldiers would bash in each others' heads with clubs and rifle butts, behead each other with sharpened spades or bayonet each others' bellies.

Thankfully the artillery barrage had not included gas shells and the defenders had suffered relatively few casualties. There were a number of deaths and numerous heavy casualties from the artillery fire, soldiers who had lost arms or legs. A full hit into the entry of a dugout had caused the majority of casualties, as soldiers had been buried alive and suffocated before they could be dug out. The incident, which was as common as it was inconsequential, did not cause major interest and was soon forgotten.

You will find countless descriptions like these in the regimental chronicles that were published hundreds of times in the 1920s to 1940s, usually by veterans' associations.

Real photo card of a German war cemetery. The cross on the right marks the last resting place of *Wehrmann* (militiaman) Albert Stielow. He served in the 3rd West Prussian Infantry Regiment 129 and died aged 28 years old on 18 July 1916. *Musketier* (musketeer) Josef Freimer is resting to his left. He was born on 13 August 1895 and also fell in July 1916.

Chapter 11

Dead, Wounded, Taken Prisoner or Missing

Even today it is impossible to give an accurate number of the victims claimed by the First World War, and it will not likely be any more possible in the future, as all sources give different numbers. The most reliable are those of the Western Front, but the numbers of casualties and prisoners of war on the Eastern Front, in the Balkans, the Caucasus, the Middle East and Africa vary widely. This is also true for the victims among the civilian population.

Self-mutilation

Compared to the dangers of being killed, severely wounded or taken prisoner, a light injury was the best that could happen to a soldier on the front. It had to be severe enough to require treatment far behind the lines, but not bad enough to make a full recovery impossible. The British soldiers called it a 'blighty wound', with Blighty meaning Britain in the soldiers' slang. For the Germans, an injury which resulted in a ticket home was known as '*Heimatschuss*' (literally: home shot).

Many soldiers were willing to pay a high price to be transferred to a hospital behind the front, and would hold a hand above the parapet or shoot themselves. As self-mutilation carried heavy penalties, you had to make sure you did not leave any obvious signs. In the German Army, rumour had it that you had to fire through

Cliché Chusseau-Flaviens
1914.. Blessés Anglais à la défense d'Anvers
10me Série 1914.. English wounded from Attwerp s defense (E|D)

1914... English wounded from Attwerp's [sic] defense.

In addition to Belgian soldiers, this picture postcard from the first months of the war also shows two British, one of them with a head wound. The picture was taken in the Antwerp area, where the Allies held out until 10 October 1914. A number of real photo cards were produced at this time from pictures taken directly behind the front, which showed 'normal' situations and events without any additions or manipulation. However the publisher was not as lucky in translating the name of the place.

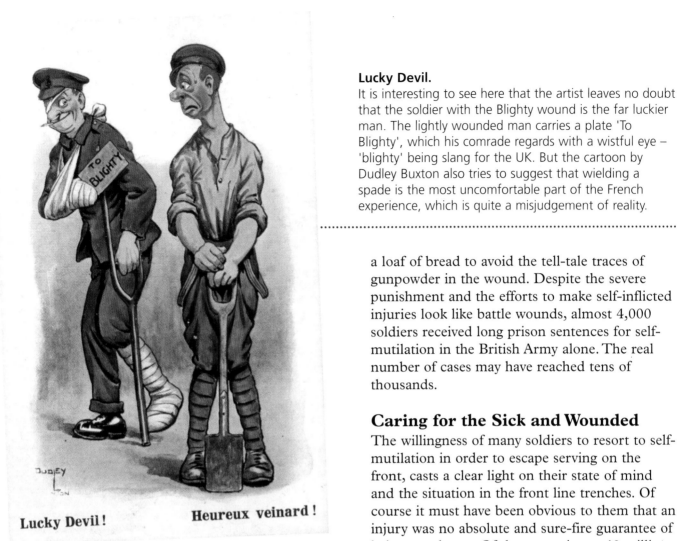

Lucky Devil.
It is interesting to see here that the artist leaves no doubt that the soldier with the Blighty wound is the far luckier man. The lightly wounded man carries a plate 'To Blighty', which his comrade regards with a wistful eye – 'blighty' being slang for the UK. But the cartoon by Dudley Buxton also tries to suggest that wielding a spade is the most uncomfortable part of the French experience, which is quite a misjudgement of reality.

Lucky Devil !   **Heureux veinard !**

a loaf of bread to avoid the tell-tale traces of gunpowder in the wound. Despite the severe punishment and the efforts to make self-inflicted injuries look like battle wounds, almost 4,000 soldiers received long prison sentences for self-mutilation in the British Army alone. The real number of cases may have reached tens of thousands.

Caring for the Sick and Wounded

The willingness of many soldiers to resort to self-mutilation in order to escape serving on the front, casts a clear light on their state of mind and the situation in the front line trenches. Of course it must have been obvious to them that an injury was no absolute and sure-fire guarantee of being sent home. Of the approximate 40 million

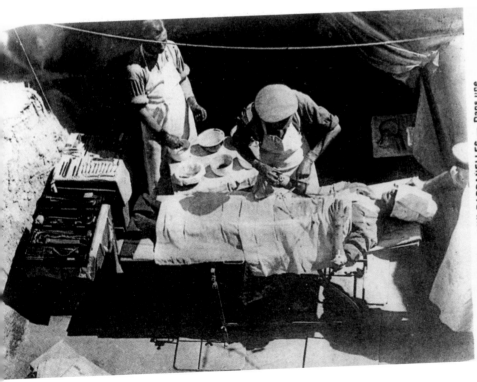

1914-15... AUX DARDANELLES — Dans une ambulance, un chirurgien au travail
1914-15... IN THE DARDANELLES - A surgeon at work in a field hospital

1914-15... In the Dardanelles. A surgeon at work in a field hospital.
A surgeon is operating on an injury on a soldier's right forearm. The operating theatre consists of a hole in the ground across which a tarpaulin can be fixed. The instruments lie prepared to the left, passed by an assistant. Behind the lines, many soldiers who were wounded at the front died of infections in their wounds, no surprise considering the circumstances of the treatment.

Prosnes (Forest of Argonne) aid post.
This French Army aid post is located underground and most likely a good stretch behind the front line trench, as the terrain has not been completely turned over by artillery barrages. A stretcher with a French Adrian helmet is visible in the foreground.

PROSNES (Argonne) - Poste d'ambulance

wounded in the First World War, roughly every fifth succumbed to his own injuries. The chances of survival were much higher on the Western Front than in the east, as nearly every second wounded soldier there died due to insufficient medical care or logistical problems.

A soldier who was wounded on the Western Front and was lucky enough not to be overlooked, or to lie in an inaccessible place, was evacuated from the combat zone and taken behind the lines by his comrades or medics. At first he would receive minimal care at an aid post, but these were mostly improvised and involved working under incredibly unfavourable hygienic conditions. If the soldier survived and was not sent back to the front, he would go on to a dressing station, getting there by either limping, or riding in a horse cart, hand cart or

We have to help each other.
This French soldier has suffered an injury to his feet and is therefore brought behind the lines by a medic in a non-regulation means of transportation. Despite his injuries he still is among the lucky ones who were not forgotten on the battlefield and had to hold out, out of reach of their comrades. He was likewise not treated in one of the horrible forward aid posts in the front lines. The picture was most likely taken in September 1914.

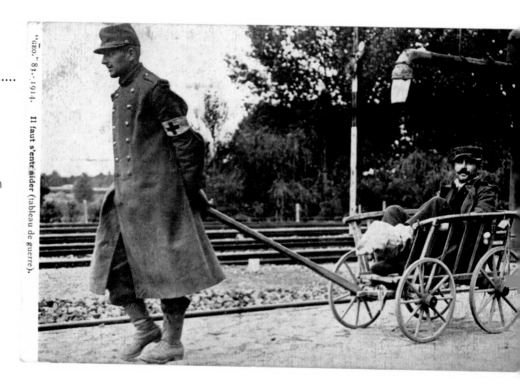

1914. . Chien ambulancier découvrant un blessé | Ambulance dog discovering a wonded

10me Série

truck to a dressing station. The dressing stations were located from a few hundred to several kilometres behind the front line, either in tents or empty buildings. If he was lucky, the soldier would carry on by ambulance, meaning either an automobile or a horse-drawn carriage, to a casualty clearing station about 20km behind the front line. Here he would receive further medical care or, depending on the severity of his injuries, would be moved by rail to a base hospital behind the lines, or even to a hospital at home. Due to the incredibly high numbers of wounded soldiers, emergency hospitals were established in schools, meeting halls, factories, monasteries and many other buildings all over Europe.

A wounded soldier who fell into the hands of the enemy was completely at their mercy, and there are a number of cases on record where wounded soldiers were killed or simply left

War of 1914. German wounded in the courtyard of the school at Varreddes.
Heavy engagements took place close to Varreddes (near Meaux) in September 1914, as part of the Battle of the Marne. A couple of German wounded are resting under a roof in the courtyard of the school. The floor is covered with straw and the men have woollen blankets, but there does not seem to be any more care. The prisoners are guarded by Gendarmes.

14. GUERRE DE 1914 — Blessés allemands dans le préau des écoles de Varreddes   A. R.

1914... Ambulance transportant des blessés
traversant la forêt de Laigue
7me Série

Ambulance transporting wounded
through Laigue forest

(E|D)

1914... Ambulance transporting wounded through Laigue forest.

The picture dates to the autumn of 1914 and shows a horse-drawn ambulance near Compiègne. The driving seat is occupied by medics and the roof by lightly wounded, as the inside is reserved for the severely wounded. Horse-drawn ambulances were a common means of casualty transportation, automobiles would be used in higher numbers only over the course of the war.

behind. On the other hand there are many reports by soldiers who received good treatment from enemy medics and doctors. Here again, the odds of survival were better for a soldier injured on the Western Front than in the other areas ravaged by war.

The medical services, which grew to enormous numbers during the war, were mainly intended to keep the army in a fighting condition. In this they were very successful, as ninety per cent of the patients returned to the front sooner or later. As an individual, the soldier once more took second place, as the men were returned to service at the front and sent back to their units as soon as possible. This meant that not only soldiers with insufficiently cured physical and mental injuries were released from care prematurely, but also patients suffering from diseases, which were far more common than injuries.

A British hospital tent.

Apparently the tents have only been pitched a short time ago, as it still is rather quiet. After the big field battles during the last weeks of August and first weeks of September, hundreds of thousands of casualties needed medical care and the military hospitals soon reached their limits. To extend their capacities, emergency hospitals were established in all countries, which sometimes continued their service beyond the end of the war. Altogether an estimated 40 million soldiers were wounded in the First World War.

8. - GUERRE EUROPÉENNE 1914
Une tente d'Hôpital Anglais

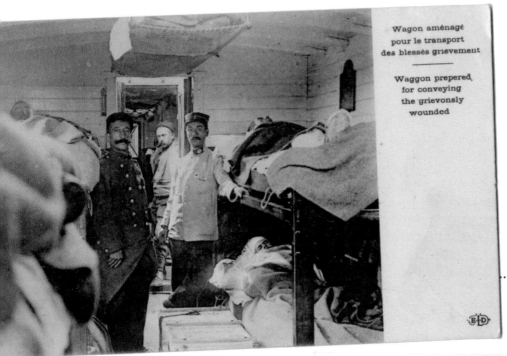

Wagon aménagé
pour le transport
des blessés grievement

Waggon prepered,
for conveying
the grievonsly
wounded

Waggon prepared for conveying the grievously wounded.

Trains that brought soldiers and supplies to the front would transport wounded soldiers and prisoners of war on their way back. Most wounded travelled in regular freight or passenger carriages, but there were also fully equipped hospital trains for difficult cases.

Ludendorff Donation Fund

An illustration by Ludwig Hohlwein (1874-1949), one of the leading representatives of artistic advertisements from the end of the nineteenth century onwards, who worked for many large enterprises in Germany and abroad. This picture postcard was published for the benefit of the *Ludendorff-Spende für kriegsbeschädigte* (Ludendorff Donation Fund for Disabled Servicemen), a foundation helping soldiers disabled in the war. All countries had charitable organisations like this, some of them only saw to very specific groups, for example the French 'Friends of the blind soldiers' (*Les Amis des soldats aveugles*).

LUDENDORFF-SPENDE

This ghastly drawing by the French artist, Pierre Dukercy, was published by a foundation for severely wounded and maimed soldiers. A wounded soldier, dazed and more dead than alive, is leaning against a tree stump on the battlefield. Scenes like this with maimed soldiers actually happened quite often, but they were rarely captured in a picture and even more rarely published and distributed.

War invalid 1914-1918.
Due to the great numbers of disabled servicemen, men on crutches or in wheelchairs, missing limbs, or those who were paralysed or blind, were a common sight on European streets in the 1920s and 1930s. A group of victims who were not so present in the public eye, were the men whose faces had been cruelly disfigured by severe injuries. In France they called themselves 'Geulles cassées', the 'broken faces'. Some were so disfigured that they only left the house wearing specially made masks.

Among the most common were scabies, tuberculosis, trench fever, sexually transmitted diseases (in some units up to 20 per cent of the men were affected), gangrene, blood poisoning and pneumonia. Despite suffering from any of these, anybody who could work was sent back to their unit as fit for service.

Regardless of the efforts to send as many soldiers back to the front as possible, even the strictest doctors could not avoid declaring a greater number of men as being unfit for service. They were the severely maimed and disfigured, who had lost one or more limbs, had their lungs heavily damaged from poison gas or had gone blind. All in all there were hundreds of thousands of men who were not killed by the war, but still had their life basically ended by massive bodily impairments.

Another group that has to be considered on its own included the soldiers who returned from the war with massive psychological problems and were wrongly diagnosed with 'shell shock.' At first the assumption was that the brain and nerves had been damaged by exploding shells, causing speech impairments, memory loss and paralysis. It was only later that they discovered it was the unending horrors the soldiers had been exposed to, which was the cause of the mental breakdowns.

A German soldier who survived the war but whose life was destroyed. He seems to be almost completely paralysed and is fixed to a chair with belts. He has only the use of his right arm remaining, but he still proudly wears his Iron Cross 2nd Class. Hundreds of thousands of soldiers were so heavily injured by the war, physically as well as psychologically, that they could not find a way back to their old lives.

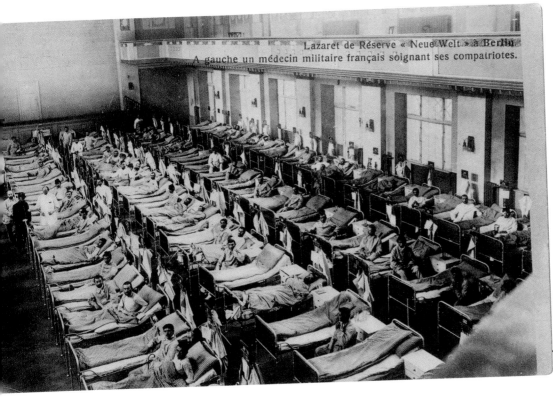

Lazaret de Réserve « Neue Welt » à Berlin.
A gauche un médecin militaire français soignant ses compatriotes.

Reserve hospital *'Neue Welt'* at Berlin. On the left a French doctor gives care to his compatriots.
This card was published by the International Committee of the Red Cross as No 5 'Germany' in its 'Prisoner of War Camps' series. Today the *'Neue Welt'* would be called an amusement park, and the reserve hospital was housed in the theatre and concert hall. Wounded French prisoners of war were treated by their own doctors here.

Unfortunately this led to treatments that would reward a patient for getting better, but also punish him if his symptoms did not fade. Quite a number of these 'shell-shocked' soldiers, who were in fact suffering from combat stress reactions, were summarily executed, often after a short court martial.

About six months before the end of the war, the Spanish Flu epidemic began to spread. Its origins were most likely in America, but it received is nickname as Spanish newspapers were the first to run reports of the disease. Unlike other forms of influenza, this strain hit young adults the hardest. In August 1918, half of the American soldiers in Europe were sick and tens of thousands would die from the effects of the influenza. Worldwide, almost 40 million people died of the virus in 1918/19.

Dead or Missing

About 10 million soldiers fell in the First World War, with the German Empire suffering the

Dozens if not hundreds of bodies cover the ground in this forest. Most likely they are fallen Russians and the location is on the eastern border of Prussia. The intact trees and lack of shell holes seem to point to machine guns being responsible for the high number of casualties. With a firing speed of 600 rounds per minute (or 10 per second), only two of these weapons could cause devastating damage like this. There is proof that machine-gun crews would sometimes stop firing as they could not bear the enormous number of casualties.

A picture from the funeral of fallen German soldiers. The honour guard is firing a three volley salute at high port. The picture was most likely taken in the eastern theatre and away from the front line, as a little boy is watching the spectacle on the left side of the picture and apart from the chaplain, there also is a nurse present on the right. The shakos seem to indicate that this is a Jäger light infantry battalion.

heaviest losses at 2 million, followed by Russia with 1.8 million, France with 1.4 million and Austria-Hungary with 1.1 million soldiers. On average about 15 per cent of mobilised soldiers lost their lives, and the percentages were even higher in France and Germany. Most of the victims were young men around 20-24 years old.

Approximately 60 to 70 percent of the deaths

Most soldiers who fell during the large battles on the Western Front were buried anonymously in mass graves, as pictured here. After the war many of the graves were reopened, the soldiers identified and buried in individual graves. But not all mass graves could be found and may remain lost forever, sometimes due to them being located close to the front line and destroyed by artillery fire in later engagements.

This postcard shows another photograph that has been tacked onto a wooden board. German soldiers have placed several casualties on the rim of a giant crater. Most likely they were killed by a mine blast. In this type of underground warfare practised by all warring factions, one tunnelled underneath the enemy positions as silently as possible, set up a huge amount of explosives and then detonated them.

were caused by the roughly 750 million artillery shells fired during the war. Two million died from rifle and machine gun bullets and about 100,000 were victims of poison gas. The others died from illness, thrust and cut wounds caused by bayonets, clubs, coshes or spades, whilst others drowned in water-filled shell holes or suffocated after being buried in dugouts.

The luckier ones had a quick death, catching a bullet or shrapnel to the head or vital organs, or being torn apart by an explosion. A severe stomach wound or extensive burns led to suffering beyond words. Breathing in poison gas, which was not immediately lethal, and a multitude of other injuries caused a slow but certain death, especially if the victim lay in no-man's-land for hours or even days, or was caught in a wire obstacle and had to endure a wretched death. Many wounded died of injuries that would not have been fatal if they had been treated in time. But some were simply not

After the battle, the bodies of fallen comrades were collected and brought to mass graves on horse-drawn carts. This task was often performed by prisoners of war, which was considered 'the normal course of events'. After a short time at the front pictures like this and even more gruesome sights were nothing out of the ordinary for most soldiers. The deportment and the facial expressions of the four men speak of routine, despite their grisly task.

found, or had to be left behind as they were lying within range of enemy fire, or their numbers simply overwhelmed the capacities of doctors and medics.

Not all of the dead were immediately recovered, and those bodies in front of the front line especially would stack up for days or even weeks without anyone being able to take them away. The stench of decay was brutal. If a contested section of the front line was hit by artillery, the bodies were scattered all over the ground and the soldiers literally lived upon and among the dead. To reduce the danger of diseases the bodies were covered in chemicals.

The fallen were buried as quickly as possible, usually in rather small cemeteries near where they died, and were divided by units not far from the front line. If possible they would be buried in individual graves, but mass graves were often used after larger engagements which resulted in many casualties, and especially if the enemy took care of the burials. This task was mostly performed by prisoners of war. After the war many of the smaller burial places were cleared and the remains buried in larger war cemeteries.

If a soldier was reported as missing then his fate was unknown. In the best cases, this meant that he had lost contact with his unit, was absent without leave or perhaps had deserted. But he could also have been taken prisoner or possibly be dead. If the soldier did not reappear and there were no reports received saying that he was in the hands of the enemy (these reports were exchanged via neutral parties), he would be declared dead after a certain amount of time, which was usually six months. As many casualties were severely disfigured or literally torn apart and others were buried without identification, the number of soldiers reported missing was very high. After the Battle of Passchendaele, the British Empire alone reported 90,000 soldiers missing in this section of the front. The names of 54,896 soldiers who died here up until 16 August 1917 and whose last resting place is unknown, are listed on the Menin Gate Memorial to the Missing and are a symbol of the millions who shared their fate.

Prisoners of War

Considering the conditions at the front and the good chance of falling ill, getting wounded or even killed, being taken prisoner was not the worst outcome for a soldier, especially on the Western Front. Even though it happened again and again that soldiers who had already surrendered were shot, these cases were usually the result of adrenalin flowing in the heat of

1. GUERRE DE 1914 — L'insolence des officiers prussiens. — Officiers de Uhlans capturés par nos alliés
L'un d'eux, avant d'entrer en prison, lance une insulte à un officier anglais A. R.

The war of 1914. The insolence of the Prussian officers.
Prussia was the symbol of German militarism and, being its representatives, Prussian officers were especially disliked. The rest of the text on this card explains that on his way into captivity, the Prussian Uhlan officer insulted the British officer. The captured Germans are in fact cavalry, but they are enlisted men.

Aus einem unserer mohammedanischen Gefangenenlager   Beim Verlassen der Moschee

One of our Mohammedan prisoner of war camps. Leaving the mosque.
With its alliance with Turkey and an eye on the large number of Islamic citizens in the British Empire, Germany tried to start a 'holy war' against the Allies. This also included publicising its excellent treatment of Muslim prisoners of war (mainly soldiers from the French overseas territories). There is no record, however, in which prisoner of war camp this splendid mosque was to be found.

battle. Usually prisoners of war were not treated badly. The simple soldiers often felt that they were all in the same boat anyhow, and as the First World War was not ideologically motivated, the enemy was not universally hated or despised, although this was not true for all theatres of the war.

In the Balkans, for example, the struggle between multi-ethnic Austria-Hungary and Bulgaria on one side, and the Serbs and Montenegrins on the other, took the form of a civil war and martial law was constantly and severely broken. The British and Americans were also often more moderate when dealing with the Germans than the French were, on whose territory the war was fought.

Altogether about 8 million soldiers were taken prisoner during the war. The Central Powers took around 5 million prisoners (among them 3.5 million Russians, roughly 500,000 Italians

FRITZ CARRIES IN ONE OF CANADA'S WOUNDED

Fritz carries in one of Canada's wounded.
Prisoners of war were often tasked with difficult, uncomfortable and dangerous missions closely behind the front line. This included the recovery and burial of fallen soldiers, or transporting wounded from the battlefield to the dressing stations, such as depicted here on this picture from the 'The *Daily Mirror* Canadian Official Series'. Incidentally, the nickname 'Fritz' carried a far less disparaging connotation than 'hun' or 'boche'.

Captured Senegalese riflemen. Year of the war 1914-15.
One of the many German cards showing captured French colonial troops, who look quite the picture in their traditional uniforms. The uncommonly tall *Tirailleur Sénégalais* on the left, was apparently interesting enough to be found on various cards. The prisoners are guarded by a field grey soldier and a member of the *Feldgendarmerie* military police, who were recruited from well-proven ex-army servicemen.

Two German officers lead their men into the Canadian camp – as prisoners.
Another card from the 'The *Daily Mirror* Canadian Official Series'. It shows a picture taken in the second half of the war, as can be identified by the uniforms and steel helmets worn by both the Canadians and the Germans. Although a rather large number of POWs are guarded by only a few Canadians, the situation nevertheless seems quite relaxed. As far as the prisoners are concerned, their war is over now, and they are still alive.

TWO GERMAN OFFICERS LEAD THEIR MEN INTO THE CANADIAN CAMP-AS PRISONERS.

PoWs of unknown nationality hunting lice in an unspecified camp, most likely in the eastern theatre. For millions of soldiers in all theatres of war, lice were a constant scourge. Prisoners of war who had a lot of time on their hands could give themselves some relief, especially in fair weather, by searching their clothing and bodies and killing as many of the insects as possible.

European war 1914. Coetquidan-Bellevue. German prisoners work on repairing streets.
All warring nations tasked prisoners of war with work detail, sometimes forcibly, sometimes by choice, to make up for the lack of labourers. For the prisoners, working meant leaving the camp, having some variety and often having better provisions, too. On principle, officers only worked if they volunteered.

and about 480,000 Frenchmen). On the Allied side, 3 million soldiers (2.2 million Austrian-Hungarian soldiers alone and almost 620,000 Germans) were taken prisoner. The treatment of prisoners of war had already been agreed upon years before the war and excepting for Turkey, all larger warring nations had signed the treaty.

The agreement was usually honoured, but sometimes the numbers of prisoners were so high that there were simply not the means to house and feed everybody. Therefore the treatment and feeding of prisoners was at its worst at the beginning of the war, as no preparations had been made yet for handling the interned. Near the end of the war the situation once more deteriorated in Germany and Austria-Hungary, as food shortages also hit the prisoner of war camps.

Perhaps one of the most depressing examples of there being no attempt made to treat prisoners of war decently, is the death march of the British and Indian soldiers who were taken prisoner by the Ottoman Empire at Kut-al-Amara, Mesopotamia, in Spring 1916. More than half of the 13,000 men died whilst being forced to march across the

Interior view of a barrack building in Hammelburg, Lower Franconia. This real photo card was sent home by a French prisoner of war, and is stamped on the reverse with *Geprüft. Lager Hammelburg IV* ('Passed. Hammelburg IV POW camp') by the censor in charge. The standard barrack building of a German prisoner of war camp was home to around 250 men. At the end of 1918 there were several hundred camps in Germany with around 2.5 million prisoners of war interned there.

« Ti viens voir sauvages ? »
Tirailleur Sénégalais en faction à la barrière
d'un camp de prisonniers allemands.

240   A.N
                                                          PARIS

His triumphant entry into Paris.
A captured German soldier is escorted by four armed
Frenchmen. This is supposed to mock the German
Emperor Wilhelm II – who the prisoner shows a certain
likeness to. Wilhelm would certainly have very much
liked to march into Paris as a victorious commander.

Have you come to see savages?
The *Tirailleur Sénégalais* is guarding a fenced-in camp for
German prisoners of war. This is a satirical French card, as
the black colonial soldier, whom German military circles
would often call a 'savage', is now guarding the captured
'savages'. Lucien Jonas (1880-1947) was a well-known
artist. He was drafted in 1914 but from 1915 onwards
served as an official war painter for the *Musée de l'Armée*.

desert without food, water or shelter.

After being taken prisoner, a soldier would
usually be searched and his prized personal
possessions would most likely be stolen. He
would then be interrogated and afterwards led to
a collection point behind the front. From here he
was transported to the rear, passing through
several transit camps, until he finally reached the
prisoner of war camp where he would stay
interned until the end of the war.

In September 1918 almost 2.5 million prisoners
of war were held in Germany, distributed across
several hundred camps. They were housed in large
barracks, each accommodating around 250 men.
Many prisoners were scheduled for work duty on
farms or in industry, where they took over the jobs
of those men sent to the front. Working gave them

more liberties, better provisions and helped them
fight the boredom. Officers were encamped in
more comfortable officers' camps and were granted
additional privileges, as they could not be required
to work.

Near the end of the war food rationing became
ever more severe in Germany, so that the
prisoners had to rely on food sent from home
more and more. These comforts were
transported and handed out by charitable
organisations such as the Red Cross.
Correspondingly, mortality was higher among
prisoners who did not receive such parcels,
especially Russians and Italians, than among the
British and French.

Chapter 12

The Home Front and the Neutral States

One reason why the First World War is called a total war is the fact that it was not only fought on the battlefield, but also had far reaching effects on the political, economic and social development of the warring countries and even those of the neutral states.

Politics and the Economy

In many European countries the interior situation was marked by schisms and contradictions, often fuelled by the rise of socialist and social democratic parties. When war broke out these political differences were, however, almost immediately buried in favour of national unity. Emperor Wilhelm II announced before the German Reichstag: 'Henceforth I know no parties, I know only Germans' and the so-called 'Burgfrieden' (originally a medieval concept of keeping peace inside the castle walls) was made. In France the President called on the parties to form a *union sacrée* and in the UK the suffragettes paused their campaign for equal (political) rights for women until further notice. These demonstrations of national unity would be universally maintained until the end of the war.

Ranks were closed not only politically, but the population was also asked to contribute to the national war effort on an economic level. Immediately after the outbreak of the war, the French president addressed his public appeal to the female population (*Aux femmes Françaises*), asking them to take over the work on the farms and bring in the harvest in the autumn. This was only the first in a number of drastic but unavoidable measures, as the military side of war

Kaiser Wilhelm II.

„Ich kenne keine Parteien mehr, kenne nur noch Deutsche".

Emperor Wilhelm II. 'Henceforth I know no parties, I know only Germans.'
Immediately after the war broke out, political factions and parties closed ranks in all countries. Political aims were no longer discussed and only national issues were important. Germany called this the 'Burgfrieden', France spoke of the 'Union sacrée'.

POUR LA FRANCE
VERSEZ VOTRE OR

L'Or Combat Pour La Victoire

LES MONNAIES D'OR SONT ÉCHANGÉES A LA BANQUE DE FRANCE

For France. Donate your gold. Gold fights for victory.
The enormous costs of the war effort were mainly paid for by the citizens of the countries involved. The national governments repeatedly published war bonds and invited the population to sign them. This card asks all French citizens to hand in their gold coins to allow the state to finance purchases made abroad.

for the war had hardly been given a thought. There were few stocks and supplies and no plans to integrate civilian factories into the defence industry. In addition, many workers and engineers in leading positions had been drafted and were at the front. Once it became apparent that this clash of arms would not be the short campaign everybody had expected, the whole economy had to be adapted to the war.

The demand for weapons, ammunition, provisions and other supplies tied up the majority of the available economic power and these problems were aggravated by the developments in the operational theatres. France was especially effected, as the occupied part of its territory was the one where coal and iron ore were mined, whereas the UK, Germany and Austria-Hungary suffered from the attempts to cut each other's naval supply lines. All warring countries tried to raise money from war bonds to cover the bigger part of their expenses. France

had been carefully planned in terms of the mobilisation and deployment of armies numbering millions, but economical preparations

This photograph taken at the onset of the war shows Bavarian soldiers being given a farewell by the population of Munich, before they march off to the front. Apart from a few exceptions, neither the soldiers nor the civilians look especially joyful or enthusiastic. The majority of the men going to war in 1914 would not survive it. The location is in front of the Hotel Wolff, which still exists directly beside the main station, and is where the troop transportations left from.

THESE SUPPLY TRAINS WILL CONTINUE MOVING AS LONG AS YOU FOLKS BUY BONDS

These supply trains will continue moving as long as you folks buy bonds.
This picture postcard was supposed to make the American population invest in war bonds. It was postmarked by the 'U.S. Military Postal Express Service' on 16 October 1918, less than four weeks before the Armistice, and also carries two censoring marks, one of which reads 'Passed by Base Censor 15. AEF' (American Expeditionary Force).

and the UK borrowed enormous sums from the US and in doing so meant they were already supported by the country even before the Americans actually entered the war. The costs of war were also dizzying in financial terms: the UK, Germany and the USA each spent about 50 billion dollars.

The Civilian Population

About 10 million civilians died from direct or indirect effects of the war, about the same number as fallen soldiers. Most non-combatants died in the eastern theatres; the Balkans, the Caucasus and the Middle East.

The effects of the war on the civilian population were severe, although of course not everybody was equally affected. The families who grieved for dead or severely injured loved ones were certainly hit the hardest, whether this meant that the father, spouse, son or brother had died in battle as a soldier or that other family members had been hurt in the fighting in one way or another. Many citizens had also seen their homes and possessions destroyed, commandeered or looted and were now fighting for sheer survival as refugees.

5. NOS MUNITIONS — Entrepôts Généraux.
Vue d'une Galerie

General store. View into a hallway.
Not only did the plans made before the beginning of the war hugely underestimate its duration, but estimates regarding the amount of ammunition needed by the artillery were also a long way from the actual demands. In some cases the whole ammunition supply for a gun was spent within a few days, leading to a substantial increase in the production of ammunition in many new factories.

Original picture from the theatre of war. Refugees on the way with their possessions.
The first streams of war refugees began in Belgium as they fled in front of the advancing German units. They were also in East Prussia, where Prussian citizens tried to escape the invading Russians. The people pictured here have most likely lost their house, as they are obviously in an area that has already seen heavy fighting.

Northern emigrants passing through Compiègne.
At the beginning of the war, the German Army managed to occupy most parts of Belgium and northern France. There were assaults against the civilian population and rumours of outright massacres were spread, making millions of inhabitants flee from the occupied areas. Here an endless convoy of horse-drawn carts passes through the town of Compiègne, indicating that this picture was most likely taken in mid-August. If the engagements allowed it, many of the refugees returned to their houses once the front lines had settled down.

Once upon a time.
A sailor nostalgically points out a picture on the wall, showing him during better times and with a box full of tasty food. This is a typical example of a 'hunger card', which decried the increasingly bad food situation and was therefore banned by the authorities. These cards were circulated from the end of 1916 onwards, after the British blockade had seriously impacted food supplies and some foods became difficult or even impossible to obtain.

Both: 'Boy, the way you look!'
Fritz Schoen (1871-?), a German interior designer, painter, cartoonist and advertisement artist, shows the estrangement between the civilian population and the men at the front. The front line soldiers could not share their experiences with those who had stayed at home, they were inconceivable in the truest sense of the word. This created an almost insurmountable rift between the veterans and the rest of the population.

In the occupied territories people had to live under the heel of a foreign army, had to accept enemy soldiers being billeted with them, could be taken hostage to enforce obedience, or even drafted as forced labourers for the enemy. Some of those were allowed to work close to home, but civilians were increasingly sent by rail across hundreds and thousands of kilometres to perform forced labour on farms and in industries.

Even those who were spared such blows due to living far enough away from the front, still felt the effects of the war. Often the breadwinner of the family had been drafted and those left behind lost the biggest part of their income. At the same time food and supplies became scarcer, prices went up and people increasingly suffered from hunger. The situation was similar everywhere, although (among the western states) Austria-

An orphan amidst the ruins caused by a German aerial bomb.
Millions of children lost their fathers in the war – but hundreds of thousands also lost their mothers. Many were raised in orphanages, while others were adopted. It is impossible to tell whether a real orphan is pictured here or the girl has only been used for a propaganda photo. The bombings by Zeppelins and aeroplanes, as well as the use of long range artillery against Paris and other civilian targets, caused a great deal of outrage.

Ruthenian refugees in Bukovina.
The population of eastern Europe also tried to flee the violence of the conflict. Today Ruthenia forms part of the Ukraine, but it was in Austro-Hungarian territory until 1918. Bukovina, located south of Ruthenia, was also part of Hungary, and today its southern part lies in Romania and the northern half in the Ukraine.

RUTHENISCHE FLÜCHTLINGE IN DER BUKOWINA

Hungary and Germany were hit the hardest due to the impact of the Allied blockade. Basic supplies like grain, fertilisers and coal were already in short supply by the early months of 1915, and bread had to be rationed. The situation deteriorated quickly, and from 1916 onwards, the population, and in particular those living in major cities, suffered from cold and hunger due to bad harvests and a severe winter. The people were weakened and mortality rates increased. In Germany alone the privations caused by the war cost almost a million lives.

The situation was even worse for the civilian population in other theatres of war. On the Eastern Front the areas directly affected by the war were far larger than on the Western Front, and the locals expected little help from the authorities. In addition, the conflict turned into something close to a civil war in some places, e.g. the Balkans. This claimed a high number of civilian victims, similar to those claimed by the war between Russia and Turkey in the Caucasus. The Turkish genocide against the Armenians, which claimed an estimated 1 million innocent

Citizens who lived close to the front line and were not forced from their homes, could be ordered to billet soldiers. This might mean their own troops, but in occupied areas also included members of the enemy forces. This real photo card shows German soldiers, who have most likely found accommodation with a French family. As there is a Stahlhelm steel helmet on the wall, this picture must have been taken in the second half of 1916 or later. Despite the presence of a photographer, the mood seems rather depressed and nobody is smiling.

After the war has ended or a previously occupied area has been retaken, a French family returns to their farm, which has suffered heavy damage. Although the situation is certainly posed, countless families would have lived through this in some form or another. You could count yourself lucky if your home was not in close proximity to the front, as often nothing remained standing where trench warfare had been fought.

lives, marked the absolute low. Also taking place on Turkish territory were the lesser-known mass murders of the Assyrians and Pontic Greeks, in which several hundred thousand Christian civilians were killed. Another 500,000 people died from lack of food in the deserts of today's Syria, as a direct result of the war.

The Role of Women

It is hardly astonishing that women took over important and varied roles during the First World War, considering they formed about half of the world population, but until Summer 1914, this was far from given.

At the beginning of the twentieth century, women still played a subordinate role in many areas, especially in public life. Women were not allowed to vote, were practically excluded from higher learning and were not supposed to have a career. Of course, women had to work as hard or even harder than men – but usually only in the house, on the farm or in the family business. The fight for autonomy and equal rights that had begun in the second half of the nineteenth century

had gained a lot of steam by the time of the Great War. Traditional female roles and occupations gained importance, but quite a number of new ones also appeared.

A female German bus or tram conductor had her picture taken in her service dress. Women in the UK and France also often performed this job during the war. From the end of 1918 onwards, many men returned to civilian life after demobilisation, and almost all women were dismissed on short notice.

Ohé le Bourgeois!
t'en fais pas, on les aura!

PATRIOTIC
1185

Hey upstanding citizen. Don't worry, we'll get them.
The relationship between affluent French citizens and decorated front line soldiers was tense. During the course of the war, the majority of the French population became poorer; prices rose and workers and soldiers became weary of the war. At the same time, a small portion of the population earned enormous amounts of money by selling weapons, ammunition and equipment to the army a development that could also be seen in the UK and Germany.

Like the whole civilian population, women suffered from poverty, cold and hunger during the war, but they also faced sexual assaults by the (often enemy) soldiers. Dozens of cases of rape committed by members of the German occupation forces are on record in Belgium and northern France alone, and in all likelihood things were equally as bad in other areas, for which no numbers are available. Wives had to fend for themselves for the duration of the war,

and many had an invalid return home or were widowed at a young age. In some western countries war widows received financial aid, but due to the enormous numbers of casualties, this was rather modest and the surplus of women did not make it easier to remarry.

The mothers, spouses, fiancées or girlfriends had a substantial influence on the morale of the troops at the front. Their letters, postcards and parcels with 'comforts from home' were often the

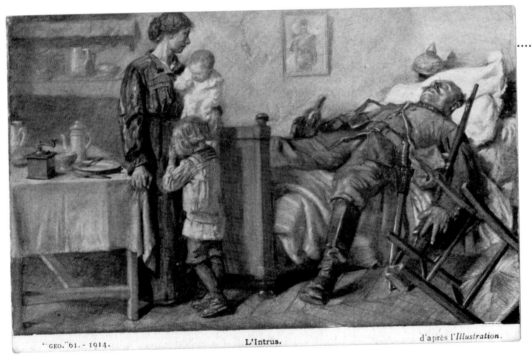

"GEO." 61. - 1914.   L'Intrus.   d'après l'*Illustration*.

The intruder.
This drawing was first published in 1914 in the French magazine *L'Illustration*. A German soldier has forced his way into the house of a French family and has fallen asleep drunk, but still armed, on the marital bed, underneath a picture of the absent head of the household in uniform. The motif refers to the German invasion in Belgium and northern France, and the soldier being in the bed may indicate a rape.

RÉQUISITIONS!
OU TRAÎTES D'ESCLAVES BELGES
PAR LES ALLEMANDS! (Fin 1916) INFAMIE!

Requisitions. The way the Germans treat Belgian slaves! (End of 1916). A disgrace!
Belgian forced labourers are packed into trains at Fosses-la-Ville station and forced to work on farms or in factories in Germany. They may also have had to work for the occupation forces behind the front line in northern France. Citizens of other states, as well as prisoners of war, shared their fate.

only connection to normal life and allowed the men a short escape from the hell of everyday front line duty. The importance of this connection is underlined by the typical French phenomenon of the 'Marraine de guerre', perhaps best translated as 'wartime godmother', which was created in Spring 1915. The idea was to 'adopt' as pen pals soldiers who had no family or whose family was unreachable in the occupied parts of the country. In this way the 'war orphans' would regularly receive mail just like the majority of their comrades. In addition, the existence of a marraine was supposed to increase the fighting spirit, as the 'adopted' soldier now had someone to fight and, if need be, even give his life for.

However sinister the motives might have been, the whole thing was a roaring success. Contact was made by newspaper advert, for example, and the marraine became a national phenomenon, appearing in books, films, plays, as well as gracing many picture postcards. The medium was perfectly suited for this, as the

La Vie chère.

Ohé! les ceux d'l'arrière; v'nez donc un peu par ici, les pruneaux y sont pour rien!

The expensive life. Hey! You at the back: come over here, plums are free of charge here.
The rising costs of food did not make life easier in wartime for the citizens, but these inconveniences were nothing compared to what the soldiers lived through at the front. 'Plums' was the name the poilus gave to the grenades which the enemy constantly fired at them.

The Woman and the War. The Godmother.
Maurice Leroy was a French book and magazine illustrator. In 1917 he published a series of ten postcards under the title *La Femme et la Guerre* showing tasks and occupations that had been mainly taken over by women. Among them were the ammunition worker, the nurse, the conductress, the foster mother and the farmer. There was also the typically French 'marraine' (godmother or foster mother), who in the minds of the soldiers and illustrators, was always young and pretty.

LEROY - La Marraine.

Lafranqui   www.delcampe.net

correspondence between men and women who did not know each other personally was not only romantic by nature, but also furthered the contact between people of very different backgrounds. Friendships between French women and soldiers from the colonial forces even resulted from this process.

Women in the Workforce

Of course the most important contribution of women to the war effort was their role as labourers. The enormous wartime economy needed far more workers in the factories than ever before, but the majority of the men were away on military service. This shortage of labour could only partially be amended by prisoners of war and forced labourers from the occupied territories, and the lion's share of the workload was shouldered by women taking over male occupations. The number of female workers in

Delivering letters also became a socially acceptable profession for women during the war. It was certainly less physically exhausting and more comfortable than working in the defence industry. Apart from the leather pouch for the letters, the service dress here consisted of a peaked cap with a metal eagle as a symbol of the *Reichspost Imperial* mail service, and a brassard with the official emblem.

Salvation Army making doughnuts under bombardment of German Guns. Front Line-France.
Like the man on the left of the picture, the women wear steel helmets and carry gas masks, which they have stored in bags in front of their bodies. Most likely this field bakery, which is set up in a ruined building, is not located immediately at the front, even though the Salvation Army did in fact work very close to the front line, and therefore was definitely subject to enemy fire.

France, for example, rose from a couple of hundred thousand in 1914 to about 6 million in 1917.

The best known were the 'munitionettes' – the women working in the ammunition factories. Their work was heavy, unhealthy, dangerous and badly paid, yet several million women still volunteered, most of them from lower social classes. Women and girls from the middle classes or of higher social standing usually volunteered to serve in civilian or military medical organisations. Here they were trained as nurses or auxiliary nurses and often worked close to the front line. What looked like a noble and peaceful occupation at first would often be a traumatising experience, as they had to treat incredible numbers of the most severely injured and maimed soldiers in the most primitive of circumstances. Hundreds of thousands of other women worked (also voluntarily) for one of the many auxiliary services as drivers, typists, telephone operators, cooks, couriers or mechanics, on the Home Front or behind the lines. The British 'Women's Army Auxiliary Corps'

This picture taken in France shows women making ammunition and checking the empty shells delivered from the turning shop. This was certainly a more comfortable task than the women who had to fill the shells with explosives. Their job was very unhealthy and dangerous, as the permanent contact with the chemicals would colour their skin yellow (hence the nick-name 'canaries'), and there were constantly explosions in the factories.

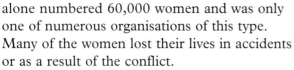

If you need us, we will be there.
A young Frenchwoman in the colourful uniform of the *Zouaves*, graces this card. It is one of a whole series of motifs, each showing a woman in various French uniforms and all carrying similar texts. They were supposed to illustrate that the female members of the population contributed an equally important share to the war effort, not that they actually wanted to take up arms and fight at the front. Only the Russians actually sent women into combat on the front line, when they fought the Austro-Hungarian troops in July 1917.

Year of the War 1915.
Four German women in their work clothes pose for the camera with artillery shells. All warring countries employed hundreds of thousands of women in the ammunition factories, not only because most men were serving at the front, but also because the numbers of shells required were immense. Wearing a skirt certainly did not help in this kind of work, but women were officially not allowed to wear trousers. On 27 January 1917 the German high command still maintained that trousers were only to be worn during physical exercise.

alone numbered 60,000 women and was only one of numerous organisations of this type. Many of the women lost their lives in accidents or as a result of the conflict.

Women who worked on the farms to maintain food supplies took up a more peaceful but equally important role. The French president made a start in late summer 1914 by asking the female citizens to bring in the harvest, a task later taken over by special organisations. In the UK this role was taken up by the 'Women's Land

Army' and the '*Frauen-Land-Armee*' in the German Empire, each numbering about 250,000 female rural workers. In the cities, professions that had previously been filled exclusively by men were increasingly taken over by women. While unimaginable before 1914, over the course of the war the number of women working as letter carriers, conductors, train guards and even in the auxiliary police rose steadily.

Excepting for a few cases, women did not serve in combat. A British female ambulance

LES TRAVAILLEUSES AGRICOLES DE LA GRANDE BRETAGNE.

L'"ARMÉE AGRICOLE" de la Grande Bretagne comprend plus de 300,000 femmes. Leurs occupations sont des plus variées ; en fait, elles font tout ce qui se rapporte aux travaux de la campagne. Divers "Collèges agricoles" ont été établis, et, à la fin de leur instruction, les femmes deviennent gérantes et instructrices. Elles apprennent non seulement à conduire les chevaux, à traire, à labourer et à accomplir les autres travaux ordinaires de la campagne, mais encore elles plantent de jeunes arbres et sont en passe de devenir d'excellentes couvreuses de chaume et expertes dans la destruction des taupes.

The female farm hands of Great Britain.
In the country, women also had to take over the lion's share of the work that had previously done by men. In addition to the rural population, this also required volunteers from the cities. The UK established the 'Women's Land Army' for this and Germany the '*Frauen-Land-Armee*'. Both organisations fielded several hundred thousand women, who played an indispensable part in providing the population with staple foods.

driver, however, managed to join the Serbian Army and rose to the rank of major, most likely as a symbol for the cooperation with the UK. The situation was different for Maria Bochkareva. She fought for the Russian Army from 1914 onwards and convinced the high command to raise a female combat unit. About 2,000 women volunteered, and in June 1917 a force of 300 women successfully fought the Austro-Hungarian Army near the town of Smorgon. Many Russian women would follow Maria Bochkareva's lead during the Second World War.

Once the war was over the situation changed abruptly. Weapons and ammunition production were reduced, the armies demobilised and some of the auxiliary organisations disbanded. Many

E. LE DELEY, Imprimeur, Paris.

Les dames ambulancières Anglaises soignant un blessé | The English nurses taking care of a wonded soldier | Cliché Chusseau, Flaviens

The English nurses taking care of a wonded soldier.
This card was published shortly after the outbreak of the war, as it was mailed on 10 October 1914. and shows female medics during an exercise. The women wear neat uniforms and discipline is strict – the woman on the left stands to attention. The UK counted five organisations that took care of the wounded during the war.

Electrical light. Factory for defence material in Lyon. Fuse workshop.
The picture shows a workbench with a number of small lathes, where women turn fuses for artillery shells. The mechanics of the fuses could be quite complicated and include small parts, perhaps this is the reason the electrical lighting is especially pointed out.

L'ÉCLAIRAGE ÉLECTRIQUE
Usine de Matériel de Guerre de Lyon

48 Atelier des Fusées

J'attends la fin de cette triste guerre
Pour te donner mes baisers de naguère

men returned home and the women lost their jobs. But the years of the war had started a development that could not be turned back. Women had worked in male professions for the first time and found themselves up to the task. For the first time, the majority of women had been financially independent and could move freely – in both the figurative and the most literal sense of the word. Skirts, corsets and long hair had given way and trousers, bras and short haircuts became acceptable. All this leaving memories that could not be erased.

In the years after the war, women were given the right to vote in many western countries, considered by some as a 'reward' for their contribution to the war effort. But not everybody shared this view, France and Italy, for example, had to go through a second world war for this.

I will wait for this sad war to end before I give you my kisses.
This romantic depiction is typical of French cards. The woman is pictured as nurse, and as a lover after the war. The great number of wounded made it impossible to meet demands with professional nurses alone, and so volunteers were also put to work. This was considered the perfect role for women, especially at the outbreak of the war, as they were considered born to take care of those in need.

'An angel in all but power is she!'
There were certainly many 'angels' among the young women from the UK, Germany or France. But they were also subject to traumatising events, witnessed terrible sights and had to cope with their experiences with severely wounded and maimed soldiers. To be able to cope with serving as a nurse, they had to distance themselves from the misery as far as possible.

The liberation is near!
This dual language postcard was published in 1916 or 1917 by the Belgian government and shows a female British labourer working a drill. The text explains that: 'Great Britain has called all able-bodied to the forces. By working without cease on the Home Front to supply sufficient ammunition to the UK and its allies, women make a contribution to this war that is no less important.'

The Neutral States

Of the fifty-four sovereign states that existed in 1914 (including the British dominions), at least thirty-four declared war up to 1918, sometimes against each other, sometimes unilaterally. Only nineteen declared themselves neutral, six of them in Europe: Denmark, the Netherlands, Norway, Spain, Sweden and Switzerland. Of course, compared to the population in the warring countries, those in the neutral states were much better off. They were not mobilised to conquer other countries, did not have to sacrifice their lives for their home country and did not have to face combat. But these states also suffered far-reaching changes to everyday life. Switzerland and the Netherlands were particularly affected, as they were surrounded by warring countries and therefore permanently at risk of being dragged into the conflict. Their forces were mobilised in 1914 and were on stand-by until after the armistice of 1918. In addition, there were huge numbers of refugees to take in and provide for, which was no small task for countries whose economy was suffering heavily from the war.

Shortly after the initial engagements many

Controrôle uitgang Kamp II — Sortie du Camp II
INTERNEERINGSKAMP BIJ ZEIST
CAMP DE ZEIST

Controls on the exit of Camp II. Internment camp near Zeist.
The rules of international law required neutral states to intern members of the forces of warring states until the war was over. Belgian soldiers from Antwerp, as well as British, Germans, French and a couple of Americans, who had voluntarily or involuntarily crossed the border into the Netherlands, were therefore detained in camps that were especially built for this purpose.

Belgians, both civilians and soldiers, had already fled to the Netherlands. According to international law, which was implemented meticulously, military personnel from warring countries had to be interned until the end of the war, and so special internment camps were erected for Belgian soldiers. A total of around 36,000 members of foreign forces were stranded in the Netherlands – mostly Belgians, but also British, German, French and a couple of US soldiers, who had either passed over the border of their own free will (escape or desertion) or involuntarily (cut off from their units or simply lost).

Most citizens of the Netherlands were happy that the war passed them by (at least for the time being?) and supported the neutrality declared by the government. But some young men objected, and as a last resort decided to serve as volunteers in the army of one of the warring nations.

Opinions amongst the population differed. A small majority were most likely pro-German and anti-British, as the UK had forced its brother nation of the Boers in South Africa under its rule

Machine gun in firing position.
When the Great War reached its pinnacle, there were still nineteen states worldwide who were neutral. Two of them were in the centre of Europe – Switzerland and the Netherlands – and therefore were completely surrounded by warring countries or contested seas. During the whole course of the war, the Netherlands Army was in a state of mobilisation to protect the Dutch territory and its neutrality. Cards like this one, published by the 'Ons Leger' society, were supposed to demonstrate the readiness of its defence against both local and foreign parties.

Pauvre petite voisine va! Hollande. **Poor little neighbour.**

Neutral states rarely appeared as motifs on the cards of warring countries. In 1916 the Frenchman, Emile Dupuis, designed a series of cards that included Greece, Norway, Portugal, the Netherlands and Switzerland as their topics. This card shows the rich and well-off Netherlands, in the form of a farmer smoking a cigar. He has plenty of milk and cheese and does not care for his poor neighbour, Belgium.

Pauvre petite Voisine va !....
Poor little Neighbour.
HOLLANDE

in the Boer War about ten years before. But on the other hand, there was indignation about the attack against Belgium, who was still neutral in 1914, and the way the German Army treated the civilian population of the neighbouring country. The artist, Louis Raemaekers, focused on this topic in particular and his drawings strongly influenced opinions at home and abroad in favour of the Allies. From late 1917 onwards, they were not only published as picture postcards, but in more than 2,000 newspapers worldwide. In the end, the Netherlands had no choice but to wait and hope that the war would be over as soon as possible.

Things deteriorated swiftly, however, in the second half of the war, and while a small part of

1914... Fugitifs d'Anvers sur la frontière Hollandaise | 1914... Fugitives from Antwerp on the Dutch frontier

16me Série

1914... Fugitives from Antwerp on the Dutch frontier.

A group of Belgian refugees, including many children, camping on the Netherlands' border. When the Germans took Antwerp on and around 10 October 1914, the stream of refugees grew to enormous proportions. An estimated 500,000 civilians and several tens of thousands of soldiers fled to the Netherlands. About 400,000 of them would return home in the following months, while the others stayed in the neutral Netherlands.

A view into one of the mess halls in the Zeist internment camp. The camp spanned an area of more 25 hectares and consisted of forty-eight barracks divided into two separate sections. It could hold around 12,000 to 15,000 people.

the population made a lot of money by selling rare supplies to Germany, the majority suffered from increasingly severe supply shortages. Imports and exports were heavily effected by the blockades enforced by both sides (Entente and Central Powers), freighters and fishing boats hit mines, were torpedoed or commandeered and many goods were considered to be of strategic importance or defence material and therefore banned from import. The economy ground to a halt and an increasing number of food and commodities had to be rationed, until finally people in the Netherlands were also suffering from hunger. Most likely, the Armistice came just in time to prevent large scale looting and public unrest.

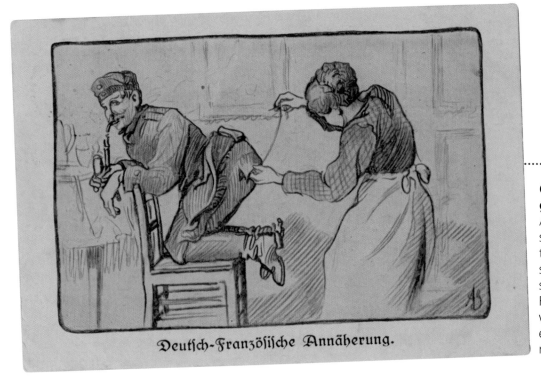

Deutsch-Französische Annäherung.

Germany and France getting closer.
A French woman is sewing the torn-up trousers of a German soldier. As many German soldiers were billeted with French families during the war, this scene might easily have happened in real life.

Mobilisé chez les Allemands! LORRAINE Enrolled in the German army.

Enrolled in the German Army.
Lorraine was among the territories annexed by the German Empire after the Franco-Prussian War of 1870/71, and was still considered an occupied territory by France. This motif shows the tragic fate of a 'Lorrainer' who considers himself a Frenchman but is drafted into the German Army to fight against France.

After hunting the *boches*, another hunt.
The enormous number of cards from all countries dealing with hunting lice illustrates that these insects must have been a universal scourge for all soldiers. Considering the many holes left by drawing pins, this picture postcard of an almost naked French soldier checking his clothing for pests, must have decorated many a wall for a long time.

Après la Chasse aux Boches, autre Chasse

Edition Rose France

Further Reading

Beer, T., *Die kaiserliche Marine auf alten Postkarten* (Hildesheim 1983).

Binder, G., *Mit Glanz und Gloria in die Niederlage. Der Erste Weltkrieg in alten Ansichtskarten aus der Sammlung von Richard Meinel* (Stuttgart 1983).

Brocks, C., *Die bunte Welt des Krieges. Bildpostkarten aus dem Ersten Weltkrieg 1914-1918* (Essen 2008).

Bryant, M., *World War I in Cartoons* (London 2006).

Clashausen, H., *Die Sonne sank im Westen. Der Erste Weltkrieg, Postkarten von 1899-1918 aus Deutschland und Frankreich* (Wülfrath 2000).

Currie, B., *The First World War in Old Picture Postcards* (Zaltbommel 1988).

Demm, E., *Der Erste Weltkrieg in der internationalen Karikatur* (Hannover 1988).

Doyle, P., *British Postcards of the First World War* (Oxford 2011).

Fanelli, G. & E. Godoli, *Art Nouveau Postcards* (London 1987).

Feith, J., *De oorlog in prent* (Amsterdam 1915).

Fischer, P., *Die propagandistische Funktion von Bildpostkarten im Ersten Weltkrieg in: S. Quandt & H. Schichtel, Der Erste Weltkrieg als Kommunikationsereignis* (Giessen 1993), pp. 63-75.

Flemming, T., *Grüße aus dem Schützengraben. Feldpostkarten im Ersten Weltkrieg aus der Sammlung Ulf Heinrich* (Berlin 2004).

Holt, T. & V., *Till the Boys Come Home. The Picture Postcards of the First World War* (London 1977).

Holzer, A., *Die andere Front. Fotografie und Propaganda im Ersten Weltkrieg* (Darmstadt 2007).

Laffin, J., *World War I in Postcards* (Gloucester 1988).

Lith, H. van, *Ik denk altijd aan jou. Prentbriefkaarten tussen front en thuisfront 1914 -1918* (Zaltbommel 2006).

Milliard, J.B. & N. Paré, *La carte postale du soldat de 1913 à 1919* (Tours 1987).

Morin, C., *La Grande Guerre des images: La propagande par la carte postale, 1914-1918* (Turquant 2012).

Philippen, J., *Geschiedenis en charme van de prentkaart* (Diest 1977).

Perault, F., *Images de poilus: La Grande Guerre en cartes postales* (Paris 2002).

Ripert, A., & C. Frère, *La Carte Postale. Son histoire, sa fonction sociale* (Paris 2001).

Roberts, A., *Postcards from the Trenches. Images from the First World War* (Oxford 2008).

Rumpf, A., *Feldpostkarten 1914-1918* (Bergisch Gladbach 1980).

Schultz-Besser, E., *Die Karikatur im Weltkriege* (Leipzig 1915).

Ruyters, H., & A., Voet, *De Nederlandse prentbriefkaart. Een selectie van de mooiste Nederlandse kaarten gerangschikt naar onderwerp* (Capelle aan de IJssel 1996).

Wery, M., *La carte postale. Témoin de l'enfer des tranchées de la Grande Guerre de 1914-1918* (Paris 2000).

Zühlke, R., *Bildpropaganda im Ersten Weltkrieg* (Hamburg 2000).

There is a great deal of information about First World War postcards on the internet. Of the countless pages dealing with collecting picture postcards, three are named here, as these gave the author important advice during the creation of this work:

www.ww1-propaganda-cards.com
www.wereldoorlog1418.nl/great-war-picture-postcards/
www.worldwar1postcards.com

You filthy liars, I'll show you!
The *Münchner Kindl* (a symbol of Munich, literally 'the Munich child') is pinching the ears of a French soldier. In its hand it carries a copy of the French newspaper *Matin* with the headline reading 'Munich bombarded by the French'. All warring nations established press information and censoring authorities. Amongst other things, their role was to write press releases for local and foreign press agencies, which contained outright false, or only partially true information, if this was considered helpful.

Index of Artists

A list of artists' names whose creations are reproduced in this book:

1914-1918. By their crusade for liberty and justice, the Allies have saved civilisation and humanity on French soil.

In France especially, the fight against the Central Powers was stylised as a war of the civilised world against the forces of darkness who tried to tumble the world into an abyss and enslave humanity. This card, which was published in late 1918, early 1919, certainly leaves no doubt about that.